Fodor's 95 San Diego

Fodor's Travel Publications, Inc.
New York • Toronto • London • Sydney • Auckland

Fodor's San Diego

Editor: Edie Jarolim
Editorial Contributors: Bob Blake, Lori Chamberlain, Jon and Noonie Corn, Echo Garrett, Edie Jarolim, Dawn Lawson, Bevin McLaughlin, Maribeth Mellin, Tracy Patruno, Mary Ellen Schultz, Kathryn Shevelow, Nancy van Itallie
Creative Director: Fabrizio La Rocca
Cartographer: David Lindroth
Illustrator: Karl Tanner
Cover Photograph: Tim Holt, Photo Researchers, Inc.

Design: Vignelli Associates

Special Sales

Fodor's Travel Publications are available at special discounts for bulk purchases for sales promotions or premiums. Special editions, including personalized covers, excerpts of existing guides, and corporate imprints, can be created in large quantities for special needs. For more information, contact your local bookseller or Special Markets, Fodor's Travel Publications, 201 East 50th Street, New York, NY 10022. Inquiries from Canada should be directed to your local Canadian bookseller or sent to Random House of Canada, Ltd., Marketing Department, 1265 Aerowood Drive, Mississauga, Ontario L4W 1B9. Inquiries from the United Kingdom should be sent to Fodor's Travel Publications, 20 Vauxhall Bridge Road, London, England SW1V 2SA.

Contents

Maps

Foreword

Many people in San Diego have been extremely helpful to the updaters of this 1995 edition, but special thanks go to Laurie Allison of the San Diego Convention & Visitors Bureau for her outstanding efficiency as an information resource; the book could not have been as effectively revised without her.

While every care has been taken to ensure the accuracy of the information in this guide, the passage of time will always bring change, and, consequently, the publisher cannot accept responsibility for errors that may occur.

All prices and opening times quoted here are based on information supplied to us at press time. Hours and admission fees may change, however, and the prudent traveler will avoid inconvenience by calling ahead.

Fodor's wants to hear about your travel experiences, both pleasant and unpleasant. When a hotel or restaurant fails to live up to its billing, let us know and we will investigate the complaint and revise our entries when the facts warrant it.

Send your letters to the editors of Fodor's Travel Publications, 201 East 50th Street, New York, NY 10022.

Highlights '95 and Fodor's Choice

Highlights '95

The downtown San Diego skyline continues to change in subtle and startling ways. Although hotel and office-tower construction seems to have peaked in this newly developed area, growth and refinement of already existing sites are continuing apace.

Designed to tie together the waterfront's many new developments, the landscaped **King Promenade,** a 12-acre park, will run along Harbor Drive from Seaport Village to the Convention Center and north to the Gaslamp Quarter. A section of the promenade near the Convention Center was completed in 1992, and the entire project is expected to be finished by early 1995.

The beginning of 1995 should also see the grand opening of the 150-acre **Arco Training Center** for Olympic athletes. Overlooking Lower Otay Lake, 10 miles east of San Diego Bay, the facility will be a warm-weather counterpart to the U.S. Olympic centers in Lake Placid, NY, and Colorado Springs, CO. Guests can survey the complex and watch athletes training for events, including archery, track, cycling, tennis, and various water-related sports; guided tours will begin at a visitor center, which will house a gift shop, interactive exhibits, and an observation deck.

Home in the past to the **America's Cup** international yacht races, San Diego is once again slated to host this hugely popular event, to be covered live around the world. Foreign and American syndicates began training here in 1994 for the best-of-seven-race series. The Defender (American) and Challenger (foreign) selection events will be held between January and April 1995, with the final, deciding race kicking off in May. A total of 14 challengers from nine nations have laid down the gauntlet for the coveted cup; America's Cup '95 will see South Africa and Russia competing in the event for the first time.

There's always something new at the **San Diego Zoo.** In the summer of 1995 a hippopotamus exhibit will be completed near the Tiger River complex. Visitors will be able to watch the antics of three African river hippos, which can weigh in excess of 3,000 pounds, from both above- and below-water viewing areas.

Public transit is finally coming to **Old Town**—en masse. If all goes as planned, the North County commuter bus line will include Old Town on its downtown route by the end of 1994, and the light rail system will have a trolley stop in place by the end of 1995. (There's also talk of an Amtrak station to follow, but it's as yet unofficial.) The money acquired by selling trolley-stop rights will help the city refurbish the McCoy House, the former residence of one of the area's original settlers; it's slated to become Old Town State Park's new visitor center by late 1995.

The building and transportation boom has spread south to Baja California, where both the Mexican government and private investors are banking on prosperity. Rosarito Beach now boasts exclusive condos and time-share resorts, and new hotels and restaurants are springing up. Ensenada is changing just as quickly, becoming much more than a weekend getaway. A new crop of tour companies specializing in Baja make the trek south hassle-free.

Fodor's Choice

No two people will agree on what makes a perfect vacation, but it's fun and helpful to know what others think. We hope you'll have a chance to experience some of Fodor's Choices yourself while visiting San Diego. For detailed information about each entry, refer to the appropriate chapters within this guidebook.

Restaurants

Dobson's, Downtown (*$$$*)

George's at the Cove, La Jolla (*$$$*)

Trattoria La Strada, Downtown (*$$–$$$*)

California Cuisine, Uptown (*$$*)

Palenque, Pacific Beach (*$–$$*)

Panda Inn, Downtown (*$–$$*)

Lodging

Le Meridien, Coronado (*$$$$*)

La Valencia, La Jolla (*$$$–$$$$*)

San Diego Princess Resort, Mission Bay (*$$$*)

Humphrey's Half Moon Inn, Shelter Island (*$$–$$$*)

Torrey Pines Inn, La Jolla (*$$*)

Ocean Manor Apartment Hotel, Ocean Beach (*$–$$*)

La Pensione, Downtown (*$*)

Favorite Zoo Exhibits

Flamingos

Koalas

Gorilla Tropics

Sun Bear Forest

Tiger River

Special Moments

Driving across the San Diego–Coronado Bridge

Evening stroll above La Jolla Cove

Spotting a gray whale spouting during the winter migration

Hiking at Cabrillo National Monument on Point Loma

Sunday picnic in Balboa Park

Beaches

La Jolla Cove

Pacific Beach

Torrey Pines State Beach

Favorite Outdoor Activities

Scuba diving off La Jolla Cove

Golfing at Torrey Pines

Roller skating at Mission Bay

Jogging along the Embarcadero

Volleyball on Ocean Beach

Windsurfing on Mission Bay

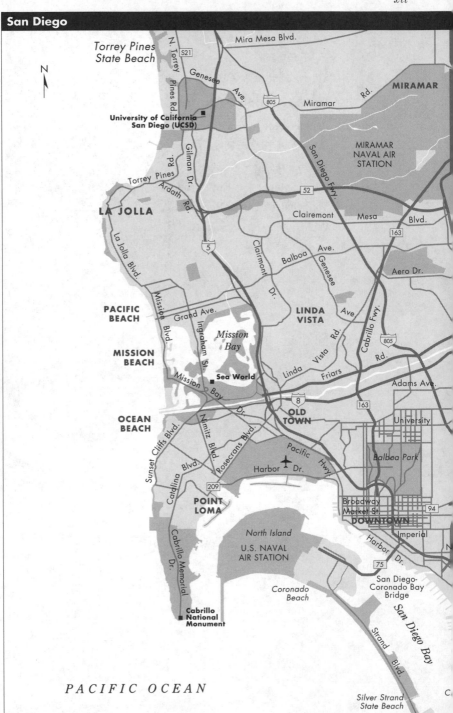

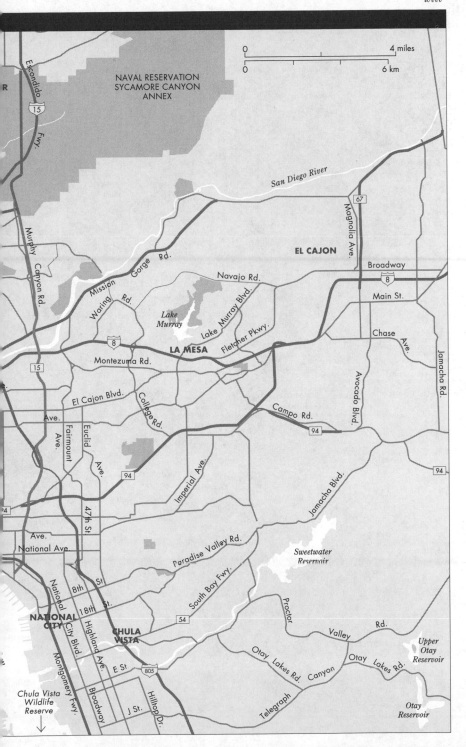

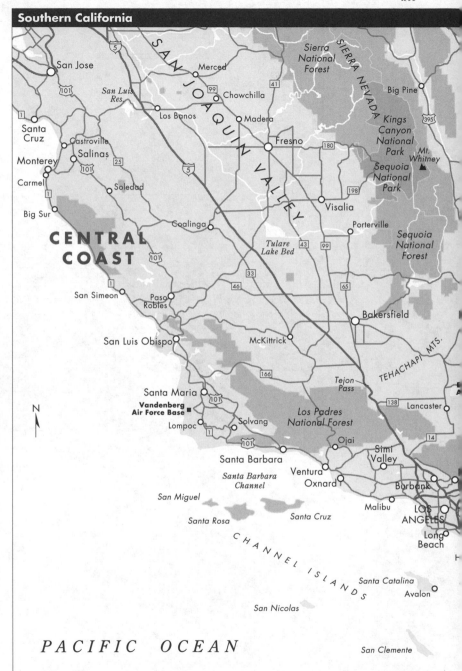

Southern California

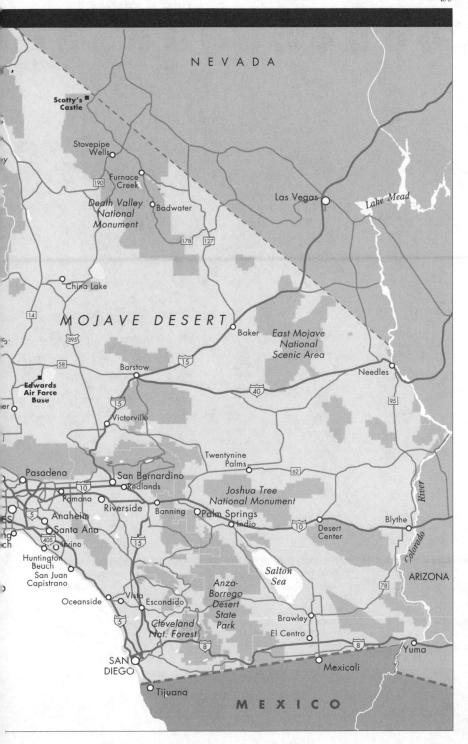

NEVADA

Scotty's
Castle

Stovepipe
Wells

Furnace
Creek

190

*Death Valley
National
Monument*

Badwater

Las Vegas

Lake Mead

178   127

China Lake

14

M O J A V E   D E S E R T

Baker

*East Mojave
National
Scenic Area*

395

58

Barstow

15

Needles

Edwards
Air Force
Base

15

Victorville

40

95

Twentynine
Palms

62

Pasadena

San Bernardino

Redlands

10

*Joshua Tree
National Monument*

Pomona

Riverside

Banning   Palm Springs

Anaheim

Santa Ana

Indio

10

Desert
Center

Blythe

405

Irvine

15

Huntington
Beach

San Juan
Capistrano

*Salton
Sea*

ARIZONA

78

Oceanside   Vista

Escondido

*Anza-
Borrego
Desert
State
Park*

Brawley

*Cleveland
Nat. Forest*

El Centro

8

8

Yuma

SAN
DIEGO

Mexicali

Tijuana

M E X I C O

Colorado River

World Time Zones

MONDAY
SUNDAY

International Date Line

+12 +13

-9

-4

-3

0

-1

25 0

-10

7

3

7

-5 -4

-3:30

4

-7

14 15

13

-11

8

-8

9

5

16

-10

6

10

17

2

12

11

18

-4

19

22

-5

-4 -3

20

23

-3

21 24

+11

+12

1

+11 +12 - -11 -10 -9 -8 -7 -6 -5 -4 -3 -2

Numbers below vertical bands relate each zone to Greenwich Mean Time (0 hrs.).
Local times frequently differ from these general indications,
as indicated by light-face numbers on map.

Algiers, **29**	Berlin, **34**	Delhi, **48**	Istanbul, **40**
Anchorage, **3**	Bogotá, **19**	Denver, **8**	Jerusalem, **42**
Athens, **41**	Budapest, **37**	Djakarta, **53**	Johannesburg, **44**
Auckland, **1**	Buenos Aires, **24**	Dublin, **26**	Lima, **20**
Baghdad, **46**	Caracas, **22**	Edmonton, **7**	Lisbon, **28**
Bangkok, **50**	Chicago, **9**	Hong Kong, **56**	London (Greenwich), **27**
Beijing, **54**	Copenhagen, **33**	Honolulu, **2**	Los Angeles, **6**
	Dallas, **10**		Madrid, **38**
			Manila, **57**

xvi

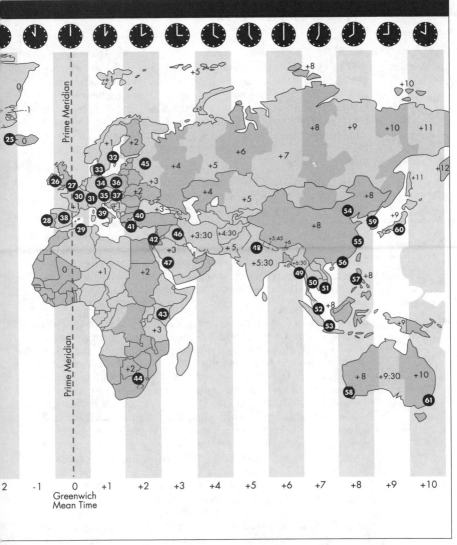

2 -1 0 +1 +2 +3 +4 +5 +6 +7 +8 +9 +10

Greenwich
Mean Time

Introduction

By Maribeth Mellin

A longtime resident of San Diego, travel writer and photographer Maribeth Mellin is a former senior editor at San Diego Magazine, the author of Fodor's Baja, and a contributor to several magazines and newspapers.

Each year, San Diego absorbs thousands of visitors who are drawn by the climate: sunny, dry, and warm nearly year-round. They swim, surf, and sunbathe on long beaches facing the turquoise Pacific, where whales, seals, and dolphins swim offshore. They tour oases of tropical palms, sheltered bays fringed by golden pampas grass, and far-ranging parklands blossoming with brilliant bougainvillea, jasmine, ice plant, and birds of paradise.

They run and bike and walk down wide streets and paths planned for recreation among the natives, who thrive on San Diego's varied health, fitness, and sports scenes. They drive by Mission Bay, a 4,600-acre aquatic park, where dozens of colorful, intricate kites fly above hundreds of picnickers lounging in the sun. They wander through the streets of downtown, where the fanciful Horton Plaza shopping center serves as a vibrant city center, with theaters, restaurants, and shops drawing crowds from nearby steel-and-glass office towers.

San Diego County is the nation's sixth largest—larger than nearly a dozen U.S. states—with a population of more than 2.5 million. It sprawls east from the Pacific Ocean through dense urban neighborhoods to outlying suburban communities that seem to sprout on canyons and cliffs overnight. Its eastern boundaries are the Cleveland National Forest, where the pines and manzanita are covered with snow in the winter, and the Anza-Borrego Desert, where delicate pink and yellow cactus blooms herald the coming of spring. San Diegans visit these vast wildernesses for their annual doses of seasonal splendors, then return to the city, where flowers bloom year-round and the streets are dry and clean. One of the busiest international borders in the United States marks the county's southern line, where approximately 60 million people a year legally cross between Mexico's Baja California peninsula and San Diego. To the north, the marines at Camp Pendleton practice land, sea, and air maneuvers in southern California's largest coastal greenbelt, marking the demarcation zone between the congestion of Orange and Los Angeles counties and the more relaxed expansiveness of San Diego.

The city of San Diego is the state's second largest, after Los Angeles. It serves as a base for the U.S. Navy's 11th Naval District and a port for ships from many nations. A considerable number of its residents were stationed here in the service and decided to stay put. Others either passed through on vacation or saw the city in movies and TV shows and became enamored of the city and its reputation as a prosperous Sunbelt playground. From its founding San Diego has attracted a steady stream of prospectors, drawn to the nation's farthest southwest frontier. Nearly 10,000 new residents arrive in San Diego each year.

Tourism is San Diego's third-largest industry, after manufacturing and the military. In the past few years, the San Diego Convention and Visitors Bureau and other local boosters have courted and won internationally important events that have brought uncalculated tourism benefits to the city. Worldwide media events, such as the America's Cup race, keep San Diego very visible as a vacation option.

The waterfront has assumed a completely new look and ambience since the 1990 opening of the 760,000-square-foot San Diego Convention Center at the foot of 5th Avenue, its saillike rooftop thrust before downtown's skyline. The convention center's completion spurred development of the area at an unprecedented rate, and the thousands of conventioneers who visit San Diego annually are boosting the downtown business climate and image as never before. Hotel development seems to have peaked after a spate of building on what seemed every patch of available land, but San Diego's politicians, business leaders, and developers have set the city's course toward a steadily increasing influx of visitors—which gives residents pleasant attractions as well as not-so-enjoyable distractions. With growth comes congestion, even in San Diego's vast expanse.

Fortunately, there are many reminders of the city's more peaceful times. In Old Town, San Diego's original city center, the courthouse, newspaper offices, and haciendas are historical adobe buildings covered with ancient twisted vines. The village of La Jolla, often compared with Monte Carlo, has retained its gentle charm despite continual development. And Balboa Park, the city's centerpiece, is a permanent testimonial to the Spanish architecture and natural ecology that give San Diego its unique character and charisma.

If San Diego sounds just a bit too laid-back and serene, consider its proximity to Mexico. Tijuana, a typically colorful and frenetic border town and an intrinsically foreign land, is only 30 minutes away. San Diegans think of Tijuana and all the Baja peninsula as their backyard playground.

During Prohibition, Americans drove down dusty, rutted roads to the spectacular gambling halls of Tijuana, Rosarito Beach, and Ensenada, where unbridled hedonism was not only tolerated but encouraged. Hollywood stars settled in for the duration, waiting out the dry days north of the border in lavish grandeur and investing their dollars in Mexican real estate. Some of Baja's grandest hotels were built during this era, when U.S. financiers recognized the value of the peninsula's rugged coastal wilderness.

Those pleasure palaces of the past have since crumbled, but Baja is undergoing a new surge of development now that the Mexican government has targeted the area as a premier tourist destination. The coastline from Tijuana through Rosarito Beach to Ensenada is rapidly being transformed from an isolated hideaway with a few resorts and vacation-home communities into a major holiday destination. Every month brings another elegant condominium and time-share development; new, full-scale RV parks have more amenities than most hotels; and there are enough restaurants, artisans' markets, and bars to keep the on-slaught of weekend travelers content. Tijuana's main Avenida Revolución continues to attract shoppers and those looking for the border city's wild side, but such cultural attractions as Mexitlan, the outdoor museum–entertainment center, are gaining in popularity as well.

Visiting Baja is easier than ever, thanks to the San Diego–Tijuana trolley, which runs from the Santa Fe Depot in downtown San Diego to the international border in San Ysidro. The trolley travels south through the suburbs of National City and Chula Vista, where giant shipyards and fish canneries have been replaced by fancy marinas. Near San Ysidro, the trackside billboards display Spanish ads for Tijuana's shopping centers, highlighting bargains in brand-name clothing from Ralph Lauren and Guess?. Still, for all its familiarity, Tijuana could never be mistaken for an American town. Therein lies its appeal.

If you prefer more organized attractions, San Diego has its share of theme parks and specialized museums. Sea World, on the shores of Mission Bay, highlights San Diego's proximity to the sea with spectacular aquariums, whale shows, shark exhibits, and penguin habitats. The San Diego Zoo, often called the country's finest zoological-botanical park, is a must-see attraction. The Wild Animal Park, 30 minutes east of downtown, preserves the natural wonders of San Diego's chaparral country while protecting endangered wildlife from around the world. Balboa Park, site of the 1915 Panama-California Exposition, houses not only the zoo but the city's finest museums in historical Spanish-Moorish palaces set amid lush lawns and rocky canyons.

San Diego has always been recognized as an environmental paradise. As the city grows, its cultural base expands to meet more sophisticated demands. Today San Diego retains its sense of a western frontier as it develops into a major cosmopolitan centerpiece for the nation. No wonder visitors from all over the world come for vacations and decide to stay for life.

1 Essential Information

Before You Go

Tourist Information

Write to the **San Diego Convention & Visitors Bureau** (401 B St., Suite 1400, San Diego 92101) for *The San Diego Official Visitors Guide,* which contains information on accommodations, restaurants, attractions, and special events, as well as maps.

The **Visitor Information Center** (2688 E. Mission Bay Dr., San Diego 92109, tel. 619/276–8200) can make your lodging reservations and publishes a newspaper, *Pathfinder* (enclose a self-addressed, stamped envelope when requesting a copy).

You can get information about other communities within San Diego County from the visitors bureaus or chambers of commerce, including those in **Borrego Springs** (622 Palm Canyon Dr., Box 66, 92004, tel. 619/767–5555), **Carlsbad** (Box 1246, 92018, tel. 619/434–6093), **Coronado** (1111 Orange Ave., Suite A, 92118, tel. 619/437–8788 or 800/622–8300), **Del Mar** (1104 Camino del Mar, 92014, tel. 619/755–4844), **San Diego North County Convention & Visitors Bureau** (720 N. Broadway, Escondido, 92025, tel. 619/745–4741 or 800/848–3336), **Julian** (2123 Main St., Box 413, 92036, tel. 619/765–1857), **La Jolla** (1055 Wall St., Box 1101, 92038, tel. 619/454–1444), and **Oceanside** (928 N. Hill St., 92054, tel. 619/722–1534 or 800/350–7873).

The **California Office of Tourism** (801 K St., Suite 1600, Sacramento, CA 95814, tel. 916/322–2881) can answer many questions about travel in the state. You can also order a visitors guide, which includes an informative section on San Diego (free; tel. 800/862–2543).

Tours and Packages

Should you buy your travel arrangements to San Diego packaged or do it yourself? There are advantages either way. Buying packaged arrangements saves you money, particularly if you can find a program that includes exactly the features you want. You also get a pretty good idea of what your trip will cost from the outset. You have two options: fully escorted tours and independent packages. Escorted tours mean having limited free time and traveling with strangers. Escorted tours are most often via motorcoach, with a tour director in charge. Your baggage is handled, your time rigorously scheduled, and most meals planned. Escorted tours are therefore the most hassle-free way to see a destination, as well as generally the least expensive. Independent packages allow plenty of flexibility. They generally include airline travel and hotels, with certain options available, such as sightseeing, car rental, and excursions. Independent packages are usually more expensive than escorted tours, but your time is your own.

While you can book directly through tour operators, you will pay no more to go through a travel agent, who will be able to tell you about tours and packages from a number of operators. Whatever program you ultimately choose, be sure to find out exactly what is included: taxes, tips, transfers, meals, baggage handling, ground transportation, entertainment, excursions, sports or recreation (and rental equipment, if necessary). Ask about the level of hotel used; its location; the size of its rooms; the kind of beds; and its amenities, such as pool, room service, or programs for children, if they're important to you. Find out the operator's cancellation penalties. Nearly everyone charges them, and the only way to avoid them is to buy trip-cancellation insurance (available from your travel agent). Also ask about the single supplement, a surcharge assessed to solo travelers. Some operators do not make you pay it if you agree to be matched up with a roommate of the same sex, even if one is not found by departure time. Remember that a program that has features you won't use may not be the most cost-wise choice.

Fully Escorted Tours Escorted tours are usually sold in three categories: deluxe, first-class, and tourist or budget class. The most important differences are the price and the level of accommodations. Some operators specialize in one category, while others offer a range. Most that include San Diego make it a one-day stop in a multidestination tour. Two deluxe tour operators are **Maupintour** (Box 807, Lawrence, KS 66044, tel. 913/843–1211 or 800/255–4266) and **Tauck Tours** (11 Wilton Rd., Westport, CT 06881, tel. 203/226–6911 or 800/468–2825). Among first-class operators are **Caravan** (401 N. Michigan Ave., Chicago, IL 60611, tel. 800/227–2862); **Collette Tours** (162 Middle St., Pawtucket, RI 02860, tel. 401/728–3805 or 800/832–4656); **Gadabout Tours** (700 E. Tahquitz Canyon Way, Palm Springs, CA 92262, tel. 619/325–5556 or 800/952–5068); and **Globus** (5301 S. Federal Circle, Littleton, CO 80123, tel. 303/797–2800 or 800/221–0090). More budget-minded are **Cosmos Tourama** (*see* Globus, *above*) and **Go America Tours** (733 3rd Ave., 7th floor, New York, NY 10017, tel. 212/370–5080). Others with a range of offerings include **Mayflower Tours** (1225 Warren Ave., Box 490, Downers Grove, IL 60515, tel. 708/960–3430 or 800/323–7604), **Parker Tours** (218–14 Northern Blvd., Bayside, NY 11361, tel. 718/428–7800 or 800/833–9600), **Trieloff Tours** (24301 El Toro Rd., Suite 140, Laguna Hills, CA 92653, tel. 800/248–6877 or 800/432–7125 in CA), **Talmage Tours** (1223 Walnut St., Philadelphia, PA 19178, tel. 215/923–7100 or 800/825–6243), and **Domenico Tours** (751 Broadway, Bayonne, NJ 07002, tel. 201/823–8687 or 800/554–8687).

Most itineraries are jam-packed with sightseeing, so you see a lot in a short amount of time (usually one place per day). To judge just how fast-paced the tour is, review the itinerary carefully. If you are in a different hotel each night, you will be getting up early each day to head out, travel to your next destination, do some sightseeing, have dinner, and go to bed; then you'll start all over again. If you want some free time, make sure it's mentioned in the tour brochure; if you want to be escorted to every meal, confirm that any tour you consider does that. Also, when comparing programs, be sure to find out if the motorcoach is air-conditioned and has a rest room on board. Make your selection based on price and stops on the itinerary.

Independent Packages Independent packages are offered by tour operators who may also do escorted programs (*see above*) and any number of other companies, from large, established firms to small, new entrepreneurs. In addition, most airlines that fly to San Diego offer packages that include accommodations, airfare, car rentals, and sometimes admission to the San Diego Zoo and Wild Animal Park. Consult **Alaska Airlines Vacations** (tel. 800/468–2248), **American Airlines Fly AAway Vacations** (tel. 800/321–2121), **America West Airlines' Vacation Planning Desk** (tel. 800/356–6611), **Delta Dream Vacations** (tel. 800/872–7786), **United Airlines' Vacation Planning Center** (tel. 800/328–6877), and **USAir Vacations** (tel. 800/428–4322). Also try **SuperCities** (139 Main St., Cambridge, MA 02142, tel. 617/621–0099 or 800/333–1234).

San Diego programs come in a wide range of prices based on levels of luxury and options—in addition to hotel and airfare, sightseeing, car rental, transfers, admission to local attractions, and other extras. Note that when pricing different packages, it sometimes pays to purchase the same arrangements separately, as when a rock-bottom promotional airfare is being offered, for example. Again, base your choice on what's available at your budget for the destinations you want to visit.

Special-
Interest
Travel
Adventure/
Nature

Oceanic Society Expeditions (Fort Mason Center, Bldg. E, San Francisco, CA 94124, tel. 415/441–1106 or 800/326–7491) has a Baja program that begins and ends in San Diego and includes snorkeling with sea lions, desert nature walks, and whale-watching boat trips. Naturalist-led nine-day trips from San Diego to Magdalena Bay in Baja, where the gray whales mate, are available from **Biological Journeys** (1696 Ocean Dr., McKinleyville, CA 95521, tel. 800/548–7555). **Eco Tour!** (San Diego North County Convention & Visitors Bureau, 720 N. Broadway, Escondido, CA 92025, tel. 619/745–4796 or 800/848–3336) combines familiar vacation elements with hands-on environmental activities. **Agua Caliente Band of Cahuilla Indians Reservation** (110 N. Indian Canyon Dr., Palm Springs, CA 92262, tel. 619/325–5673) has day-long excursions to three spectacular Indian canyons and trading posts.

Bicycling

Backroads (1516 5th St., Suite L101, Berkeley, CA 94710, tel. 510/527–1555 or 800/462–2848) has a weekend camping and mountain-biking trip in nearby Anza Borrego State Park. **Imagine Tours** (tel. 800/228–7041) arranges tours around the area. **Native Cycles** (70–053 Hwy. 111, Rancho Mirage, CA 92262, tel. 800/952–5068) specializes in custom excursions in the nearby desert.

Golf

Best Golf Tours (332 Forest Ave., Laguna Beach, CA 92651, tel. 714/752–8881 or 800/227–0212) and **Golf America, Inc.** (7514 Girard Ave., No. 243, La Jolla, CA 92037, tel. 800/435–5775 or 619/454–2026) have design-your-own golf packages in Palm Springs. **Golf Amtrak/Great American Vacations** (1220 Kensington, Oakbrook, IL 60521, tel. 800/872–7245 or 800/321–8684 in southern California) has several excursions.

Horseback
Riding

FITS Equestrian (685 Lateen Rd., Solvang, CA 93463, tel. 805/688–9494 or 800/666–3487) offers an eight-day, ride-all-you-want getaway at the Pavoreal Ranch, once owned by John Wayne.

Wine Tours

Burbury Wine Tour (2554 Lincoln Blvd., No. 525, Marina del Rey, CA 90291, tel. 310/208–0980) offers picnic wine tours to wineries in Temecula Valley.

Tips for British Travelers

Visitor
Information

Write or fax the **United States Travel and Tourism Administration** (Box 1EN, tel. 071/495–4466, fax 071/409–0566) for a free USA pack.

Passports
and Visas

You need a valid 10-year passport to enter the United States. A visa is not necessary unless (1) you are planning to stay more than 90 days; (2) your trip is for purposes other than vacation; (3) you have at some time been refused a visa, or refused admission to, the United States, or have been required to leave by the U.S. Immigration and Naturalization Service; or (4) you do not have a return or onward ticket. You will need to fill out the Visa Waiver Form, 1–94W, supplied by the airline.

To apply for a visa or for more information, call the U.S. Embassy's Visa Information Line (tel. 0891/200290; calls cost 48p per minute or 36p per minute cheap rate).

Customs British visitors age 21 or over may import the following into the United States: 200 cigarettes or 50 cigars or 2 kilograms of tobacco; one U.S. liter of alcohol; gifts to the value of $100. Restricted items include meat products, seeds, plants, and fruits. Never carry illegal drugs.

Returning to the United Kingdom, you may import duty-free 200 cigarettes, 100 cigarillos, 50 cigars or 250 grams of tobacco; 1 liter of spirits or 2 liters of fortified or sparkling wine; 2 liters of still table wine; 60 milliliters of perfume; 250 milliliters of toilet water; plus £36 worth of other goods, including gifts and souvenirs.

For further information or a copy of *A Guide for Travellers*, which details standard customs procedures as well as what you may bring into the United Kingdom from abroad, contact HM Customs and Excise (New King's Beam House, 22 Upper Ground, London SE1).

Insurance Most tour operators, travel agents, and insurance agents sell specialized policies covering accident, medical expenses, personal liability, trip cancellation, and loss or theft of personal property. Some policies include coverage for delayed departure and legal expenses, winter sports, accidents, or motoring abroad. You can also purchase an annual travel-insurance policy valid for every trip you make during the year in which it's purchased (usually only trips of less than 90 days). Before you leave, make sure you will be covered if you have a preexisting medical condition or are pregnant; your insurers may not pay for routine or continuing treatment or may require a note from your doctor certifying your fitness to travel.

The **Association of British Insurers,** a trade association representing 450 insurance companies, advises extra medical coverage for visitors to the United States.

For advice by phone or a free booklet, "Holiday Insurance," that sets out what to expect from a holiday-insurance policy and gives price guidelines, contact the Association of British Insurers (51 Gresham St., London EC2V 7HQ, tel. 071/600–3333; 30 Gordon St., Glasgow G1 3PU, tel. 041/226–3905; Scottish Provincial Bldg., Donegall Sq. W, Belfast BT1 6JE, tel. 0232/249176; call for other locations).

Tour Operators Tour operators offering packages to San Diego include **British Airways Holidays** (Atlantic House, Hazelwick Ave., Three Bridges, Crawley, West Sussex RH10 1NP, tel. 0293/611611), **Jetsave** (Sussex House, London Rd., East Grinstead, West Sussex RH19 1LD, tel. 0342/312033), **Key to America** (15 Feltham Rd., Ashford, Middlesex TW15 1DQ, tel. 0784/248777), **Kuoni Travel Ltd.** (Kuoni House, Dorking, Surrey RH5 4AZ, tel. 0306/76711), **Premier Holidays** (Premier Travel Center, Westbrook, Milton Rd., Cambridge CB4, 1YQ, tel. 0223/355977), and **Trailfinders** 194 Kensington High St., London W8 7RG, tel. 071/937–5400; 58 Deansgate, Manchester, M3 2FF, tel. 061/839–6969).

Airfares Fares vary enormously. Fares from consolidators are usually the cheapest, followed by promotional fares, such as APEX (advance purchase excursion). A few phone calls should reveal the current picture. When comparing fares, don't forget to figure airport taxes and weekend supplements. Once you know which airline is going your way at the right time for the least money, book immediately, since seats at the lowest prices often sell out quickly. Travel agents will generally hold a reservation for up to five days, especially if you give a credit-card number.

Some travel agencies that offer cheap fares to San Diego include **Trailfinders** (42–50 Earl's Court Rd., London W8 6EJ, tel. 071/937–5400), specialists in round-the-world fares and independent travel; **Travel Cuts** (295a Regent St., London W1R 7YA, tel. 071/637–3161), the Canadian Students' travel service; **Flightfile** (49 Tottenham Court Rd., London W1P 9RE, tel. 071/700-2722), a flight-only agency.

Flying as an on-board courier to San Diego is a possibility. Contact **Courier Travel Services** (346 Fulham Rd., London SW10 9UH, tel. 071/351–0300) for details.

Car Rental Make the arrangements from home to avoid inconvenience, save money, and guarantee yourself a vehicle. Major firms include **Alamo** (tel. 0800/272200), **Budget** (tel. 0800/181181), **EuroDollar** (tel. 0895/233300), **Europcar** (tel. 081/950–5050), and **Hertz** (tel. 081/679–1799).

In the United States, you must be 21 to rent a car; rates may be higher for those under 25. Extra costs cover child seats, compulsory for children under 5 (about $3 per day); additional drivers (around $1.50 per day); and the all-but-compulsory collision damage waiver (*see* Car Rentals, *below*). To pick up your reserved car, you will need the reservation voucher, a passport, a United Kingdom driver's license, and a travel insurance policy covering each driver.

Travelers with Disabilities Main information sources include the **Royal Association for Disability and Rehabilitation** (RADAR, 25 Mortimer St., London W1N 8AB, tel. 071/637–5400), which publishes travel information for people with disabilities in Britain, and **Mobility International** (228 Borough High St., London SE1 1JX, tel. 071/403–5688), the headquarters of an international membership organization that serves as a clearinghouse of travel information for people with disabilities.

When to Go

For the most part, any time of the year is the right time for a trip to San Diego. The climate is generally close to perfect. Typical days are sunny and mild, with low humidity—ideal for sightseeing and for almost any sport that does not require snow and ice. The annual high temperature averages 70° Fahrenheit and the low 55°, and the annual rainfall is usually less than 10 inches. Most of the rain occurs in January and February, but precipitation usually lasts for only part of the day or for a day or two at most. The rainfall during the winters of 1992 and 1993, which dampened the spirits of visitors but ended a five-year drought, was uncharacteristic.

From mid-December through mid-March, gray whales can be seen migrating along the coast. And in early spring, wildflowers transform the desert into a rainbow of colors.

Climate The following are average maximum and minimum temperatures for San Diego.

Jan.	62F	17C	May	66F	19C	Sept.	73F	23C
	46	8		55	13		62	17
Feb.	62F	17C	June	69F	21C	Oct.	71F	22C
	48	9		59	15		57	14
Mar.	64F	18C	July	73F	23C	Nov.	69F	21C
	50	10		62	17		51	11
Apr.	66F	19C	Aug.	73F	23C	Dec.	64F	18C
	53	12		64	18		48	9

Information For current weather conditions and forecasts for cities in the United
Sources States and abroad, plus the local time and helpful travel tips, call
the **Weather Channel Connection** (tel. 900/932–8437; 95¢ per
minute) from a touch-tone phone.

Festivals and Seasonal Events

February The **Buick Invitational Golf Tournament** (tel. 800/888–2842) attracts more than 100,000 people, including local and national celebrities, to the Torrey Pines Golf Course.

March The **Ocean Beach Kite Festival** (tel. 619/531–1527) is an annual kite-
decorating and -flying contest for all ages at Ocean Beach.

April The **San Diego Crew Classic** (tel. 619/488–0700) brings together
more than 2,000 athletes on college teams from across the United
States for a rowing competition at Crown Point in Mission Bay. The
Downtown ArtWalk (tel. 619/260–1313), an annual open house for
downtown's art galleries, has become a weekend-long festival in the
G Street neighborhood.

May The **Cinco de Mayo Festival** (tel. 619/299–6055) brings lively entertainment and booths to town for this yearly Mexican celebration in
Old Town State Park and the Bazaar del Mundo. The **Del Mar National Horse Show,** at the Del Mar Fairground (tel. 619/792–4288),
provides the occasion for thousands of show horses to compete. The
Pacific Beach Block Party (tel. 619/272–7282) is an annual street fair
with live music, food stands, and games.

June The **Indian Fair** (tel. 619/239–2001) attracts Native Americans from
throughout the southwest for arts, crafts, ethnic foods, and dances
at the Museum of Man in Balboa Park. The **San Diego County Fair
at Del Mar** (tel. 619/755–1161) is a classic county fair, with flower
and garden shows, a carnival, displays, and livestock shows.

July The **Old Globe Festival** (tel. 619/239–2255), which runs from July
until September, features works of Shakespeare in repertory with
other classic and contemporary plays at the Old Globe Theatre in
Balboa Park. The **Over-the-Line Tournament** (tel. 619/688–0817) is
a rowdy party that takes place over two weekends, with more than
1,000 three-person teams competing in a sport that's a cross between softball and stickball, on Fiesta Island in Mission Bay. **Sand
Castle Days** (tel. 619/424–6663), at Imperial Beach Pier, brings sand
sculptors of all ages together for one of the largest sand-castle
events in the United States.

August **America's Finest City Week** (tel. 619/542–0324) gives San Diegans a
chance to proclaim their pride with a half-marathon, parades, and
concerts. **Las Californias/Tijuana Fair** (tel. 619/298–4105 or 66/84-
05–37 in Tijuana), a south-of-the-border festival, features Mexican
arts and crafts, food booths, and lively music and dancing.

September **Street Scene** (tel. 619/557–8490) transforms the historic Gaslamp
Quarter into a rollicking two-day music festival, with 10 stages
showcasing more than 60 bands from around the world. The **Texaco
Star Mart Cup** (tel. 619/268–1250) unlimited hydroplane races draw
thunderboat enthusiasts to Mission Bay.

October **Zoo Founders Day** (tel. 619/231–1515) means that everyone has free
admission to the world-famous San Diego Zoo.

November The **Dixieland Jazz Festival** (tel. 619/297–5277) presents a weekend
filled with performances by well-known bands at the Town & Coun-
try Hotel. El Cajon's **Mother Goose Parade** (tel. 619/444–8712) is a

two-hour, nationally televised spectacular with 200 floats, bands, horses, and clowns.

December **Christmas on El Prado** (tel. 619/239–0512) is sponsored by the museums in Balboa Park. Attractions include carolers and a candlelight procession, and admission is free to all the museums. **San Diego Harbor Parade of Lights** (tel. 619/236–1212) brings colorfully lit boats through the downtown harbor.

What to Pack

Clothing San Diego's casual lifestyle and year-round mild climate set the parameters for what you'll want to pack. You can leave formal clothes and cold-weather gear behind.

Plan on warm weather at any time of the year. Cottons, walking shorts, jeans, and T-shirts are the norm at tourist attractions. Pack bathing suits and shorts regardless of the season. Casual attire is generally acceptable; only a few restaurants require a jacket and tie for men. Women may want to bring something a little dressier than their sightseeing garb.

Evenings are cool, even in summer, so be sure to bring a sweater or a light jacket. Rainfall in San Diego is not usually heavy; you won't need a raincoat except during the winter months, and even then, an umbrella may be sufficient protection. Be sure you take proved, comfortable walking shoes with you. Even if you don't walk much at home, you'll find yourself covering miles while sightseeing on your vacation.

It's always important to pack light; porters and luggage trolleys may be hard to find. Don't take more luggage than you can handle comfortably yourself.

Miscellaneous While it is true that you can buy film, sunscreen lotion, aspirin, and most other necessities almost anywhere in San Diego, it's a nuisance to have to search for staples. Take along a reasonable supply of things you know you'll be using routinely.

Sunglasses are a must in San Diego. Also remember that binoculars can be a pleasure on a trip, especially if you're in town during whale-watching season; tuck in a small pair. Bring an extra pair of eyeglasses or contact lenses in your carry-on luggage. If you have a health problem that requires a prescription drug, pack enough to last the duration of the trip—but *not* in luggage that you plan to check; your bags might go astray. Pack a list of the offices that supply refunds for lost or stolen traveler's checks.

Luggage **Regulations** Free airline baggage allowances depend on the airline, the route, and the class of your ticket; ask in advance. In general, on domestic flights you are entitled to check two bags—neither exceeding 62 inches, or 158 centimeters (length + width + height), or weighing more than 70 pounds (32 kilograms). A third piece may be brought aboard; its total dimensions are generally limited to less than 45 inches (114 centimeters), so it will fit easily under the seat in front of you or in the overhead compartment. In the United States the Federal Aviation Administration (FAA) gives airlines broad latitude for carry-on allowances and tailors limits to different aircraft and operational conditions. Charges for excess, oversize, or overweight pieces vary.

Safeguarding *Your Luggage* Before leaving home, itemize your bags' contents and their worth in case they go astray. To minimize that risk, tag them inside and out with your name, address, and phone number. (If you use your home address, cover it so that potential thieves can't see it.) Put a copy of your itinerary inside each bag, so that you can be tracked easily. At check-in, make sure that the tag attached by baggage handlers bears the correct three-letter code for your destination. If your bags do not arrive with you or if you detect damage, immediately file a written report with the airline before you leave the airport.

Insurance   In the event of loss, damage, or theft on domestic flights, airlines' liability is $1,250 per passenger, excluding valuable items such as jewelry, cameras, and others that are listed in the fine print on your ticket. Excess-valuation insurance can be bought directly from the airline at check-in. Your homeowner's policy may fill the gap; or firms such as **The Travelers Companies** (1 Tower Sq., Hartford, CT 06183, tel. 203/277–0111 or 800/243–3174) and **Wallach and Company** (107 W. Federal St., Box 480, Middleburg, VA 22117, tel. 703/687–3166 or 800/237–6615) sell baggage insurance.

Getting Money from Home

Many automated-teller machines (ATMs) are tied to international networks such as **Cirrus** and **Plus.** You can use your bank card at ATMs to withdraw money from an account and get cash advances on a credit-card account if your card has been programmed with a personal identification number, or PIN. Check in advance on limits on withdrawals and cash advances within specified periods. On cash advances you are charged interest from the day you receive the money from ATMs as well as from tellers. Transaction fees for ATM withdrawals outside your home turf may be higher than those for withdrawals at home.

For specific Cirrus locations in the United States and Canada, call 800/424–7787. For U.S. Plus locations, call 800/843–7587 and press the area code and first three digits of the number you're calling from (or of the calling area where you want an ATM).

Wiring Money   You don't have to be a cardholder to send or receive a **MoneyGram from American Express** for up to $10,000. Go to a MoneyGram agent in retail and convenience stores and American Express travel offices, and pay up to $1,000 with a credit card and anything over that in cash. You are allowed a free long-distance call to give the transaction code to your intended recipient, who needs only to present identification and the reference number to the nearest MoneyGram agent to pick up the cash. MoneyGram agents are in more than 70 countries (call 800/926–9400 for locations). Fees range from 3% to 10%, depending on the amount and your method of payment.

You can also use **Western Union.** To wire money, take either cash or a cashier's check to the nearest office or call and use MasterCard or Visa. Money sent from the United States or Canada will be available for pickup at agent locations in 78 countries within minutes. Once the money is in the system it can be picked up at *any* of 22,000 locations (call 800/325–6000 for the one nearest you).

Traveling with Cameras, Camcorders, and Laptops

Film and Cameras   If your camera is new or if you haven't used it for a while, shoot and develop a few test rolls of film before you leave home. Store film in a cool, dry place—never in a car's glove compartment or on the shelf under its rear window.

Airport security X-rays generally aren't harmful to film with ISO below 400. To protect your film, carry it with you in a clear plastic bag and ask for a hand inspection. Such requests are honored at U.S. airports. Don't depend on a lead-lined bag to protect film in checked luggage—the airline may increase the radiation to see what's inside.

Camcorders Before your trip, put camcorders through their paces, invest in a skylight filter to protect the lens, and check all the batteries.

Videotape Videotape is not damaged by X-rays, but it may be harmed by the magnetic field of a walk-through metal detector, so ask for a hand-check. Airport security personnel may ask you to turn on the camcorder to prove that it's what it appears to be, so make sure the battery is charged.

Laptops Security X-rays do not harm hard-disk or floppy-disk storage, but you may request a hand-check, at which point you may be asked to turn on the computer to prove that it is what it appears to be. (Check your battery before departure.) Most airlines allow you to use your laptop aloft except during takeoff and landing (so as not to interfere with navigational equipment).

Traveling with Children

Publications
Local Guides *San Diego Family Press,* a monthly magazine for parents, is filled with listings of events and resources; it is available by mail (Box 23960, San Diego 92193, tel. 619/685–6970) for $2.50, which covers postage and handling, or free in San Diego at Longs drugstores, Boney's grocery stores, and local libraries. *Places to Go with Children in Southern California,* by Stephanie Kegan ($9.95; Chronicle Books, 275 5th St., San Francisco, CA 94103, tel. 415/777–7240), gives you suggestions for traveling with kids in this area.

Newsletter *Family Travel Times,* published 10 times a year by **Travel With Your Children** (TWYCH, 45 W. 18th St., 7th Floor Tower, New York, NY 10011, tel. 212/206–0688; annual subscription $55), covers destinations, types of vacations, and modes of travel. TWYCH also publishes *Cruising with Children* and *Skiing with Children.*

Books *Great Vacations with Your Kids,* by Dorothy Jordan and Marjorie Cohen ($13; Penguin USA, 120 Woodbine St., Bergenfield, NJ 07621, tel. 800/253–6476), and *Traveling with Children—And Enjoying It,* by Arlene K. Butler ($11.95 plus $3 shipping per book; Globe Pequot Press, 6 Business Park Rd., Box 833, Old Saybrook, CT 06475, tel. 800/243–0495 or 800/962–0973 in CT), help you plan your trip with children, from toddlers to teens. From the same publisher are *Recommended Family Resorts in the United States, Canada, and the Caribbean,* by Jane Wilford with Janet Tice ($12.95), and *Recommended Family Inns of America* ($12.95).

Tour Operators **Grandtravel** (6900 Wisconsin Ave., Suite 706, Chevy Chase, MD 20815, tel. 301/986–0790 or 800/247–7651) offers international and domestic tours for people traveling with their grandchildren. The catalogue, as charmingly written and illustrated as a children's book, positively invites armchair traveling with lap-sitters aboard. **Rascals in Paradise** (650 5th St., Suite 505, San Francisco, CA 94107, tel. 415/978–9800 or 800/872–7225) specializes in adventurous, exotic, and fun-filled vacations for families to carefully screened resorts and hotels around the world.

Getting There *Airfares*	On domestic flights, children under 2 not occupying a seat travel free, and older children currently travel on the "lowest applicable" adult fare.

Baggage The adult baggage allowance applies for children paying half or more of the adult fare.

Safety Seats The FAA recommends the use of safety seats aloft and details approved models in the free leaflet "**Child/Infant Safety Seats Recommended for Use in Aircraft**" (available from the Federal Aviation Administration, APA–200, 800 Independence Ave. SW, Washington, DC 20591, tel. 202/267–3479; Information Hotline, tel. 800/322–7873). Airline policy varies. U.S. carriers allow FAA-approved models bearing a sticker declaring their FAA approval. Because these seats are strapped into regular passenger seats, airlines may require that a ticket be bought for an infant who would otherwise ride free.

Facilities Aloft Some airlines provide other services for children, such as children's meals and freestanding bassinets (only to those with seats at the bulkhead, where there's enough legroom). Make your request when reserving. The annual February/March issue of *Family Travel Times* details children's services on dozens of airlines ($10; *see above*). "Kids and Teens in Flight" (free from the U.S. Department of Transportation's Office of Consumer Affairs, R-25, Washington, DC 20590, tel. 202/366–2220) offers tips for children flying alone.

Hints for Travelers with Disabilities

Wheelchair accessibility of attractions in San Diego varies. At the **San Diego Zoo** (tel. 619/231–1515), some enclosures are accessible; others are dangerous for wheelchairs because there are steep hills. The **San Diego Wild Animal Park** (tel. 619/480–0100) in Escondido is almost completely accessible. Careful advance planning will eliminate most unpleasant surprises.

Local Information The **Access Center of San Diego** (Information and Referrals, 1295 University Ave., Suite 10, San Diego 92103, tel. 619/293–3500, TDD 619/293–7757) publishes lists of hotels, motels, and restaurants with access for the disabled. **Accessible San Diego** (2466 Bartell St., San Diego 92123, tel. 619/279–0704) has a visitor information center and telephone hot line, makes hotel referrals, and provides guides to San Diego's attractions for visitors with mobility problems.

Organizations Several organizations provide travel information for people with disabilities, usually for a membership fee, and some publish newsletters and bulletins. Among them are the **Information Center for Individuals with Disabilities** (Fort Point Pl., 27–43 Wormwood St., Boston, MA 02210, tel. 617/727–5540 or 800/462–5015 in MA between 11 and 4, or leave message; TTY 617/345–9743); **Mobility International USA** (Box 10767, Eugene, OR 97440, tel. and TTY 503/343–1284, fax 503/343–6812), the U.S. branch of an international organization based in Britain (*see below*) that has affiliates in 30 countries; **MossRehab Hospital Travel Information Service** (tel. 215/456–9603, TTY 215/456–9602); the **Travel Industry and Disabled Exchange** (TIDE, 5435 Donna Ave., Tarzana, CA 91356, tel. 818/344–3640, fax 818/344–0078); and **Travelin' Talk** (Box 3534, Clarksville, TN 37043, tel. 615/552–6670, fax 615/552–1182).

In the United Kingdom Important information sources include the **Royal Association for Disability and Rehabilitation** (RADAR, 25 Mortimer St., London W1N 8AB, tel. 071/637–5400), which publishes travel information for people with disabilities in Britain, and **Mobility International**

(228 Borough High St., London SE1 1JX, tel. 071/403–5688), an international clearinghouse of travel information for people with disabilities.

Travel Agencies and Tour Operators
Flying Wheels Travel (143 W. Bridge St., Box 382, Owatonna, MN 55060, tel. 507/451–5005 or 800/535–6790) is a travel agency specializing in domestic and worldwide cruises, tours, and independent travel itineraries for people with mobility problems. Adventurers should contact **Wilderness Inquiry** (1313 5th St. SE, Minneapolis, MN 55414, tel. and TTY 612/379–3838), which orchestrates action-packed trips such as white-water rafting, sea kayaking, and dog sledding for people with disabilities. Tours are designed to bring together people who have disabilities and those who don't.

Publications
Two free publications are available from the U.S. Consumer Information Center (Pueblo, CO 81009): "New Horizons for the Air Traveler with a Disability" (include Dept. 608Y in the address), a U.S. Department of Transportation booklet describing changes resulting from the 1986 Air Carrier Access Act and from the 1990 Americans with Disabilities Act, and the Airport Operators Council's *Access Travel: Airports* (Dept. 5804), which describes facilities and services for people with disabilities at more than 500 airports worldwide.

Travelin' Talk Directory (*see* Organizations, *above*) was published in 1993. This 500-page resource book ($35 check or money order with a money-back guarantee) is packed with information for travelers with disabilities. **Twin Peaks Press** (Box 129, Vancouver, WA 98666, tel. 206/694–2462 or 800/637–2256) publishes the *Directory of Travel Agencies for the Disabled* ($19.95), listing more than 370 agencies worldwide, and *Wheelchair Vagabond* ($14.95), a collection of personal travel tips. Add $2 per book for shipping. **The Sierra Club** publishes *Easy Access to National Parks* ($16 plus $3 shipping; 730 Polk St., San Francisco, CA 94109, tel. 415/776–2211). Fodor's publishes *Great American Vacations for Travelers with Disabilities*, detailing services and accessible attractions, restaurants, and hotels in San Diego and other U.S. destinations (available in bookstores, or call 800/533–6478).

Getting Around
About one-third of the bus lines are served by buses with elevator ramps. The **San Diego Trolley** (tel. 619/231–3004), which goes as far as the Mexican border, has lifts for wheelchairs. Round-the-clock wheelchair transportation throughout San Diego is available through **Self-Reliance Shuttle** (Box 90458, San Diego 92169, tel. 619/272–4117).

Hints for Older Travelers

Many discounts are available to older travelers: Meals, lodging, entry to various attractions, car rentals, tickets for buses and trains, and campsites are among the prime examples. Some discounts are given solely on the basis of age, without membership requirement; others require membership in an organization. In California, the state park system, which includes more than 200 locations, provides a $2 discount on campsites for anyone 62 or over and others in the same private vehicle; ask for this discount when you make reservations.

If you are 50 or older, ask about senior discounts even if there is no posted notice. A 10% cut on a bus ticket and $2 off a pizza may not seem like major savings, but they add up, and you can cut the cost of a trip appreciably if you remember to take advantage of these options.

Organizations   The **American Association of Retired Persons** (AARP, 601 E St. NW, Washington, DC 20049, tel. 202/434–2277) provides independent travelers who are members of the AARP (open to those age 50 or older; $8 per person or couple annually) with the Purchase Privilege Program, which offers discounts on lodging, car rentals, and sightseeing, and the AARP Motoring Plan, which furnishes domestic trip-routing information and emergency road-service aid for an annual fee of $39.95 per person or couple ($59.95 for a premium version). AARP also arranges group tours, cruises, and apartment living through AARP Travel Experience from American Express (400 Pinnacle Way, Suite 450, Norcross, GA 30071, tel. 800/927–0111 or 800/745–4567).

Two other organizations offer discounts on lodgings, car rentals, and other travel products, along with such nontravel perks as magazines and newsletters: the **National Council of Senior Citizens** (1331 F St. NW, Washington, DC 20004, tel. 202/347–8800; membership $12 annually) and **Mature Outlook** (6001 N. Clark St., Chicago, IL 60660, tel. 800/336–6330; $9.95 annually).

Note: For reduced rates, mention your senior-citizen identification card when booking hotel reservations, not when checking out. At restaurants, show your card before you're seated; discounts may be limited to certain menus, days, or hours. If you are renting a car, ask about promotional rates that might improve on your senior-citizen discount.

Educational Travel   The nonprofit **Elderhostel** (75 Federal St., 3rd floor, Boston, MA 02110, tel. 617/426–7788) has offered inexpensive study programs for people 60 and older since 1975. Held at more than 1,800 educational institutions, courses cover everything from marine science to Greek myths and cowboy poetry. Participants usually attend lectures in the morning and spend the afternoon sightseeing or on field trips; they live in dorms on the host campuses. Fees for programs in the United States and Canada, which usually last one week, run about $300, not including transportation.

Tour Operators   The following tour operators specialize in older travelers: If you want to take your grandchildren, look into **Grandtravel** (*see* Traveling with Children, *above*); **Saga International Holidays** (222 Berkeley St., Boston, MA 02116, tel. 800/343–0273) caters to those over age 60 who like to travel in groups. **SeniorTours** (508 Irvington Rd., Drexel Hill, PA 19026, tel. 215/626–1977 or 800/227–1100) arranges motorcoach tours throughout the United States and Nova Scotia, as well as Caribbean cruises.

Publications   *The 50+ Traveler's Guidebook: Where to Go, Where to Stay, What to Do* by Anita Williams and Merrimac Dillon ($12.95; St. Martin's Press, 175 5th Ave., New York, NY 10010) is available in bookstores and offers many useful tips. "The Mature Traveler" (Box 50820, Reno, NV 89513, tel. 702/786–7419; $29.95 annually), a monthly newsletter, contains many travel deals.

Hints for Gay and Lesbian Travelers

The gay-and-lesbian scene in San Diego is concentrated in Hillcrest, an artsy neighborhood just north of downtown where you'll find the **Gay Center for Social Services** (3916 Normal St., tel. 619/692–4297). This is the place to pick up copies of *Update, Gay and Lesbian Times,* and *Bravo*, the city's main gay publications, as well as a map listing all the gay and lesbian bars and restaurants in the area.

Organizations The **International Gay Travel Association** (Box 4974, Key West, FL 33041, tel. 800/448–8550), which has 700 members, will provide you with names of travel agents and tour operators that specialize in gay travel. The **Gay & Lesbian Visitors Center of New York Inc.** (135 W. 20th St., 3rd floor, New York, NY 10011, tel. 212/463–9030 or 800/395–2315; $100 annually) mails a monthly newsletter, valuable coupons, and more to its members.

Travel Agencies and Tour Operators The dominant travel agency in the market is **Above and Beyond** (3568 Sacramento St., San Francisco, CA 94118, tel. 415/922–2683 or 800/397–2681). Tour operator **Olympus Vacations** (8424 Santa Monica Blvd., No. 721, West Hollywood, CA 90069, tel. 310/657–2220) offers gay and lesbian resort holidays. **Skylink Women's Travel** (746 Ashland Ave., Santa Monica, CA 90405, tel. 310/452–0506 or 800/225–5759) handles individual travel for lesbians all over the world and conducts two international and five domestic group trips annually.

Publications The premiere international travel magazine for gays and lesbians is **Our World** (1104 N. Nova Rd., Suite 251, Daytona Beach, FL 32117, tel. 904/441–5367; $35 for 10 issues). **Out & About** (tel. 203/789–8518 or 800/929–2268; $49 for 10 issues, full refund if you aren't satisfied) is a 16-page monthly newsletter with extensive information on resorts, hotels, and airlines that are gay-friendly.

Further Reading

There is no better way to establish the mood for your visit to Old Town San Diego than by reading Helen Hunt Jackson's 105-year-old romantic novel, *Ramona*, a best-seller for more than 50 years and still readily available. The Casa de Estudillo in Old Town has been known for many years as Ramona's Marriage Place because of its close resemblance to the house described in the novel. Richard Henry Dana, Jr.'s *Two Years Before the Mast* (1869), based on the author's experiences as a merchant sailor, provides a masculine perspective on early San Diego history.

Other novels with a San Diego setting include Raymond Chandler's mystery about the waterfront, *Playback*; Wade Miller's mystery, *On Easy Street*; Eric Higgs's gothic thriller, *A Happy Man*; Tom Wolfe's satire of the La Jolla surfing scene, *The Pump House Gang*; and David Zielinski's modern-day story, *A Genuine Monster.*

Arriving and Departing

From North America by Plane

Flights are either nonstop, direct, or connecting. A **nonstop** flight requires no change of plane and makes no stops. A **direct** flight stops at least once and can involve a change of plane, although the flight number remains the same; if the first leg is late, the second waits. This is not the case with a **connecting** flight, which involves a different plane and a different flight number.

Airlines Lindbergh Field (tel. 619/231–2100), just 3 miles northwest of downtown, has regular service to and from many U.S. and Mexican cities via most major and regional carriers, including **Aeromexico** (tel. 800/237–6639), **Alaska Airlines** (tel. 800/426–0333), **America West**

(tel. 800/247–5692), **American** (tel. 800/433–7300), **Arizona Airways** (tel. 800/274–0662), **Continental** (tel. 800/525–0280), **Delta** (tel. 800/221–1212), **Mark Air** (tel. 800/627–5247), **Midwest Express** (tel. 800/452–2022), **Morris Air** (tel. 800/444–5660), **Northwest** (tel. 800/225–2525), **Reno Air** (tel. 800/736–6247), **Sky West** (tel. 800/453–9417), **Southwest** (tel. 800/435–9792), **Trans World Airlines** (tel. 800/221–2000), **United** (tel. 800/241–6522), and **USAir** (tel. 800/428–4322).

Cutting Costs The Sunday travel section of most newspapers is a good source of deals. When booking, particularly through an unfamiliar company, call the Better Business Bureau and your local or state Consumer Protection Bureau to find out whether any complaints have been registered against the company, pay with a credit card if you can, and consider trip-cancellation and default insurance.

Promotional Less expensive fares, called promotional or discount fares, are
Airfares round-trip and involve restrictions, which vary according to the route and season. You must usually buy the ticket in advance (7, 14, or 21 days are usual), although some of the major airlines have added no-frills, cheap flights to compete with new bargain airlines on certain routes.

With the major airlines, the cheaper fares generally require minimum- and maximum-stays (for instance, over a Saturday night or at least seven and no more than 30 days). Airlines generally allow some return-date changes for a $25–$50 fee, but most low-fare tickets are nonrefundable. Only a death in the family would prompt the airline to return any of your money if you chose to cancel a nonrefundable ticket. However, you can apply an unused nonrefundable ticket toward a new ticket, again with a small fee. The lowest fare is subject to availability, and only a small percentage of the plane's total seats will be sold at that price. Contact the **U.S. Department of Transportation's Office of Consumer Affairs** (I–25, Washington, DC 20590, tel. 202/366–2220) for a copy of "Fly-Rights: A Guide to Air Travel in the U.S." *The Official Frequent Flyer Guidebook* by Randy Petersen (4715-C Town Center Dr., Colorado Springs, CO 80916, tel. 719/597–8899, 800/487–8893, or 800/485–8893; $14.99, plus $3 shipping and handling) yields valuable hints on getting the most for your air-travel dollars.

Consolidators Consolidators or bulk-fare operators—"bucket shops"—buy blocks of seats on scheduled flights that airlines anticipate they won't be able to sell. They pay wholesale prices, add a markup, and resell the seats to travel agents or directly to the public at prices that still undercut the airline's promotional or discount fares. Moreover, some consolidators sometimes give you your money back. Carefully read the fine print detailing penalties for changes and cancellations. If you doubt the reliability of a company, call the airline once you've made your booking and confirm that you do indeed have a reservation on the flight.

Discount Travel clubs offer members unsold space on airplanes, cruise ships,
Travel Clubs and package tours at as much as 50% below regular prices. Membership may include a regular bulletin or access to a toll-free hot line giving details of available trips departing from three or four days to several months in the future. Most also offer 50% discounts off hotel rack rates, but double-check with the hotel to make sure it isn't offering a better promotional rate independent of the club. Clubs include **Discount Travel International** (114 Forrest Ave., Suite 203, Narberth, PA 19072, tel. 215/668–7184; $45 annually, single or family), **Entertainment Travel Editions** (Box 1014, Trumbull, CT

06611, tel. 800/445–4137; $28–$48), **Great American Traveler** (Box 27965, Salt Lake City, UT 84127, tel. 800/548–2812; $29.95 annually), **Moment's Notice Discount Travel Club** (425 Madison Ave., New York, NY 10017, tel. 212/486–0503; $45 annually, single or family), **Privilege Card** (3391 Peachtree Rd. NE, Suite 110, Atlanta, GA 30326, tel. 404/262–0222 or 800/236–9732; domestic annual membership $49.95, international $74.95), **Travelers Advantage** (CUC Travel Service, 49 Music Sq. W, Nashville, TN 37203, tel. 800/548–1116; $49 annually, single or family), and **Worldwide Discount Travel Club** (1674 Meridian Ave., Miami Beach, FL 33139, tel. 305/534–2082; $50 annually for family, $40 single).

Publications The newsletter "Travel Smart" (40 Beechdale Rd., Dobbs Ferry, NY 10522, tel. 800/327–3633; $44 annually) has a wealth of travel deals in each monthly issue.

Smoking Since February 1990, smoking has been banned on all domestic flights of less than six hours' duration; the ban also applies to domestic segments of international flights aboard U.S. and foreign carriers.

Between the Airport and Center City **San Diego Transit** Route 2 buses leave every 10 to 15 minutes Monday through Friday and every 15 to 20 minutes Saturday and Sunday, from the front of East Terminal's USAir section; the first bus leaves at 5:26 AM and the last at 1:11 AM during the week. The buses go along Broadway, downtown. The fare is $1.50 per person, 75¢ for senior citizens. Taxi fare is $6–$8 plus tip to most center-city hotels. **Super Shuttle** (tel. 619/278–8877 or 800/974–8885 in San Diego) and **Public Shuttle** (tel. 619/990–8770) will take you directly to your destination, often for less than a cab would cost. Numerous hotels and motels offer their guests complimentary transportation. If you have rented a car at the airport, you can take Harbor Drive, at the perimeter of the airport, to downtown, only about 3 miles away.

By Car

Interstate 5 stretches from Canada to the Mexican border and bisects San Diego. Interstate 8 provides access from Yuma, Arizona, and points east. Drivers coming from Nevada and the mountain regions beyond can reach San Diego on I–15. Avoid rush-hour periods, when the traffic can be jammed for miles.

Car Rentals

A car is essential for San Diego's sprawling freeway system and comes in handy for touring Baja California, although it's not necessary in Tijuana. The airport in San Diego is a five-minute drive from downtown, and rates are equivalent in both areas, so an airport rental may be your best bet. Most major car-rental companies are represented in San Diego, including **Alamo** (tel. 800/327–9633), **Avis** (tel. 800/331–1212 or 800/879–2847 in Canada), **Budget** (tel. 800/527–0700), **Dollar** (tel. 800/800–4000), **Hertz** (tel. 800/654–3131 or 800/263–0600 in Canada), and **National** (tel. 800/227–7368). Unlimited-mileage rates range from $32 per day for an economy car to $41 for a large car; weekly unlimited-mileage rates range from $145 to $192. This does not include tax, which in San Diego is 7.75% on car rentals. Budget companies serving San Diego include **General** (tel. 800/327–7607) and **Rent-A-Wreck** (tel. 800/243–3523). For higher-end options, *see* Getting Around by Limousine, *below.*

Extra Charges Picking up the car in one city and leaving it in another may entail substantial drop-off charges or one-way service fees. The cost of a collision or loss-damage waiver (*see below*) can also be high. Some rental agencies will charge you extra if you return the car *before* the time specified on your contract. Ask before making unscheduled drop-offs. Fill the tank when you turn in the vehicle to avoid being charged for refueling at what you'll swear is the most expensive pump in town.

Rental companies are beginning to allow their cars to be taken across the Mexican border, but you must ask permission and purchase Mexican auto insurance. **Avis** (tel. 800/331–1212) and **Courtesy** (tel. 619/497–4800) offer this option.

Cutting Costs Major international companies have programs that discount their standard rates by 15%–30% if you make the reservation before departure (anywhere from 24 hours to 14 days), rent for a minimum number of days (typically three or four), and prepay the rental. More-economical rentals may come as part of fly/drive or other packages, even bare-bones deals that combine only the rental and an airline ticket (*see* Tours and Packages, *above*).

Insurance and Collision Damage Waiver Before you rent a car, find out exactly what coverage, if any, is provided by your personal auto insurer and by the rental company. Don't assume that you are covered. If you do want insurance from the rental company, secondary coverage may be the only type offered. You may already have secondary coverage if you charge the rental to a credit card. Only Diner's Club (tel. 800/234–6377) provides primary coverage in the United States and worldwide.

In general, if you have an accident, you are responsible for the automobile. Car-rental companies may offer a collision damage waiver (CDW), which ranges in cost from $4 to $14 a day. You should decline the CDW only if you are certain you are covered through your personal insurer or credit-card company. California, New York, and Illinois have outlawed the sale of CDW altogether.

Note: You need Mexican auto insurance for travel in Mexico whether or not you purchase the CDW.

By Train

Amtrak trains (tel. 800/872–7245) from Los Angeles arrive at Santa Fe Depot (1050 Kettner Blvd., corner of Broadway, near the heart of downtown, tel. 619/239–9021). There are additional stations in Del Mar (tel. 619/481–0114) and Oceanside (tel. 619/722–4622), both in north San Diego County. Eight trains operate daily in either direction.

By Bus

Greyhound (tel. 619/239–8082 or 800/231–2222) operates more than 20 buses a day between the downtown terminal at 120 West Broadway and Los Angeles, connecting with buses to all major U.S. cities. Many buses are express or nonstop; others make stops at coastal towns en route.

Staying in San Diego

Important Addresses and Numbers

Tourist Information Stop in at the **International Visitor Information Center** (11 Horton Plaza, at 1st Ave. and F St., tel. 619/236–1212; open Mon.–Sat., 8:30–

5 year-round, Sun. 11–5 June–Aug.) at the **Balboa Park Visitors Center** (1549 El Prado, in Balboa Park, tel. 619/239–0512; open daily 9–4), or at the **Mission Bay Visitor Information Center** (2688 E. Mission Bay Dr., off I–5 at the Mission Bay Dr. exit, tel. 619/276–8200; open Mon.–Sat. 9–5, Sun. 9:30–4:30 winter, open later in summer).

San Diego City Beach and Weather Conditions Information Line (tel. 619/221–8884).

Weather Forecast (tel. 619/289–1212).

Emergencies   **Police, ambulance,** and **fire** departments can all be reached by dialing 911. For the **Poison Control Center,** call 619/543–6000 or 800/876–4766.

Doctor   Hospital emergency rooms, with physicians on duty, are open 24 hours. Major hospitals are **Mercy Hospital and Medical Center** (4077 5th Ave., tel. 619/294–8111), **Scripps Memorial Hospital** (9888 Genesee Ave., La Jolla, tel. 619/457–4123), **Veterans Administration Hospital** (3350 La Jolla Village Dr., La Jolla, tel. 619/552–8585), and **UCSD Medical Center** (200 W. Arbor Dr., Hillcrest, tel. 619/543–6222).

Doctors on Call (tel. 619/275–2663) offers 24-hour medical service to San Diego hotels.

Dentist   The **San Diego County Dental Society** (tel. 619/275–0244) can provide referrals to those with dental emergencies.

Getting Around

Many attractions, such as the Gaslamp Quarter, Balboa Park, and La Jolla, are best seen on foot. A variety of public transportation will bring travelers to any major tourist and shopping area, but it is best to have a car for exploring more remote coastal and inland regions. The International Visitor Information Center (*see above*) provides maps of the city.

By Bus   Fares on **San Diego Transit** buses are $1.50, $1.75 on express buses; senior citizens pay 75¢ on all buses. A free transfer is included in the fare, but you must request it when you board. Buses to most major attractions leave from 4th Avenue or 5th Avenue and Broadway. The **San Diego Transit Information Line** (tel. 619/233–3004, TTY/TDD 619/234–5005; open daily 5:30 AM–8:30 PM) can provide details on getting to and from any location. The **Day Tripper Transit Pass** is good for unlimited trips on the same day on buses and on the trolley and the ferry for $4; there's also a four-day pass for $12. Passes are available at the **Transit Store** (449 Broadway, tel. 619/234–1060) as well as at the ferry landing and the downtown Amtrak station.

Regional bus companies that service areas outside the city include **ATC Van Co.** (tel. 619/427–5660), for Coronado, the Silver Strand, and Imperial Beach; **Chula Vista Transit** (tel. 619/233–3004), for Bonita and Chula Vista; **National City Transit** (tel. 619/474–7505), for National City; **North County Transit District** (tel. 619/722–6283), for the area bound by the ocean, east to Escondido, north to Camp Pendleton, and south to Del Mar; and **Northeast Rural Bus System** (tel. 619/765–0145) or **Southeast Rural Bus System** (tel. 619/478–5875), for access to rural county towns.

By Taxi   Taxi fares are regulated at the airport—all companies charge the same rate (generally $2 for the first mile, $1.40 for each additional mile). Fares vary among companies on other routes, however, including the ride back to the airport. Cab companies that serve most areas of the city are **Coast Shuttle** (tel. 619/477–3333), **Co-op Silver Cabs** (tel. 619/280–5555), **Coronado Cab** (tel. 619/435–6211), **La Jolla Cab** (tel. 619/453–4222), **Orange Cab** (tel. 619/291–3333), and **Yellow Cab** (tel. 619/234–6161).

By Trolley The **San Diego Trolley** (tel. 619/233–3004) travels from downtown to within 100 feet of the U.S.–Mexican border, stopping at 21 suburban stations en route. The basic fare is $1.75 one way. The trolley also travels from downtown to Encanto, Lemon Grove, La Mesa, and El Cajon in East County. Tickets must be purchased before boarding. Ticket-vending machines, located at each station, require exact change. Trolleys operate daily, approximately every 15 minutes, 5 AM–9 PM, the every 30 minutes until 1 AM. The Bayside line serves the Convention Center and Seaport Village; lines to Old Town, Mission Valley, and North County are under construction.

By Train **Amtrak** (tel. 800/872–7245) makes nine trips daily, in each direction, between San Diego, Del Mar, and Oceanside. The round-trip fare from San Diego to Del Mar or Oceanside is $10 ($6 one way). Seats are nonreserved, but tickets should be purchased before boarding.

By Ferry The **San Diego-Coronado** Ferry (tel. 619/234–4111) leaves from the Broadway Pier daily, every hour on the hour, 9 AM–9:30 PM Sunday–Thursday, until 10:30 PM Friday and Saturday. The fare is $2 each way. The **Harbor Hopper** (tel. 619/488–5022, 619/488–2720, or 800/300–7447) is a water-taxi service that shuttles passengers around Mission Bay. The fare is $4 each way, $6 round-trip. Hours and days of operation change with the season; call ahead for information.

By Limousine Limousine companies offer airport shuttles and customized tours. Rates vary and are per hour, per mile, or both, with some minimums established. Companies that offer a range of services include **Advantage Limousine Service** (tel. 619/563–1651), **La Jolla Limousines** (tel. 619/459–5891), **Limousines by Linda** (tel. 619/234–9145), and **Olde English Livery** (tel. 619/232–6533).

By Horse-Drawn Carriage **Cinderella Carriage Co.** (tel. 619/239–8080) will take parties of two to four people through the Gaslamp Quarter, the waterfront, and downtown. The cost is $75 for one hour, $40 for a half-hour ride, and $55 for 45 minutes.

Guided Tours

Orientation **Gray Line Tours** (tel. 619/491–0011 or 800/331–5077) and **San Diego Mini Tours** (tel. 619/477–8687) offer two daily sightseeing excursions for about $25.

Old Town Trolley (tel. 619/298–8687) travels to almost every attraction and shopping area on open-air trackless trolleys. Drivers double as tour guides. You can take the full two-hour, narrated city tour or get on and off as you please at any of the nine stops. An all-day pass costs $16 for adults, $7 for children 6–12. The trolley, which leaves every 30 minutes, operates daily 9–5:30 in the summer, 9–4:30 in winter.

Free two-hour trolley tours of the downtown redevelopment area, including the Gaslamp Quarter, are hosted by **Centre City Development Corporation's Downtown Information Center** (tel. 619/235–2222). Groups of 35 passengers leave from 255 G Street, downtown, the first and third Saturday of each month at 10 AM. Reservations are necessary. The tour may be canceled if there aren't enough passengers.

Special- **Civic Helicopters** (tel. 619/438–8424 or 800/438–HELI) has helicop-
Interest ter tours starting at $69 per person per half-hour.

San Diego Harbor Excursion (tel. 619/234–4111) and **Hornblower Invader Cruises** (tel. 619/234–8687) sail on narrated cruises of San Diego Harbor, departing from Broadway Pier. Both companies offer one-hour cruises ($10), departing several times daily, and a two-hour tour ($15) each day at 2 PM (additional tours in summer). No reservations are necessary, and both vessels have snack bars on board. **Mariposa Sailing Cruises** (tel. 619/224–0800) has morning and afternoon tours of the harbor and San Diego Bay for $40 per person.

Balloon Six-passenger hot-air balloons lift off from San Diego's North Country. Most flights are at sunrise or sunset and are followed by a traditional champagne celebration. Companies that offer daily service, weather permitting, are **Air Affaire** (tel. 619/560–6373 or 800/331–1979), **Pacific Horizon** (tel. 619/756–1790 or 800/244–1790), and **Skysurfer** (tel. 619/481–6800 or 800/660–6809 in CA). Balloon flights average $145 per person for early morning or late afternoon.

Whale- Gray whales migrate south to Mexico and back north from mid-De-
Watching cember to mid-March. As many as 200 whales pass the San Diego coast each day, coming within yards of tour boats. During whale-watching season, ***The Apollo*** (tel. 619/221–8500), a luxury motor yacht, offers narrated tours twice a day. **Mariposa Sailing Cruises** (tel. 619/224–0800) tailors whale-watching expeditions for up to six people. **H&M Landing** (tel. 619/222–1144) and **Seaforth Sportfishing** (tel. 619/224–3383) have daily whale-watching trips in large party boats.

Walking **The Gaslamp Quarter Foundation** (410 Island Ave., tel. 619/233–5227) leads 1½-hour architectural tours of the restored downtown historic district on Saturday at 11 AM ($5 adults, $3 senior citizens and students). Self-guided tour brochures are available at the office, weekdays 10–4:30.

On weekends, the State Park Department (tel. 619/220–5422) gives free walking tours of **Old Town.** Groups leave from 4002 Wallace Street at 2 PM daily, weather permitting.

Walkabout (tel. 619/231–7463) offers several different free walking tours throughout the city each week.

Credit Cards

The following credit card abbreviations are used throughout this guide: AE, American Express; D, Discover; DC, Diners Club; MC, MasterCard; V, Visa.

2 Portrait of San Diego

Idylling in San Diego

By Edie
Jarolim

Edie Jarolim
is a New
York–born
freelance
writer and
editor who
recently
moved to
Tucson, which
is within easy
driving
distance of
San Diego.

I've never been to Sea World; performing fish give me the willies. And during the two years I lived within striking distance of Balboa Park, I had to take visiting friends to the zoo so many times I began having nightmares about koalas. But if I came to dislike various theme-park aspects of the city, I nevertheless loved San Diego. At first sight.

A typical easterner, I went out to San Diego in the late 1970s expecting to find a smaller version of Los Angeles. The freeways were there, along with a fair share of traffic congestion, but so was an oceanscape of surprisingly pristine beauty. The first drive I took from the University of California, where I was doing graduate research, knocked me for a loop: I rounded a curve on La Jolla Shores Drive to confront a coastline that could match any on the French Riviera.

I was also taken by the distinctiveness of the many shoreline communities. For one thing, the beaches tend to get funkier as you head south from the old-money enclave of La Jolla: Pacific Beach, with its Crystal Pier, is an aging Victorian resort taken over by teenagers, while transients and surfers share the turf at Ocean Beach. To the north, Del Mar has a strip of shops that rival those of Rodeo Drive, while Carlsbad and Oceanside show the democratizing influence of nearby Camp Pendleton.

Unlike Los Angeles, San Diego is still strongly defined by its relationship to the ocean—to some degree by default. During the latter half of the 19th century, the town was banking on a rail link to the east. A building boom in the 1880s was largely based on the assumption that San Diego would become the western terminus of the Santa Fe Railroad line; the city hoped in this way to compete with Los Angeles, which was already connected by rail to San Francisco and thus to the national railroad network. The link was completed in 1885, but it proved unsuccessful for a variety of reasons, including the placement of the line through Temecula Canyon, where 30 miles of track were washed out repeatedly in winter rainstorms. The Santa Fe soon moved its West Coast offices to San Bernardino and Los Angeles, and to this day there is no direct rail service from San Diego to the eastern part of the United States.

Instead, San Diego's future was sealed in 1908, when President Theodore Roosevelt's Great White Fleet stopped here on a world tour to demonstrate U.S. naval strength. The navy, impressed during that visit by the city's excellent harbor and temperate climate, decided to build a destroyer base on San Diego Bay in the 1920s; the newly developing aircraft industry soon followed (Charles Lindbergh's plane *Spirit of St. Louis* was built here). Over the years San Diego's economy became largely dependent on the military and its attendant enterprises, which provided jobs as well as a demand for local goods and services by those stationed here.

San Diego's character—conservative where Los Angeles's is cutting edge—was formed in large part by the presence of its military installations, which now occupy more than 165,000 acres of land in the area. And the city conducts most of its financial business in a single neighborhood, the district fronting San Diego Bay, in this way resembling New York more than its economic rival up the coast. San Diego has set some of its most prestigious scientific facilities on the water—Scripps Institute of Oceanography, naturally, but also Salk Institute. Jonas Salk didn't need the Pacific marine environment for his research, but his regular morning runs along Torrey Pines Beach no doubt cleared his head.

San Diego also has the ocean to thank for its near-perfect weather. A high-pressure system from the north Pacific is responsible for the city's sunshine and dry air; moderating breezes off the sea (caused by the water warming and cooling more slowly than the land) keep the summers relatively cool and the winters warm and help clear the air of pollution. In the late spring and early summer the difference between the earth and water temperatures generates coastal fogs. This phenomenon was another of San Diego's delightful surprises: I never tired of watching the mist roll in at night, wonderfully romantic, as thick as any I'd ever seen in London and easier to enjoy in the balmy air.

If I loved San Diego from the start, I had a hard time believing in its existence. It was difficult to imagine that a functioning American city could be so attractive, that people lived and worked in such a place every day. Although I'd never considered myself a Puritan, I quickly came to realize that I'd always assumed work and leisure environments had to be separate, that one was supposed to toil in unpleasant surroundings in order to earn the time spent in idyllic settings.

I found that I could get used to working on sunny days, but that it was impossible to remain unaffected by the city's physical presence. Rampant nature conspires in a variety of ways to force you to let your guard down here. In northern East Coast cities, plants are generally orderly and prim: shrubs trimmed, roses demurely draped around railings, tulips set in proper rows. Even the famed cherry blossoms of Washington, D.C., are profuse in neat columns. In San Diego, the flora, whimsical at best, sometimes border on obscenity. The ubiquitous palms come in comedic pairs: Short, squat trees that look like overgrown pineapples play Mutt to the Jeff of the tall, skinny variety. The aptly named bottle-brush bushes vie for attention with bright red flame trees, beaky orange birds of paradise, and rich purple bougainvillea spilling out over lush green lawns. Only in Hawaii had I previously encountered anthurium, a waxy red plant with a protruding white center that seems to be sticking its tongue out at you. "We're still on the mainland," I felt like telling them all on some days: "Behave yourselves."

Ironically, it was the Victorians who were largely responsible for this indecorous natural profusion. Difficult as it is to imagine now, it's the sparse brown vegetation of San Diego's undeveloped mesas that accurately reflects the climate of the region, technically a semiarid steppe. When Spanish explorer Juan Rodríguez Cabrillo sailed into San Diego Bay in 1542, looking for a shortcut to China, he and his crew encountered a barren, desolate landscape that did not inspire them to settle here, or even stop for very long.

It wasn't until the late 19th century, when the Mediterranean in general and Italy in particular were all the rage among wealthy residents, that the vegetation now considered characteristic of southern California was introduced to San Diego. In 1889, money raised by the Ladies Annex to the Chamber of Commerce was used to plant trees in Balboa Park, and between 1892 and 1903 a wide variety of exotic foliage was brought into the city: eucalyptus, cork oak, and rubber trees, to name a few. As homeowners in the area can attest, most of the landscaped local vegetation couldn't survive if it were not watered regularly.

No doubt both the natural setting and the relentlessly fine weather help contribute to the clash of cultures that exists here. The conservative traditionalism of the military presence in town is posed against the liberal hedonism of visiting sunseekers, as well as a large local student population. Nude bathing is popular at Black's Beach in La Jolla, a spot that's reasonably private because it's fairly inaccessible: You have to hike down steep cliffs in order to get to the water. Rumor has it that every year a few navy men are killed when they lose their footing on the cliffs, so intent are they at peering through their binoculars.

But I suspect it's the rare person of any political persuasion who can confront the southern California attitude toward nudity with equanimity. I hadn't wanted to believe all the stereotypes, but the first time I went to a dinner party in town, the host asked the group if we wanted to adjourn to the hot tub after we ate. I hadn't brought my bathing suit, so I declined.

The next day, I consulted a local expert in matters of whirlpool etiquette. "What does one do?" I asked. "Undress in front of a group of relative strangers and jump into the water with them? Does one rip off one's clothes with abandon? Fold them carefully afterward? Or go into another room and come out in the raw?" "All that's up to the individual," she answered. "Do whatever you feel comfortable with." "None of it," I asserted. "Where I come from, when people of different genders take their clothes off together, they tend to have sex." "That's optional, too," she said.

Nods to certain So-Cal conventions notwithstanding, San Diego has never come close to approaching the much-touted libertinism of Los Angeles. It has the porno theaters and sleazy clubs you'd expect in a liberty port, but little entertainment of a more sophisticated nature. Celebrities who came down from Hollywood in the 1920s and '30s sought out suites at the La Valencia

Hotel and other chic La Jolla locales for the privacy, not the nightlife; the gambling they did at Del Mar racetrack to the north was of the tony, genteel sort. Those who sought thrills— and booze during Prohibition—headed farther south, to Mexico. Raymond Chandler, who spent most of his last 13 years in La Jolla and died there in 1959, wrote a friend that the town was "a nice place . . . for old people and their parents."

For all its conservatism, the one thing San Diego didn't conserve was its past—in some cases because there was little to save. When Father Junipero Serra arrived in 1769 to establish the first of the California missions, he did not find the complex dwellings that characterized so many of the Native American settlements he had encountered in Mexico. Nor did his fellow Spaniards improve much upon the site during their stay; the town that the Mexicans took over in 1822 was rudimentary, consisting mostly of rough adobe huts. The mission church had been moved to a new site in 1774, and the original Spanish presidio, abandoned in the 1830s, was in ruins by the next decade; some grass-covered mounds and a giant cross built in 1913 on Presidio Hill, incorporating the tiles of the original structure, are all that's left of it.

Though a romanticized version of the city during the Mexican period (1822–49), today's Old Town district gives a rough idea of San Diego's layout at that time, when somewhat more impressive structures, such as Casa Estudillo and the Bandini House, were built. San Diego didn't really begin to flourish, however, until 1850, the year that California became a state. At that point the dominant architectural influence came from the East Coast; their enthusiasm for becoming American caused San Diegans to reject their Spanish and Mexican roots as inappropriately "foreign." Thus the first brick structure in the state, the Whaley House (1856), was built in typical New England nautical style. Most of the original Old Town was destroyed by fire in 1872, and a good deal of what was left fell victim to the construction of I-5.

During the Victorian era (1880–1905), the site of the city's development moved south; entrepreneur Alonzo Horton may have miscalculated the success of the rail link to the East Coast, but when he bought up a huge lot of land in 1867 for his "Addition," he knew the city's future lay on the harbor. It was in this area, now the city's financial district, that many of the neo-Gothic structures characteristic of the period were built. Perhaps it's perversely fitting that a number of the Victorian relics in downtown San Diego were removed in conjunction with the 15-block Horton Redevelopment Project, of which the huge Horton Plaza shopping complex is the center.

San Diego finally began to reject the East Coast architectural style at the turn of the century, and at the Panama–California Exposition of 1915 the city celebrated its Spanish roots—as well as a Moroccan and Italian past it never had—with a vengeance. The beautiful Spanish-style structures built for the occasion fit right into the Mediterranean landscape that had been cultivated in Balboa Park during the Victorian era; today these buildings house most of the city's museums. San Diego became even more thoroughly Hispanicized during the 1920s and '30s as Spanish colonial–style homes became popular in new suburbs, such as Mission Hills and Kensington, as well as in the beach communities that were developing. Downtown buildings began looking like Italian palaces and Moorish towers.

San Diego's landscape of ravines and hills is partly responsible for the city's sprawling development in the 20th century, and the popularization of the automobile in the 1930s helped ensure its continuing growth in an outward direction. The physical barriers have been overcome by an ever-expanding highway system—though not by a viable public transportation network—but the discrete, individual neighborhoods created by them remain, if their populations sometimes shift. For example, Kearny Mesa, formerly a middle-class suburban neighborhood, is now one of the many Southeast Asian communities in the city.

In some ways, as residents and visitors alike have long feared, San Diego is coming to look more like Los Angeles. Faceless developments are cropping up all over once-deserted canyons and mesas, and the huge, castlelike Mormon temple built along I–5 north of La Jolla wouldn't look out of place in Disneyland. But in the years since I lived there, San Diego has also become more like a city—that is, what easterners know to be the city in its divinely ordained form.

As recently as the early 1980s, virtually no one went downtown unless required to. It was a desolate place after dark, and people who worked there during the day never stayed around in the evening to play. Gentrification of sorts began in the mid-1970s, as the low rents attracted artists and real-estate speculators. At about the same time the city designated the formerly rough Stingaree neighborhood as the Gaslamp Quarter, but revitalization, in the form of street-level shops and art galleries, didn't really take until Horton Plaza was completed in 1985. For many years the newly installed gaslights illuminated only the homeless.

The poor and disenfranchised are still here—indeed, many lost their homes to various redevelopment projects—but now the staff at the recently renovated historic U.S. Grant Hotel offers to accompany its guests across the street to Horton Plaza at night so they won't be bothered by vagrants. For the first time there's a concentration of good restaurants, and a serious art and theater scene is developing in the district, too.

The area is also a terminus for the San Diego Trolley. This inexpensive transportation link to Mexico has, among other things, allowed Mexican artists to bring their works to a wider market and fostered a cultural as well as a touristic exchange with Tijuana, which has cleaned up its own act considerably in recent years.

I like the infusion of life into downtown San Diego, and I even like Horton Plaza, which, with its odd angles and colorful banners, looks like it was designed by Alice in Wonderland's Red

Queen. But maybe I miss that spot of unadulterated blight that once helped me to believe in San Diego's reality.

Reality seems to be setting in on a large scale these days. San Diego's bad neighborhoods still don't look like slums as I know them, but gang-related crime is on the increase in the southeast part of the city. In recent years, sewage spills have closed a number of southern beaches, and the problem is likely to grow, since neither San Diego nor Tijuana has enacted any large-scale programs for effective waste disposal. Friends tell me that even the weather is changing for the worse, a fact they attribute to global warming.

Would I move back to San Diego? In a minute. Like many temporary residents, I left the city vowing to return; unlike many, I've never managed to do more than visit. I used to think that if I had the chance I'd live in Hillcrest, a close-knit inland community with lots of ethnic restaurants and theaters that show foreign films, but I've come to realize that would only be transplanting my East Coast life into the sun. Now I think I'll wait until I'm rich and can afford to move to La Jolla; no doubt I'll be old enough by then to fit in, so I'll fully enjoy that suite in the La Valencia Hotel overlooking the cove.

3   Exploring San Diego

By Maribeth Mellin

Revised by Edie Jarolim

Exploring San Diego is an endless adventure, limited only by time and transportation constraints, which, if you don't have a car, can be considerable. San Diego is more a chain of separate communities than a cohesive city. Many of the major attractions are at least 5 miles away from one another. The streets are fun for getting an up-close look at how San Diegans live, but true southern Californians use the freeways, which crisscross the county in a sensible fashion. Interstate 5 runs a direct north–south route through the county's coastal communities to the Mexican border. Interstates 805 and 15 do much the same inland, with I–8 as the main east–west route. Highways 163, 52, and 94 act as connectors.

If you are going to drive around San Diego, study your maps before you hit the road. The freeways are convenient and fast most of the time, but if you miss your turnoff or get caught in commuter traffic, you'll experience a none-too-pleasurable hallmark of southern California living—freeway madness. Southern California drivers rush around on a complex freeway system with the same fervor they use for jogging scores of marathons each year. They particularly enjoy speeding up at interchanges and entrance and exit ramps. Be sure you know where you're going before you join the freeway chase. Better yet, use public transportation or tour buses from your hotel and save your energy for walking in the sun.

If you stick with public transportation, plan on taking your time. San Diego's bus system covers almost all the county, but it does so slowly. Since many of the city's major attractions are clustered along the coast, you'll be best off staying there or in the Hotel Circle/Mission Valley hotel zone. Downtown and Fashion Valley Shopping Center in Mission Valley are the two major transfer points. Some buses have bicycle racks in the back, and a bike is a great mode of transportation here. The bike-path system, although never perfect, is extensive and well marked. Taxis are expensive, given the miles between various sights, and are best used for getting around once you're in a given area.

We have divided San Diego into seven exploring sections, organized around neighborhoods (*see* the Exploring San Diego map for the location of each tour). Downtown's main thoroughfares are Harbor Drive, running along the waterfront; Broadway, through the center of downtown; and 6th Avenue to Balboa Park. The numbered streets run roughly north–south; the lettered and named streets (Broadway, Market, Island, and Ash) run east–west. Only Broadway, Market Street, and Island Avenue have two-way traffic. The rest alternate one-way directions.

There are large, reasonably priced ($3.50–$7 per day) parking lots along Harbor Drive, Pacific Highway, and lower Broadway and Market Street. Meters cost 50¢ an hour and are usually good for two hours. Don't plan on beating a ticket by rushing back and throwing quarters in your meter every so often. The space is limited to two hours—if you stay longer, no matter how much money is in your meter, you can get a ticket.

Balboa Park, Sea World, Cabrillo National Monument, and Mission Bay all have huge parking lots, and it is rare not to find a space, though it may seem as if you've parked miles away from your destination. Parking is more of a problem in Old Town, where the free lots fill up quickly, and in La Jolla and Coronado, where you generally need to rely on hard-to-find street spots or expensive, by-the-hour parking lots.

Exploring San Diego

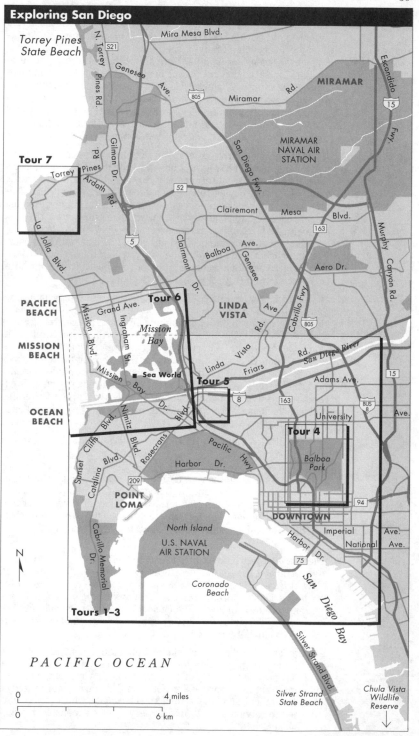

Torrey Pines
State Beach

Mira Mesa Blvd.

N. Torrey Pines Rd.

S21

Genesee

Ave.

805

MIRAMAR

Miramar

Rd.

Escondido Fwy.

15

MIRAMAR
NAVAL AIR
STATION

San Diego Fwy.

Tour 7

Torrey

Pines

Rd.

Ardath Rd.

Gilman Dr.

52

Clairemont

Mesa

Blvd.

163

5

La Jolla Blvd.

Clairemont

Dr.

Balboa

Ave.

Genesee

Aero Dr.

Murphy Canyon Rd.

Cabrillo Fwy.

805

PACIFIC
BEACH

Tour 6

Grand Ave.

Ingraham St.

Mission Blvd.

Mission Bay

LINDA
VISTA

Ave.

Rd.

Vista

MISSION
BEACH

Linda

Friars

Rd.

San Diego River

15

Sea World

Tour 5

Adams Ave.

Mission

Bay

8

163

BUS
8

OCEAN
BEACH

Nimitz Blvd.

Sunset Cliffs Blvd.

Catalina Blvd.

Dr.

Blvd.

Rosecrans

Pacific

Hwy.

University

Ave.

Tour 4

209

Harbor

Dr.

Balboa
Park

94

POINT
LOMA

North Island
U.S. NAVAL
AIR STATION

DOWNTOWN

Harbor

Dr.

Imperial

Ave.

Cabrillo Memorial Dr.

75

National

Ave.

N

Coronado
Beach

San Diego Bay

Tours 1–3

Silver Strand Blvd.

PACIFIC OCEAN

Silver Strand
State Beach

Chula Vista
Wildlife
Reserve

0 ——————— 4 miles

0 ——————— 6 km

Highlights for First-time Visitors

Cabrillo National Monument (*see* Tour 3)

Horton Plaza (*see* Tour 1)

Hotel Del Coronado (*see* Tour 2)

La Jolla Cove (*see* Tour 7)

Old Town State Historic Park (*see* Tour 5)

Reuben H. Fleet Space Theater and Science Center (*see* Tour 4)

San Diego Zoo (*see* Tour 4)

Sea World (*see* Tour 6)

Seaport Village (*see* Tour 1)

Tour 1: Downtown and the Embarcadero

Numbers in the margin correspond to points of interest on the Tours 1–3: Central San Diego map.

Downtown San Diego, just 3 miles south of the international airport, is changing and growing rapidly, gaining status as a cultural and recreational center for the county's residents and visitors alike.

San Diego's politicians and business leaders have made a concerted effort to draw San Diegans to an area long ignored or avoided by the local populace. Thanks to a decade-long redevelopment effort, elegant hotels, upscale condominium complexes, and swank, trendy cafés now attract newcomers and natives to a newly developed center city that has retained an outdoor character. Mirrored office and banking towers reflect the nearly constant blue skies and sunshine.

Downtown's natural attributes were easily evident to its original booster, Alonzo Horton, who arrived in San Diego in 1867. Horton looked at the bay and the acres of flatland surrounded by hills and canyons and knew he had found San Diego's center. Though Old Town, under the Spanish fort at the Presidio, had been settled for years, Horton understood that it was too far away from the water to take hold as the commercial center of San Diego. He bought 960 acres along the bay at 27½¢ per acre and literally gave away the land to those who would develop it or build houses. Within months, he had sold or given away 226 city blocks of land; settlers camped on their land in tents as their houses and businesses rose.

The transcontinental train arrived in 1885, and the land boom was on. Although the railroad's status as a cross-country route was short-lived, the population soared from 5,000 to 35,000 in less than a decade—a foreshadowing of San Diego's future. In 1887, the Santa Fe Depot was constructed at the foot of Broadway, two blocks from the water. Freighters chugged in and out of the harbor, and by the early 1900s, the navy had moved in.

As downtown grew into San Diego's transportation and commercial hub, residential neighborhoods blossomed along the beaches and inland valleys. The business district gradually moved farther away from the original heart of downtown, at 5th Avenue and Market Street, past Broadway, up toward the park. Downtown's waterfront

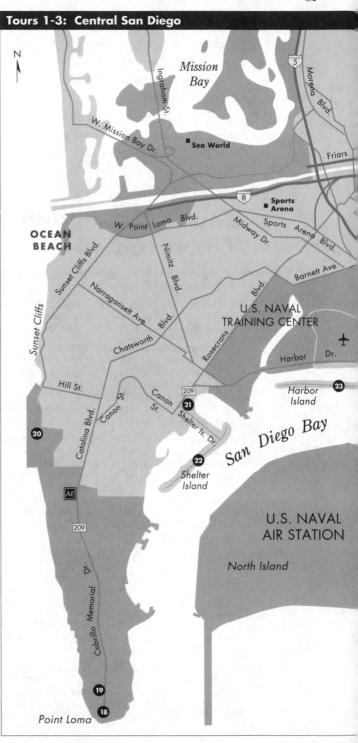

Tours 1-3: Central San Diego

Time Out   In the Central Plaza, **Upstart Crow & Co.,** a combination bookstore and coffeehouse, serves fancy nonalcoholic coffee drinks and great pastries and cakes. You can leaf through some of the store's books—there's an excellent selection of volumes on San Diego—in an upstairs reading lounge.

Seaport Village's center reaches out onto **Embarcadero Marine Park North,** an 8-acre grassy point into the harbor where kite-fliers, roller-skaters, and picnickers hang out in the sun. Seasonal celebrations with live music and fireworks are held here throughout the year.

The mirrored towers of the San Diego Marriott Hotel and Marina mark the end of Seaport Village, but the waterfront walkway continues past the hotel's marina, where hotel guests moor their enormous, extravagant yachts. Just beyond the Marriott is the striking **⑤ San Diego Convention Center,** designed by Arthur Erickson; its nautical lines are complemented by the backdrop of blue sky and sea. The center often holds trade shows that are open to the public, and tours of the building are available.

Just south of the convention center, at the **Embarcadero Marina Park South,** the San Diego Symphony (tel. 619/699-4205) presents its annual Summer Pops concert series, complete with fireworks finales that light up the bay. These musical extravaganzas, increasingly popular in recent years, have gone upscale, offering cabaret seating as well as food and bar service.

One way to reach the heart of downtown is to walk up Market Street from Seaport Village. The **Olde Cracker Factory,** at Market and State streets, houses antiques and collectibles shops. Continue two blocks to Front Street and turn south one block to Island to reach the new facility of the **Children's Museum of San Diego** (*see* Chapter 4, San Diego for Children).

Another way to approach the central business district is to walk up Broadway from the Broadway Pier. Two blocks to the west of Harbor Drive, at Kettner Boulevard, you'll come to the Mission Revival–**⑥** style **Santa Fe Depot,** built in 1915 on the site of the original 1887 station. The terminal for north- and south-bound Amtrak passengers, the graceful, tile-domed depot hosts an unattended tourist information booth with bus schedules, maps, and brochures. Formerly an easily spotted area landmark, the depot is now overshadowed by **1 America Plaza** next door. At the base of this massive 34-story office tower, designed by architect Helmut Jahn, is a transit center that links the train, trolley, and city bus systems. (The Greyhound bus station is just a few blocks away at 120 West Broadway.) The building's signature crescent-shaped glass-and-steel canopy arching out over the trolley tracks calls attention to the new Sculpture Plaza that fronts the downtown branch of the **San Diego Museum of Contemporary Art,** opened in early 1993. The two-story building adjoining the transit center, with four small galleries, is the main locus for contemporary art exhibits in San Diego while the original facility in La Jolla undergoes expansion. *1001 Kettner Blvd., tel. 619/234-1001. Admission: $2 adults, $1 students, senior citizens, children under 13; free Thurs. 5-9 PM. Open Tues., Wed, and Fri.-Sun. 11 AM-6 PM, Thurs. 11 AM-9 PM.*

Six blocks farther east, at the corner of 1st Avenue and Broadway, **⑦** downtown begins to come alive. Here you'll pass the **Spreckels Theater,** a grand old stage that presents pop concerts and touring **⑧** plays these days. Another block down and across the street, the **U. S.**

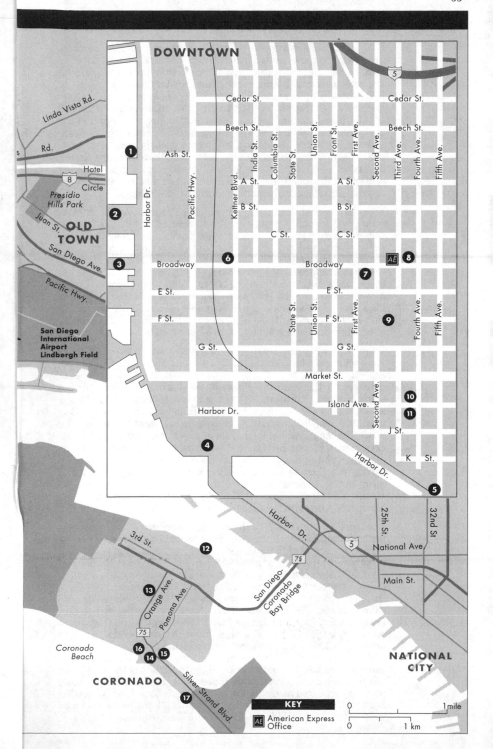

fell into bad times during World War I, when sailors, gamblers, and prostitutes were drawn to one another and the waterfront bars.

But Alonzo Horton's modern-day followers, city leaders intent on prospering while preserving San Diego's natural beauty, have reclaimed the downtown area. Replacing old shipyards and canneries are hotel towers and waterfront parks; the Martin Luther King, Jr., Promenade project is slated to put 12 acres of greenery along Harbor Drive from Seaport Village to the convention center by the end of 1995. Nineteen ninety-two saw the completion of the part of the park near the $160 million, 760,000-square-foot San Diego Convention Center, which hosted its first events in early 1990. And a few blocks inland, the hugely successful Horton Plaza shopping center, opened in 1985, led the way for the hotels, restaurants, shopping centers, and housing developments that are now rising on every square inch of available space in downtown San Diego.

Your first view of downtown, regardless of your mode of transportation, will probably include the **Embarcadero,** a waterfront walkway on Harbor Drive lined with restaurants, sea vessels of every variety—cruise ships, ferries, tour boats, houseboats, and naval destroyers—and a fair share of seals and sea gulls. Many boats along the Embarcadero have been converted into floating gift shops, and others are awaiting restoration. If you plan to spend a good portion of your day in the area, either strolling or taking a harbor excursion, it's a good idea to park at the huge municipal lot ($4 per day) along the south side of the B Street Pier building; much of the parking along Harbor Drive is limited to two-hour meters.

To get some historical perspective on your Embarcadero visit, begin your tour two blocks north of the parking lot at the foot of Ash Street, where the *Berkeley,* an 1898 riverboat, is moored. It's headquarters for the **Maritime Museum,** a collection of three restored ships that may be toured for one admission price. The *Berkeley,* which served the Southern Pacific Railroad at San Francisco Bay until 1953, had its most important days during the great earthquake of 1906, when it carried thousands of passengers across San Francisco Bay to Oakland. Its carved wood paneling, stained-glass windows, and plate-glass mirrors have been restored, and its main deck serves as a floating museum, with exhibits on oceanography and naval history. Anchored next to the Berkeley, the small Scottish steam yacht *Medea,* launched in 1904, may be boarded but has no interpretive displays.

The most interesting of the three ships is the ***Star of India,*** a beautiful windjammer built in 1863 and docked at the foot of Grape Street. The ship's high wooden masts and white sails flapping in the wind have been a harbor landmark since 1926. Built at Ramsey on the Isle of Man, the *Star of India* made 21 trips around the world in the late 1800s, when she traveled the East Indian trade route, shuttled immigrants from England to Australia, and served the Alaskan salmon trade. The ship languished after she was retired to San Diego Harbor, virtually ignored until 1959. Then a group of volunteers, organized by the Maritime Museum, stripped the wooden decks, polished the figurehead, and mended the sails. On July 4, 1976, the *Star of India* commemorated the bicentennial by setting sail in the harbor. The oldest iron sailing ship afloat in the world, she has made short excursions five times since then, but for the most part stays moored at the pier and open to visitors. *1306 N. Harbor Dr., tel. 619/234–9153. Admission: $6 adults, $4 senior citizens and students 13–17, $2 children 6–12, $12 families. Ships open daily 9–8.*

A cement pathway runs south from the *Star of India* along terfront to the pastel **B Street Pier,** used by ships from majo lines as both a port of call and a departure point. The caverno building has a cruise-information center and a small, cool b gift shop.

Another two blocks south on Harbor Drive brings you to the f Broadway and **Broadway Pier,** a gathering spot for day-trip ready to set sail. A cluster of storefront windows sell tickets fo harbor tours and whale-watching trips that leave from the doc January and February, when the gray whales migrate from Pacific Northwest to southern Baja. One of the most traditional, a delightful, boat trips to take from the pier is the **Bay Ferry** to Co nado Island (*see* Tour 2: Coronado, *below,* for details).

Time Out   Those waiting for their boats can grab a beer or ice cream at th diner-style **Bay Cafe** and sit on the upstairs patio or on benches along the busy pathway; it's a good vantage point for watching the sailboats, paddle wheelers, and yachts vie for space. Another option is to buy some fish-and-chips and perch on an outdoor stool at **Anthony's Fish Grotto and Fishette,** the most casual of the three Embarcadero restaurants owned by the Anthony Ghio family.

The navy's Eleventh Naval District has control of the next few waterfront blocks to the south, and a series of destroyers, submarines, and carriers cruise in and out, some staying for weeks at a time. On weekends, the navy usually offers tours of these floating cities (call 619/532–1431 for information on hours and types of ships). A steady stream of joggers, bicyclists, and serious walkers on the Embarcadero pathway picks up speed at **Tuna Harbor,** the hub of San Diego's commercial tuna fishing, one of the city's earliest industries.

Seaport Village (tel. 619/235–4013 for recorded events information or 619/235–4014) is the next attraction you'll reach if you continue south on Harbor Drive. It was a wise developer who saw the good fortune in this stretch of prime waterfront that now connects the harbor with the hotel towers and convention center. Spread out across 14 acres are three connected shopping plazas, designed to reflect the architectural styles of early California, especially New England clapboard and Spanish Mission. A ¼-mile wooden boardwalk that runs along the bay, as well as 4 miles of simulated dirt-road and cobblestone paths, leads to a bustling array of specialty shops, snack bars, and restaurants—more than 75 in all. You can browse through a shell shop, a rubber-stamp shop, and a shop devoted to left-handed people and nosh to your heart's delight on everything from fast Greek, Mexican, and French fare to seafood in nautical-style indoor restaurants. Seaport Village's shops are open daily 10–9 (10–10 in summer); a few eateries open early for breakfast, and many have extended nighttime hours, especially in summer.

Almost as many adults as children enjoy riding the hand-carved, hand-painted steeds on the **Broadway Flying Horses Carousel,** created by I.D. Looff in Coney Island in 1890. The ride was moved from its next home, Salisbury Beach in Massachusetts, and faithfully restored for Seaport Village, where it began operating in the West Plaza on the July 4 weekend of 1980; tickets are $1. Strolling clowns, mimes, musicians, and magicians are also on hand throughout the village to entertain kids; those not impressed by such pretechnological displays can duck into the Sega family entertainment center near the carousal and play video games.

Grant Hotel, built in 1910, is far more formal than most other San Diego lodgings; the massive marble lobby, gleaming chandeliers, and white-gloved doormen hearken back to the more gracious time when it was built.

The theme of shopping in adventureland carries over from Seaport Village to downtown San Diego's centerpiece, **Horton Plaza** (tel. 619/238–1596). Completed in 1985, this shopping, dining, and entertainment mall fronts Broadway and G Street from 1st to 4th avenues and covers more than six city blocks. The **International Visitor Information Center,** operated in the complex by the San Diego Convention and Visitors Bureau, is the traveler's best resource for information on the city. The staff members and volunteers who run the center speak an amazing array of languages and are well acquainted with the myriad needs and requests of tourists. They dispense information on hotels, restaurants, and tourist attractions, including Tijuana. *11 Horton Plaza, street level at the corner of 1st Ave. and F St., tel. 619/236–1212. Open year-round, Mon.–Sat. 8:30–5; June–Aug., also open Sun. 11–5.*

Designed by Jon Jerde, Horton Plaza is far from what one would imagine a shopping center—or city center—to be. A collage of pastels with elaborate, colorful tile work on benches and stairways, cloth banners waving in the air, and modern sculptures marking the entrances, Horton Plaza rises in uneven, staggered levels to six floors, offering great views of downtown from the harbor to Balboa Park and beyond. The complex's innovative architecture has strongly affected the rest of downtown's development, and new apartment and condominium complexes along G and Market streets mimic its brightly colored towers and cupolas.

Horton Plaza has a large, multilevel parking garage; the long lines of cars in search of a place to land show just how successful the complex has become. The first three hours of parking are free with validation (you needn't purchase anything to get a shop to validate your ticket) and, to encourage people to stay downtown at night, there's unlimited free parking after 5 PM. If you use this garage, be sure to remember where you leave your car. The lot is notoriously confusing, and the various levels, coded by fruits and vegetables, don't quite match up with the levels the shops are on.

Robinson's, Nordstrom, the Broadway, and Mervyn's department stores anchor the shopping sections, with an eclectic assortment of 120 clothing, sporting goods, jewelry, book, and gift shops flanking them. A movie complex, restaurants, and a long row of take-out ethnic food shops and dining patios line the uppermost tier. On the lowest level, facing 1st Avenue, is the Farmers Market, an upscale grocery with fresh, gourmet meats, seafood, and produce. The San Diego Repertory Theater, one of the longest-burning and brightest lights in San Diego's explosive theater scene, has two stages below ground level. Most of the shops close weekdays at 9 PM and weekends at 6 PM, but the restaurants and theaters stay open later.

Time Out Dining options at Horton Plaza are extensive—everything from pungent burritos to Peking duck. **La Salsa,** on the uppermost dining level, has wonderful marinated pork tacos and blue corn chips—darker in color and stronger in flavor than traditional corn chips. **Galaxy Grill** is a '50s-style diner with great burgers and shakes.

Opened in 1992 across from Horton Plaza on 1st Avenue between G and F streets, **The Paladion** (tel. 619/232–1627) is the most recent addition to the thriving downtown retail scene. This ultrahaute complex features a collection of toney boutiques such as Cartier, Tiffany, and Gucci.

Before Horton Plaza became the bright star on downtown's redevelopment horizon, the nearby **Gaslamp Quarter** was gaining attention and respect. A 16-block National Historic District, centered on 5th and 4th avenues from Broadway to Market Street, the quarter contains most of San Diego's Victorian-style commercial buildings from the late 1800s, when Market Street was the center of early downtown. At the farthest end of the redeveloped quarter, the ⑩ **Gaslamp Quarter Association** is headquartered in the William Heath Davis House (410 Island Ave., tel. 619/233–5227), one of the first residences in town. Davis was a San Franciscan whose ill-fated attempt to develop the waterfront area preceded the more successful one of Alonzo Horton. In 1850, Davis had this prefab saltbox-style house shipped around Cape Horn and assembled in San Diego. Walking tours of the historic district leave from here on Saturdays at 11; they cost $5 for adults, $3 for senior citizens and students. If you can't make the tour, stop by the house between 10 and 4:30 Monday through Friday and pick up a self-guiding brochure and map.

In the latter part of the 19th century, businesses thrived in this area, but at the turn of the century, downtown's commercial district moved farther west toward Broadway, and many of San Diego's first buildings fell into disrepair. During the early 1900s, the quarter became known as the Stingaree district. Prostitutes picked up sailors in lively area taverns, and dance halls and crime flourished here; the blocks between Market Street and the waterfront were best avoided.

As the move for downtown redevelopment emerged, there was talk of destroying the buildings in the quarter, literally bulldozing them and starting from scratch. In 1974, history buffs, developers, architects, and artists formed the Gaslamp Quarter Council. Bent on preserving the district, they gathered funds from the government and private benefactors and began the painstaking, expensive task of cleaning up the quarter, restoring the finest old buildings, and attracting businesses and the public back to the heart of New Town. Some two decades later, their efforts have paid off. Former flophouses have become choice office buildings, and the area is dotted with characterful shops and restaurants.

Across the street from the Gaslamp Quarter Association's head-⑪ quarters, at the corner of Island and 3rd avenues, is the **Horton Grand Hotel.** In the mid-1980s, this ornate, quintessentially Victorian hostelry was created by joining together two historic hotels, the Kahle Saddlery and the Grand Hotel, built in the boom days of the 1880s; Wyatt Earp stayed at the Kahle Saddlery (then called the Brooklyn Hotel) while he was in town speculating on real estate ventures and opening gambling halls. Doomed to demolition and purchased from the city for $1 each, the two hotels were dismantled and painstakingly reconstructed on a new site, about four blocks from their original locations. A small Chinese Museum serves as a tribute to the surrounding Chinatown district, a collection of modest homes that once housed Chinese laborers and their families.

Many of the quarter's landmark buildings are located on 4th and 5th avenues, between Island Avenue and Broadway. Among the nicest are the Backesto Building, the Louis Bank of Commerce, and the Mercantile Building, all on 5th Avenue, and the Keating Building on F Street. Johnny M's 801, at the corner of 4th Avenue and F

Street, is a magnificently restored turn-of-the-century tavern with a 12-foot mahogany bar and a spectacular stained-glass domed ceiling.

As more and more artists—and art entrepreneurs—move to the area, the section of G Street between 6th and 9th avenues has become a haven for galleries; stop in at any one of them to pick up a map of the downtown arts district. The three-story brick Pannikin Building, at the corner of 7th Avenue and G Street, houses Ariba, an international folk-art boutique, and a coffee importer and roasting plant.

Time Out   Fifth Avenue between F and G streets is lined with restaurants, a number of them offering outdoor patios; **Trattoria La Strada** (702 5th Ave.) is a good place to sit out on a fine afternoon with a glass of wine and an antipasto. Many hip coffeehouses have also sprung up in the Gaslamp Quarter; you can nurse a double espresso at **Lulu's** (419 F St.) for hours.

Tour 2: Coronado

Coronado Island, an incorporated city unto itself, is a charming, peaceful community. The Spaniards called the island Los Coronados, or "the Crowned Ones," in the late 1500s and the name stuck. Today's residents, many of whom live in grand Victorian homes handed down for generations, tend to consider their island to be a sort of royal encampment, safe from the hassles and hustle of San Diego proper.

North Island Naval Air Station was established in 1911 on the island's north end, across from Point Loma, and was the site of Charles Lindbergh's departure on his flight around the world. Today high-tech air- and seacraft arrive and depart continually from North Island, providing a real-life education in military armament. Coronado's long relationship with the navy has made it an enclave of sorts for retired military personnel.

The streets of the island are wide, quiet, and friendly, with lots of neighborhood parks where young families mingle with the island's many senior citizens. Grand old homes face the waterfront and the Coronado Municipal Golf Course, with its lovely setting under the bridge, at the north end of Glorietta Bay; it's the site of the annual Fourth of July fireworks. Community celebrations and live-band concerts take place in Spreckels' Park on Orange Avenue.

Coronado is visible from downtown and Point Loma and accessible via the arching blue 2.2-mile-long San Diego–Coronado Bridge, a landmark just beyond downtown's skyline. There is a $1 toll for crossing the bridge into Coronado, but cars carrying two or more passengers may enter through the free car-pool lane. The bridge handles more than 20,000 cars each day, and rush hour tends to be slow, which is fine, since the view of the harbor, downtown, and the island is breathtaking, day and night. Until the bridge was completed in 1969, visitors and residents relied on the Coronado Ferry, which ran across the harbor from downtown. When the bridge was opened, the ferry closed down, much to the chagrin of those who were fond of traveling at a leisurely pace. In 1987, the ferry returned, and with it came the island's most ambitious development in decades. Coronado's residents and commuting workers have quickly adapted to this traditional mode of transportation, and the ferry has become quite popular with bicyclists, who shuttle their bikes across the harbor and ride the island's wide, flat boulevards for hours.

You can board the Bay Ferry (tel. 619/234–4111) at downtown San Diego's Embarcadero from the Broadway Pier, at Broadway and Harbor Drive. Boats depart hourly from 9 AM to 9:30 PM Sunday through Thursday, until 10:30 PM Friday and Saturday; the fare is

12 $2 each way. In Coronado, you will disembark at the **Old Ferry Landing,** which is actually a new development on an old site. Its buildings resemble the gingerbread domes of the Hotel del Coronado, long the island's main attraction. The Old Ferry Landing is similar to Seaport Village, with small shops and restaurants and lots of benches facing the water. Nearby, the elegant Le Meridien Hotel accommodates many wedding receptions and gala banquets.

13 A trackless trolley runs from the landing down **Orange Avenue,** the island's version of a downtown. It's easy to imagine you're on a street in Cape Cod when you stroll along this thoroughfare: The clapboard houses, small restaurants, and boutiques—many of them selling nautical paraphernalia—are in some ways more characteristic of New England than they are of California. But the East Coast illusion tends to dissipate as quickly as a winter fog here when you catch sight of one of the avenue's many citrus trees—or realize it's February and the sun is warming your face.

14 At the end of Orange Avenue, the **Hotel Del Coronado** is the island's most prominent landmark. Selected as a National Historic Site in 1977, the Del (as natives say) celebrated its 100th anniversary in 1988. Celebrities, royalty, and politicians marked the anniversary with a weekend-long party that highlighted the hotel's colorful history, integrally connected with that of the island itself.

The Del was the brainchild of wealthy financiers Elisha Spurr Babcock, Jr., and H.L. Story, who, in 1884, saw the potential of the island's virgin beaches and its view of San Diego's emerging harbor. The next year, they purchased a 4,100-acre parcel of land for $110,000 and threw a lavish Fourth of July bash for prospective investors in their hunting and fishing resort. By the end of the year, they had roused public interest—and had an ample return on their investment. The hotel was completed in 1888, and Thomas Edison himself threw the switch as the Del became the world's first electrically lighted hotel. It has been a dazzler ever since.

The Del's ornate Victorian gingerbread architecture is recognized all over the world because the hotel has served as a set for many movies, political meetings, and extravagant social happenings. It is said that the Duke of Windsor first met Wallis Simpson here. Eight presidents have been guests of the Del, and the film *Some Like It Hot,* starring Marilyn Monroe, was filmed at the hotel. Today, lower-level corridors are lined with historic photos from the Del's early days.

A red carpet leads up the front stairs to the main lobby, with its grand oak pillars and ceiling, and out to the central courtyard and gazebo. To the right is the Crown Room, a cavernous room with an arched ceiling made of notched sugar pine and constructed without nails. Enormous chandeliers sparkle overhead.

Time Out   The most popular meal on the island is the lavish Sunday brunch in the **Crown Room.** Pianists and harpists play soothing melodies from the curved balconies. The room can seat more than 1,000 diners, but it would be wise to make reservations in advance if you're dining with a group, particularly on holidays. Brunch is served from 9 to 2 and costs $21.95 for adults, $16.95 children 6–10, and $5.95 for children 2–5.

The Grand Ballroom overlooks the ocean and the hotel's long white beach. The patio surrounding the sky-blue swimming pool is a great place for just sitting back and imagining what the bathers looked like during the '20s, when the hotel rocked with good times. More rooms have been added in high-rise towers beside the original 400-room building, which is still the most charming place to stay. *1500 Orange Ave., tel. 619/435–6611. Guided tours ($10) from the lobby Thurs.–Sat. 10 and 11 AM.*

Coronado's other main attraction is its 86 historic homes—many of them turn-of-the-century mansions—and sites. The **Glorietta Bay Inn,** across the street from the Del, was the residence of John Spreckels, the original owner of North Island and the property on which the Hotel Del Coronado now stands. On Tuesday, Thursday, and Saturday morning at 11, the inn is the departure point for a walking tour of the area's historical homes. Sponsored by the Coronado Historical Association, the tour includes some spectacular mansions along with the Meade House, where L. Frank Baum wrote *The Wizard of Oz.* The cost is $5; call 619/435 5892 or 619/435 5444 for more information.

You can start your own tour at nearby **Star Park** on Loma Avenue, the hub for five streets that have been designated historic sites. But before you set out, stop in at the **Coronado Beach Historical Museum,** opened by the Coronado Historical Association in April 1993. Housed in a beautifully restored Cape Cod–style cottage built by an East Coast family in 1898, the museum illustrates the island's history with photographs and displays of its major formative events and sites: the Hotel del Coronado (including an original chamber pot from one of the rooms); Tent City, a summer resort just south of the Del developed by John Spreckels at the turn of the century; the early ferry boats; and the North Island Naval Air Station. It also hosts a small gift shop and a cozy sun porch. *1126 Loma Ave., tel. 619/435–7242. Admission free (donations accepted). Open Wed.–Sun. 10–4.*

Silver Strand Beach State Park runs along Silver Strand Boulevard from the Del to Imperial Beach. The view from the shore to Point Loma is lovely, and the long, clean beach is a perfect family gathering spot, with fire rings, rest rooms, and lifeguards. Across from the strand is the Coronado Cays, an exclusive community, popular with yacht owners and celebrities, and the Loews Coronado Bay Resort, which opened in 1991.

Tour 3: Point Loma, Shelter Island, and Harbor Island

Point Loma curves around the San Diego Bay west of downtown and the airport, protecting the center city from the Pacific's tides and waves. Although a number of military installations are based here and some main streets are cluttered with motels and fast-food shacks, Point Loma is an old and wealthy enclave of stately family homes for military officers, successful Portuguese fishermen, and political and professional leaders. Its bayside shores front huge estates, with sailboats and yachts packed tightly in private marinas.

Take Catalina Drive all the way down to the tip of Point Loma to reach **Cabrillo National Monument,** named after the Portuguese explorer Juan Rodríguez Cabrillo. Cabrillo, who had earlier gone on voyages with Cortés, was the first European to come to San Diego, which he called San Miguel, in 1542. In 1913, government grounds were set aside to commemorate his discovery. Today his monument, a 144-acre preserve of rugged cliffs and shores and outstanding overlooks, is one of the most frequently visited of all National Park Service sites.

Begin your tour at the visitor center, where films and lectures about Cabrillo's voyage, the sea-level tidal pools, and the gray whales migrating offshore are presented frequently. The center has an excellent shop with an interesting selection of books about nature, San Diego, and the sea; maps of the region, posters of whales, flowers, shells, and the requisite postcards, slides, and film are also on sale. Visitors who are unable to do much hiking around the site should inquire here about the park shuttle service. Rest rooms and water fountains are plentiful along the paths that climb to the monument's various viewpoints, but, except for a few vending machines at the Visitor Center, there are no food facilities. Exploring the grounds consumes time and calories; bring a picnic and rest on a bench overlooking the sailboats headed to sea.

Signs along the walkways that edge the cliffs explain the views, with posters depicting the various navy, fishing, and pleasure craft that sail into and fly over the bay. Directly south across the bay from the visitor center is the North Island Naval Air Station on the west end of Coronado Island. Directly left on the shores of Point Loma is the Naval Ocean Systems Center and Ballast Point; nuclear-powered submarines are now docked where Cabrillo's small ships anchored in 1542.

A statue of Cabrillo overlooks downtown from the next windy promontory, where visitors gather to admire the stunning panorama over the bay, from the snowcapped San Bernardino Mountains, some 200 miles northeast, to the hills surrounding Tijuana. The stone figure standing on the bluff looks rugged and dashing, but he is a creation of an artist's imagination—no portraits of Cabrillo are known to exist.

The 2-mile Bayside Trail winds through cliffside chaparral, curving under the clifftop lookouts and bringing you ever closer to the bayfront scenery. You cannot reach the beach from this trail and must stick to the path to protect the cliffs from erosion and yourself from poisonous plants. Along the way, you'll see prickly pear cactus and yucca, black-eyed Susans, fragrant sage, and maybe a lizard or a hummingbird. The climb back is long but gradual, leading up to the old lighthouse.

The oil lamp of the **Old Point Loma Lighthouse** was first lit in 1855. The light, sitting in a brass-and-iron housing above a painstakingly refurbished white wooden house, shone through a state-of-the-art lens from France and was visible from the sea for 25 miles. Unfortunately, it was too high above the cliffs to guide navigators trapped in southern California's thick offshore fog and low clouds. In 1891, a new lighthouse was built on the small shore under the slowly eroding 400-foot cliffs. The old lighthouse is open to visitors, and the coast guard still uses the newer lighthouse and a mighty foghorn to guide boaters through the narrow channel leading into the bay.

The western and southern cliffs of Cabrillo Monument are prime whale-watching territory. A sheltered viewing station offers a tape-recorded lecture describing the great gray whales' migration from the Bering Sea to Baja, and high-powered viewers help you focus on the whales' water spouts. The whales are visible on clear days in January and February, mostly in early morning.

More accessible sea creatures can be seen in the tidal pools at the foot of the monument's western cliffs. Drive north from the visitor center to the first road on the left, which winds down to the coast guard station and the shore. When the tide is low (check with the ranger), you can walk on the rocks around saltwater pools filled with starfish, crabs, anemones, octopuses, and hundreds of other sea creatures and plants. The pools are protected by law, so the creatures are off-limits. *Cabrillo National Monument, Box 6670, San Diego 92166, tel. 619/557–5450. Admission: $4 per car, $2 per person entering on foot, or by bicycle or bus. Golden Age Passport holders, people with disabilities, and children 16 and under free. Park open daily 9–5:15, Old Lighthouse 9–5, Bayside Trail 9–4, tidal-pool areas 9–4:30 in winter; in summer, the park is open until sunset, and other areas have extended hours.*

⑲ More than 40,000 white headstones in **Fort Rosecrans National Cemetery** overlook both sides of the point just north of the monument as you head back into the neighborhoods of Point Loma. The navy has various centers along Rosecrans Street, which also leads to the U.S. Marine Corps Recruit Depot.

Continue north on Catalina Boulevard to Hill Street and turn left **⑳** to reach **Sunset Cliffs Park,** at the western side of Point Loma near Ocean Beach. The cliffs are aptly named, since their main attraction is their vantage point as a fine sunset-watching spot. The dramatic coastline here seems to have been carved out of ancient rock. Certainly the waves make their impact, and each year more sections of the cliffs sport caution signs. Don't ignore these warnings: It's easy to lose your footing and slip in the crumbling sandstone, and the surf can get very rough. Small coves and beaches dot the coastline and are popular with surfers drawn to the pounding waves and locals from the neighborhood who name and claim their special spots. The homes along Sunset Cliffs Boulevard are lovely examples of southern California luxury, with pink stucco mansions beside shingle Cape Cod–style cottages.

Return to Catalina Boulevard and backtrack south for a few blocks to reach Canon Street, which leads toward the peninsula's eastern **㉑** (bay) side. Almost at the shore, you'll see **Scott Street,** which runs along Point Loma's waterfront from Shelter Island to the Marine Corps Recruiting Center on Harbor Drive. Lined with deep-sea fishing charters and whale-watching boats, this is a good spot from which to watch fishermen (and women) haul marlin, tuna, and puny mackerel off their boats.

Time Out   The freshest and tastiest fish to be found along Point Loma's shores comes from **Point Loma Sea Foods,** off Scott Street at Emerson Street, behind the Vagabond Inn. A fish market sells specialties fresh from the boat, and locals and tourists alike crowd the adjacent take-out counter for seafood cocktails and salads, great ceviche, and wonderful crab and shrimp sandwiches made with freshly baked sourdough bread. There are a couple of places to sit outside, but most folks squeeze into tables in the small dining area behind the store.

㉒ Scott Street is bisected by Shelter Island Drive, which leads to **Shelter Island,** actually a peninsula that sits in the narrow channel between Point Loma's eastern shore and the west coast of Coronado. In 1950, the port director thought there should be some use for the soil dredged to deepen the ship channel. Why not build an island?

His hunch paid off. Shelter Island's shores now support towering mature palms, a cluster of mid-range resorts, restaurants, and side-by-side marinas. It is the center of San Diego's yacht-building industry, and boats in every stage of construction are visible in the yacht yards. A long sidewalk runs from the landscaped lawns of the **San Diego Yacht Club** (tucked down Anchorage Street off Shelter Island Drive), past boat brokerages to the hotels and marinas, which line the inner shore, facing Point Loma. On the bay side, fishermen launch their boats or simply stand on shore and cast. Families relax at picnic tables along the grass, where there are fire rings and permanent barbecue grills, while strollers wander to the huge Friendship Bell, given to San Diegans by the people of Yokohama in 1960.

㉓ Go back up Shelter Island Drive, turn right on Rosecrans Street, and make another right on North Harbor Drive to reach **Harbor Island,** a peninsula adjacent to the airport that was created out of 3.5 million tons of rock and soil from the San Diego Bay. Again, hotels and restaurants line the inner shores, but here, the buildings are many stories high, and the views from the bayside rooms are spectacular. The bay shore has pathways, gardens, and picnic spots for sightseeing or working off the calories from the island restaurants' fine meals. On the west point, Tom Ham's Lighthouse restaurant has a coast guard–approved beacon shining from its tower.

Tour 4: Balboa Park

Numbers in the margin correspond to points of interest on the Tour 4: Balboa Park map.

Straddling two mesas overlooking downtown and the Pacific Ocean, Balboa Park is set on 1,400 beautifully landscaped acres. Hosting the majority of San Diego's museums and a world-famous zoo, the park serves as the cultural center of the city, as well as a recreational paradise for animal lovers and folks who want to spend a day picnicking or strolling in a lush green space.

Many of the park's ornate Spanish-Moorish buildings were intended to be temporary structures housing exhibits for the Panama–California International Exposition of 1915. Fortunately, city leaders realized the buildings' value and incorporated them in their plans for Balboa Park's acreage, which had been set aside by the city founders in 1868. The Spanish theme first instituted in the early 1900s was carried through in new buildings designed for the California Pacific International Exposition of 1935–36. El Prado, the courtyard and walkway first created for the 1915 exposition, now passes through San Diego's central museum district, with pathways forking off to other attractions.

The Laurel Street Bridge, also known as Cabrillo Bridge, is the park's official gateway; it leads over a vast canyon, filled with downtown commuter traffic on Highway 163, to El Prado, which, beyond the art museum, becomes the park's central pedestrian mall. At

Tour 4: Balboa Park

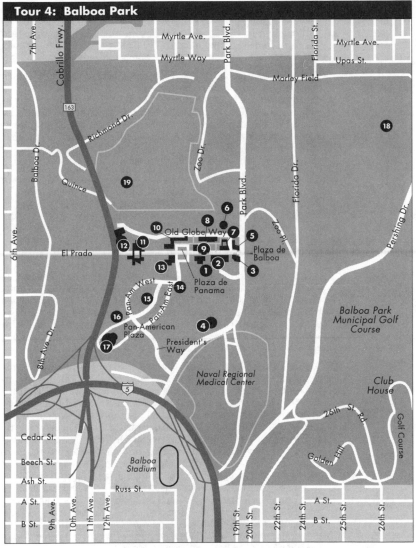

Botanical Building, **8**
Casa del Balboa, **2**
Casa del Prado, **7**
Centro Cultural de la Raza, **4**
House of Pacific Relations, **15**
Morley Field, **18**
The Museum of Man, **11**
Park Information Center, **1**

Reuben H. Fleet Space Theater and Science Center, **3**
San Diego Aerospace Museum and International Aerospace Hall of Fame, **17**
San Diego Art Institute, **13**
San Diego Automotive Museum, **16**
San Diego Museum of Art, **10**

San Diego Natural History Museum, **5**
San Diego Zoo, **19**
Simon Edison Center for the Performing Arts, **12**
Spanish Village Arts and Crafts Center, **6**
Spreckels Organ Pavilion, **14**
Timken Art Gallery, **9**

Christmas the bridge is lined with colored lights; bright pink blossoms on rows of peach trees herald the coming of spring. The 100-bell carillon in the California Tower tolls the hour. Figures of California's historic personages decorate the base of the 200-foot spire, and a magnificent blue-tiled dome shines in the sun.

Parking near Balboa Park's museums is no mean accomplishment, especially on fine summer days when the lots fill up quickly. If you're driving in via the Laurel Street Bridge, the first parking area you'll come to is off the Prado to the left, going toward Pan American Plaza. Don't despair if there are no spaces here; you'll see more lots as you continue down along the same road. If you end up parking a bit far from your destination, just consider the stroll back through the greenery part of the day's recreational activities.

Most of the park's museums are open daily 10–4; during the summer, a number are open late on Thursday—phone ahead to ask. It's impossible to cover the entire park in one day, so decide before you head out what you'd like your focus to be. If your interests run to the aesthetic, the Museum of Photographic Arts and the San Diego Museum of Art are must-sees. Those with a penchant for natural and cultural history shouldn't miss the San Diego Natural History Museum or the Museum of Man; those oriented toward space and technology should visit the Reuben H. Fleet Space Theater and Science Center and the San Diego Aerospace Museum. If you don't choose to go inside, you'll be entertained by the street performers who gather along the Prado and delighted by the park's many gardens, representing a variety of natural landscapes. What follows are some highlights of the park's attractions, rather than a complete rundown of the sights and activities available here.

❶ A good place to begin a visit is at the **Balboa Park Visitors Center.** Maps and pamphlets—as well as the friendly volunteers who run the center—can help you decide what you'd like to see. The office sells the Passport to Balboa Park, which has reduced-price coupons to the museums—worthwhile if you want to visit a number of them and aren't entitled to the other discounts that many give to children, senior citizens, and military personnel. On Tuesdays, the museums offer free admission on a rotating basis; inquire here about the schedule. Also available at the office is a schedule and route map for the free trams that operate around the park, giving you an alternative way to get back to your car or bus if all that culture has tired you. From April through September, trams run 9:30–5:30, approximately every 8–12 minutes; the rest of the year, service is 11–5 and frequency is 12–24 minutes. *In the House of Hospitality, on the Prado just past its junction with Pan American Plaza Rd., tel. 619/239–0512. Open daily 9–4.*

❷ Next door to the House of Hospitality, the **Casa de Balboa** houses four museums: the San Diego Hall of Champions Sports Museum, the Museum of Photographic Arts, the San Diego Historical Society–Museum of San Diego History, and the San Diego Model Railroad Museum. Starting from the left as you enter, the **Museum of San Diego History** features rotating exhibits on local urban history after 1850, when California became part of the United States. The society's research library is in the building's basement. *Tel. 619/232–6203. Admission: $3 adults. Open Wed.–Sun. 10–4:30.*

Down the hall, the **San Diego Sports Museum Hall of Champions** celebrates local heroes with a vast collection of memorabilia, uniforms, paintings, photographs, and computer and video displays. An amusing bloopers film is screened at the Sports Theater. *Tel.*

619/234–2544. Admission: $3 adults, $1 children 6–17. Open daily 10–4:30.

The **Museum of Photographic Arts,** one of the few in the country dedicated solely to photography, celebrated its 10th anniversary in 1993. World-renowned classic photographers, such as Ansel Adams, Imogen Cunningham, Henri Cartier-Bresson, and Edward Weston, are represented by the museum, along with relatively obscure contemporary artists. Volunteers lead tours through the exhibits, which change every six weeks. Gallery talks are given on weekends. *Tel. 619/239–5262. Admission: $3. Open daily 10–5.*

Below MOPA, in the basement of the Casa de Balboa, is the **San Diego Model Railroad Museum.** The room is filled with the sounds of chugging engines, screeching brakes, and shrill whistles when the six model-train exhibits are in operation. *Tel. 619/696–0199. Admission: $3 adults. Open Wed.–Fri. 11–4, weekends 11–5.*

If you continue walking down El Prado, you'll come to the Plaza de Balboa and a large central fountain. Just past the fountain, El Prado ends in a bridge that crosses over Park Boulevard to a perfectly tended rose garden and a seemingly wild cactus grove. From here, you can see across the canyon to even more parkland, with picnic groves, sports facilities, and acres of ranging chaparral.

To the right of the Plaza de Balboa fountain, on the same side of the ❸ road as the Casa de Balboa, the **Reuben H. Fleet Space Theater and Science Center** features clever interactive exhibits that teach children and adults about scientific principles. On a huge, domed overhead screen at the Omnimax Theater, informative and exhilarating films about nature and space (shown regularly throughout the day) seem to lift the viewer right into the action. The center's gift shop is akin to a museum, with toys and gadgets that inspire the imagination. At night, the Laserium presents laser shows set to rock music. *Tel. 619/238–1233. Science Center admission: $2.25 adults, $1 children 5–15 or included with price of theater ticket. Space Theater tickets: $5.50 adults, $4 senior citizens, $3 children 5–15; laser shows: $7.50 adults, $5 children 5–15. Open Sun.–Tues. 9:30 AM–6 PM, Wed. and Thurs. 9:30 AM–9:30 PM, Fri. and Sat. 9:30 AM–10:30 PM.*

To the south, past the parking lots of the Reuben H. Fleet Space ❹ Theater, is the **Centro Cultural de la Raza,** an old water tower converted into a cultural center focusing on Mexican arts. Attractions include a gallery with rotating exhibits and a theater, as well as a permanent collection of mural art, a fine example of which may be seen on the tower's exterior. *Tel. 619/235–6135. Admission free. Open Wed.–Sun. noon–5.*

Across the Plaza de Balboa fountain from the Reuben H. Fleet Space Theater and Science Center, a short flight of steps will take ❺ you up to the **San Diego Natural History Museum,** which features displays on the plants and animals of southern California and Mexico. Children seem particularly impressed by the dinosaur bones and the live-insect zoo. The Hall of Mineralogy hosts an impressive collection of gems. Near the museum entrance, the 185-pound brass Foucault Pendulum, suspended on a 43-foot cable, demonstrates the earth's rotation. The museum frequently schedules nature walks, films, and lectures. *Tel. 619/232–3821. Admission: $6 adults, $5 senior citizens, $2 children 6–17. Open daily 9:30–4:30.*

North of the natural history museum, on the way to the zoo, is the ❻ **Spanish Village Arts and Crafts Center.** Built for the 1935–36 exposition, the village houses are now used as arts-and-crafts studios.

The sculptors, photographers, jewelers, and other artists who rent space here demonstrate their skills and their wares—most available for sale—to the public. *No phone. Admission free. Open daily 11–4.*

Behind the village, a 48-passenger **miniature train** runs a half-mile loop through eucalyptus groves. Nearby, riders on the antique **carousel** stretch from their seats to grab the brass rings suspended an arm's length away and earn a free ride. *Tel. 619/239–4748. Admission: $1 for railroad, $1 for carousel. Open mid-June–Labor Day, daily 11–5:30; the rest of the year, weekends and school holidays 11–4:30.*

7 If you head back east along the Prado from the San Diego Natural History Museum, you'll come to the **Casa del Prado**, which houses classes, group meetings, and special events. The San Diego Floral Association (tel. 619/232–5762) has a small gift shop, research library, and offices here. Be sure to wander through—you may chance upon a show of orchids, bonsai, or ikebana, the Japanese art of flower arranging.

8 The action gets lively in the next section of El Prado, where mimes, jugglers, and musicians perform on long lawns beside the Lily Pond in front of the graceful **Botanical Building.** Built for the 1915 exposition, the latticed, open-air nursery houses more than 500 types of tropical and subtropical plants. The orchid collection is stunning, and there are benches beside cool, miniature waterfalls for resting in the shade. The Lily Pond, filled with giant koi fish and blooming water lilies, is popular with photographers. *Admission free. Open Tues.–Sun. 10–4.*

9 On the other side of the Lily Pond is the only privately owned building in the park, operated by the Putnam Foundation. The small **Timken Art Gallery** houses a selection of minor works by major European and American artists, as well as a fine collection of Russian icons. *Tel. 619/239–5548. Admission free. Open Oct.–Aug., Tues.–Sat. 10–4:30, Sun. 1:30–4:30. Closed Sept.*

10 Just behind the Timken Gallery on the Plaza de Panama, the **San Diego Museum of Art** is known primarily for its Spanish Baroque and Renaissance paintings, including works by El Greco, Goya, Rubens, and Van Ruisdale. The museum also has strong holdings of Southeast Asian art and Indian miniatures, and its Baldwin M. Baldwin wing displays more than 100 pieces by Toulouse-Lautrec. The museum's latest acquisition is a large collection of contemporary California art. An outdoor Sculpture Garden exhibits both traditional and modernistic pieces in a striking natural setting. *Tel. 619/232–7931. Admission: $5 adults, $4 senior citizens, $2 students with current ID and children 6–17. Open Tues.–Sun. 10–4:30.*

Time Out Take a break from museum-hopping with a cup of freshly brewed coffee or a glass of California chardonnay in the San Diego Museum of Art's **Sculpture Garden Café,** which also offers a small selection of tasty—if rather pricey—gourmet lunches.

11 If you get back on El Prado and continue east, you'll come to the **Museum of Man,** located under the California Tower. One of the finest anthropological museums in the country, it houses an extensive collection first assembled for the 1915 exposition and amplified over the years. Exhibits focus on Southwestern, Mexican, and South American cultures; the latest acquisition, in 1993, was a collection of ancient Egyptian artifacts. In the "Lifestyles and Ceremonies" section, high-tech gadgetry is employed in displays on biology, reproduction, and culture, offering a fascinating look at the costumes and rituals of San Diego's many ethnic communities. Weddings are sometimes held at the Chapel of St. Francis, a model of a typical early California hacienda chapel viewed by appointment only. *Tel. 619/239–2001. Admission: $4 adults, $2 children 13–18, $1 children 6–12. Open daily 10–4:30.*

⑫ The **Simon Edison Centre for the Performing Arts** (tel. 619/239–2255), including the Cassius Carter Centre Stage, the Lowell Davies Festival Theatre, and the Old Globe, sits beside the Museum of Man under the California Tower. Originally devoted to Shakespearean theater, the Globe now also holds first-rate productions by other playwrights, too. All three theaters are small and intimate, and evening performances on the outdoor stages are particularly enjoyable during the summer.

⑬ Across the Prado and back toward the Museum of Art, the **House of Charm** is the permanent home of the San Diego Art Institute. Currently closed for renovations, it's scheduled to reopen sometime in 1995. In the interim, the Art Institute is holding its shows in Mission Valley Center (1640 Camino del Rio N, Suite 1368, tel. 619/220–4800 for information on hours).

Next to the House of Charm, the **Alcazar Garden** was designed to replicate the gardens surrounding the Alcazar Castle in Seville. The flower beds are ever-changing horticultural exhibits, with bright orange and yellow poppies blooming in the spring and deep rust and crimson chrysanthemums appearing in the fall. The benches by the tiled fountains are nice spots to rest.

At the Plaza de Panama parking lot, west of the Art Institute, another road heads south from El Prado. It's divided by a long island
⑭ of flowers as it curves around the **Spreckels Organ Pavilion** and the 5,000-pipe Spreckels Organ, believed to be the largest outdoor pipe organ in the world. You can hear this impressive instrument at one of the concerts offered at 2 PM on Sunday afternoons year-round. On summer evenings, local military bands, gospel groups, and barbershop quartets hold concerts, and at Christmas, the park's massive Christmas tree and life-size nativity display turn the pavilion into a seasonal wonderland. *Tel. 619/226–0819. Admission free. Open Fri.–Sun. 10–4.*

Northeast of the Organ Pavilion, the first phase of a new Japanese Friendship Garden includes an exhibit house, a traditional sand-and-stone garden, and a picnic area with a view of the canyon below. There are also a snack bar and a small gift shop. *Tel. 619/232–2780. Admission: $2 adults, $1 senior citizens, military, disabled visitors, children over 7; free Tues. Open Fri.–Sun. and Tues. 10–4.*

To the right of the organ pavilion, on Pan American West road, the
⑮ **House of Pacific Relations** is really a cluster of stucco cottages representing more than 30 foreign countries. The buildings are open on Sunday, and individual cottages often present celebrations on their country's holidays.

Farther west, in the building used as the Palace of Transportation
⑯ for the 1935–36 exposition, the **San Diego Automotive Museum** maintains a large collection of vintage cars and has an ongoing automobile restoration program. *Tel. 619/231–2886. Admission: $4 adults, $3 senior citizens, $2 children 6–17. Open daily 10–4:30.*

⑰ The southern road ends at the Pan American Plaza and the **San Diego Aerospace Museum and International Aerospace Hall of**

Fame. Looking unlike any other structure in the park, the sleek, streamlined edifice was commissioned by the Ford Motor Company for the 1935–36 exposition; at night, with a line of blue neon outlining it, the round building looks like a landlocked UFO. Exhibits about aviation and aerospace pioneers line the rotunda, and a collection of real and replicated aircraft fills the center. *Tel. 619/234–8291. Admission: $4 adults, $1 children 6–17. Open daily 10–4:30.*

Next to the aerospace center, the **Starlight Bowl** (tel. 619/544–7800 or 619/544–STAR) presents live musicals during the summer on its outdoor stage; actors freeze in their places when planes roar overhead on their way to Lindbergh Field. The Federal Building, also in the Pan American Plaza, is the home of the U.S. Olympic Volleyball Team, and the Municipal Gymnasium is used by amateur basketball and volleyball teams.

President's Way leads from the plaza to Park Boulevard, the main thoroughfare from the park to downtown. **Pepper Grove,** along the boulevard, has lots of picnic tables and a playground.

The parklands across the Cabrillo Bridge, at the west end of El Prado, have been set aside for picnics and athletics. Roller skaters perform along Balboa Drive, leading to **Marston Point,** overlooking downtown. Ladies and gents in spotless white outfits meet regularly on summer afternoons for lawn-bowling tournaments at the green beside the bridge. Dirt trails lead into pine groves with secluded picnic areas.

⑱ The far-east end of Balboa Park, across Park Boulevard and Florida Canyon on Morley Field Drive, is the park's athletic center. **The Morley Field Sports Complex** (tel. 619/692–4919) has an unusual Frisbee Golf Course, with challenging "holes" (wire baskets hung from metal poles) where players toss their Frisbees over canyons and treetops to reach their goal. Morley Field also boasts a public pool, tennis courts, an archery range, a casting pool, playgrounds, and a velodrome used for bicycle races.

⑲ Fronting Park Boulevard is Balboa Park's most famous attraction, the 100-acre **San Diego Zoo.** More than 3,200 animals of 777 species roam in expertly crafted habitats that spread down into, around, and above the natural canyons. Equal attention has been paid to the flora and the fauna, and the zoo is an enormous botanical garden with one of the world's largest collections of subtropical plants.

From the moment you walk through the entrance and face the swarm of bright pink flamingos and blue peacocks, you know you've entered a rare pocket of natural harmony. Exploring the zoo fully requires the stamina of a healthy hiker, but open-air trams that run throughout the day allow visitors to see 80% of the exhibits on their 3-mile tour. The animals are attuned to the buses and many like to show off; the bears are particularly fine performers, waving and bowing to their admirers. The Skyfari ride, which soars 170 feet above ground, gives a good overview of the zoo's layout and a marvelous panorama of the park, downtown San Diego, the bay, and the ocean, far past the Coronado Bridge.

Still, the zoo is at its best when you can wander the paths that climb through the huge enclosed Scripps Aviary, where brightly colored tropical birds swoop between branches just inches from your face. The Gorilla Tropics exhibit, beside the aviary, is the zoo's latest venture into bioclimatic zone exhibits, where animals live in enclosed environments modeled on their native habitats. Throughout the zoo, walkways wind over bridges and past waterfalls ringed with tropical ferns; giant elephants in a sandy plateau roam so close you're tempted to pet them. The San Diego Zoo houses the only koalas outside Australia and three rare golden monkeys number among its impressive collection of endangered species; a small two-headed snake named Thelma and Louise holds court in the reptile house.

The Children's Zoo is worth a visit, no matter what your age. Goats and sheep beg to be petted and are particularly adept at snatching bag lunches, while bunnies and guinea pigs seem willing to be fondled endlessly. In the nursery windows, you can see baby lemurs and spider monkeys playing with Cabbage Patch kids, looking much like the human babies peering from strollers through the glass. The exhibits are designed in size and style for four-year-olds, but that doesn't deter children of all ages from having fun. Even the rest rooms are child-size. The hardest part of being in the Children's Zoo will be getting your family to move on.

The Wedgeforth Bowl, a 3,000-seat amphitheater, holds various animal shows throughout the day, occasionally hosted by the zoo's ambassador of goodwill, Joan Embery, called "the most widely known inhabitant of the zoo." Embery's frequent appearances on Johnny Carson's *Tonight* show, usually with some charming critter to entertain the host, made the San Diego Zoo a household name among late-night viewers.

The zoo's simulated Asian rain forest, Tiger River, brings together 10 exhibits with more than 35 species of animals. As spectacular as the tigers, pythons, and water dragons are, they seem almost inconsequential among the $500,000 collection of exotic trees and plants. The mist-shrouded trails winding down a canyon into Tiger River pass by fragrant jasmine, ginger lilies, and orchids, giving the visitor the feeling of descending into a South American jungle. In Sun Bear Forest, playful cubs constantly claw apart the trees and shrubs that serve as a natural playground for climbing, jumping, and general rowdiness. Throughout the zoo, plans are under way to remodel exhibit areas into closer facsimiles of the animals' natural habitats.

Time Out   The zoo is not known for its culinary wonders, though there are plenty of food stands selling popcorn, pizza, and enormous ice-cream cones. The best restaurant in the zoo is the **Peacock and Raven,** just inside the main entrance, serving sandwiches, salads, and light meals. The views are rather better than the food at the **Treehouse Cafe** at Gorilla Tropics, but the restaurant's Swiss Family Robinson perspective is fun. The **Safari Kitchen,** left of the Flamingo Lagoon, offers reasonably good fried chicken and warm chocolate chip cookies.

In many ways also a self-sustaining habitat for humans, the zoo rents strollers, wheelchairs, and cameras; it also has a first-aid office, a lost-and-found, and an ATM. It's best to avert your eyes from the zoo's two main gift shops until the end of your visit; you can spend a half-day just poking through the wonderful animal-related posters, crafts, dishes, clothing, and toys. *Tel. 619/234–3153. Admission (including unlimited access to the Skyfari ride and the Children's Zoo): $12 adults, $4 children 3–11; tram ride: $3 adults, $2.50 children; children 11 and under enter free during the month of October. D, MC, V. Gates open fall–spring, daily 9–4 (visitors may remain until 5); summer, daily 9–5 (visitors may remain until 6).*

Tour 5: Old Town

Numbers in the margin correspond to points of interest on the Tour 5: Old Town San Diego map.

San Diego's Spanish and Mexican history and heritage are most evident in Old Town, just north of downtown at Juan Street, near the intersection of I–5 and I–8. It wasn't until 1968 that Old Town became a state historic park. Fortunately, private efforts kept the area's history alive until then, and a number of San Diego's oldest structures remain in good shape.

Although Old Town is often credited as being the first European settlement in southern California, the true beginnings took place overlooking Old Town from atop Presidio Park (*see below*). There, Father Junipero Serra established the first of California's missions, San Diego de Alcalá, in 1769. Some of San Diego's Native Americans, called the San Diegueños by the Spaniards, were forced to abandon their seminomadic lifestyle and live at the mission. They were expected to follow Spanish customs and adopt Christianity as their religion, but they resisted these impositions fiercely; of all the California missions, San Diego de Alcalá was the least successful in carrying out conversions. For security reasons, the mission was built on a hill, but it didn't have an adequate water supply, and food became scarce as the number of Native Americans and Spanish soldiers occupying the site increased.

In 1774, the hilltop was declared a Royal Presidio, or fortress, and the mission was moved to its current location along the San Diego River, 6 miles east of the original site. Losing more of their traditional grounds and ranches as the mission grew along the riverbed, the Native Americans attacked and burned it in 1775, destroying religious objects and killing Franciscan Padre Luis Jayme. Their later attack on the presidio was less successful, and their revolt was short-lived. By 1800, about 1,500 Native Americans were living on the mission's grounds, receiving religious instruction and adapting to Spanish ways.

The pioneers living within the presidio's walls were mostly Spanish soldiers, poor Mexicans, and mestizos of Spanish and Native American ancestry, many of whom were unaccustomed to farming San Diego's arid land. They existed marginally until 1821, when Mexico gained independence from Spain, claimed its lands in California, and flew the Mexican flag over the presidio. The Mexican government, centered some 2,000 miles away in Monterrey, stripped the missions of their landholdings, and an aristocracy of landholders began to emerge. At the same time, settlers were beginning to move down from the presidio to what is now called Old Town.

A rectangular plaza was laid out along today's San Diego Avenue to serve as the settlement's center. In 1846, during the war between Mexico and the United States, a detachment of marines raised the U.S. flag over the plaza on a pole said to have been a mainmast. The flag was torn down once or twice, but by early 1848, Mexico had surrendered California, and the U.S. flag remained. In 1850, San Diego became an incorporated city, with Old Town as its center.

Old Town's historic buildings are clustered around **Old Town Plaza,** bounded by Wallace Street on the west, Calhoun Street on the north, Mason Street on the east, and San Diego Avenue on the south; you can see the presidio from behind the cannon by the flagpole. These days, the plaza is a pleasant place for resting and regrouping as you

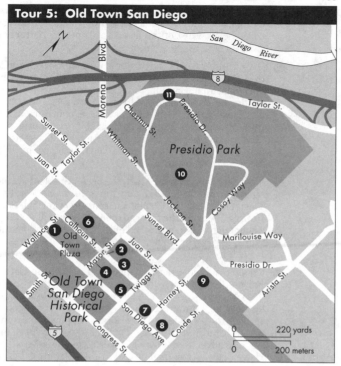

Tour 5: Old Town San Diego

plan your tour of Old Town and watch other visitors stroll by; art shows often fill the lawns around the plaza. San Diego Avenue is closed to traffic here, and the cars are diverted to Juan and Congress streets, both of which are lined with shops and restaurants. There are a number of free parking lots on the outskirts of Old Town, but they fill quickly. By the end of 1995, the San Diego trolley should stop here; in the meantime, if you plan to visit on the weekend, come early to find a spot.

A new visitor center is scheduled to open in Old Town in late 1995, but the **Old Town State Historic Park** office is currently in the **Robinson-Rose House,** on the west (Wallace Street) side of the plaza. This was the original commercial center of old San Diego, housing railroad offices, law offices, and the first newspaper press; one room has been restored and outfitted with period furnishings. Park rangers now show films and distribute information from the living room. An excellent free walking tour of the park leaves from here daily at 2 PM, weather permitting. From 10 to 1 every Wednesday and the first Saturday of the month, park staff and volunteers in period costume give cooking and crafts demonstrations at the Machado y Stewart adobe; adjacent to the Bandini House near Juan Street, you can watch a blacksmith hammering away at his anvil from 10 to 2 every Wednesday and Saturday. *4002 Wallace St., tel. 619/220–5422. Open daily 10–5. Closed Thanksgiving, Christmas, and New Year's.*

Many of Old Town's buildings were destroyed in a huge fire in 1872, but after the site became a state historic park in 1968, efforts were begun to reconstruct or restore the structures that remained. Eight of the original adobes are still intact. The tour map available at the

Robinson-Rose House gives details on all of the historic houses on the plaza and in its vicinity; a few of the more interesting ones are noted below. Most of the houses are open to visitors daily 10–4 and most do not charge admission.

❷ On Mason Street, at the corner of Calhoun Street, **La Casa de Bandini** is one of the loveliest haciendas in San Diego. Built in 1829 by a Peruvian, Juan Bandini, the house served as Old Town's social center during Mexican rule. Albert Seeley, a stagecoach entrepreneur, purchased the home in 1869, built a second story, and turned it into the Cosmopolitan Hotel, a comfortable way station for travelers on the day-long trip south from Los Angeles. These days, Casa Bandini's colorful gardens and main-floor dining rooms house a popular Mexican restaurant.

❸ Next door on Calhoun Street, the **Seeley Stables** became San Diego's stagecoach stop in 1867 and were the transportation hub of Old Town until near the turn of the century, when the Southern Pacific Railroad became the favored mode of travel. The stables now house a collection of horse-drawn vehicles, Western memorabilia, and Native American artifacts. There is a $2 admission fee for adults, $1 for children 6–17.

❹ This fee also covers admittance to **La Casa de Estudillo,** built on Mason Street in 1827 by the commander of the San Diego Presidio, Jose Maria Estudillo. The largest and most elaborate of the original adobe homes, it was occupied by members of the Estudillo family until 1887. After being left to deteriorate for some time, it was purchased and restored in 1910 by sugar magnate and developer John D. Spreckels, who advertised it in bold lettering on the side as "Ramona's Marriage Place"; the small chapel in the house was believed to be the setting for the wedding in Helen Hunt Jackson's popular novel.

❺ On Twigg Street and San Diego Avenue, the **San Diego Union Newspaper Historical Museum** is in the Casa de Altamirano, a New England-style wood-frame house prefabricated in Maine and shipped around Cape Horn in 1851. The building has been restored to replicate the newspaper's offices of 1868, when the first edition of the *San Diego Union* was printed.

Also worth exploring in the plaza area are the **Dental Museum, Mason Street School, Wells Fargo Museum,** and the **San Diego Courthouse.** Ask at the visitor center for locations.

Northwest of the plaza lies the unofficial center of Old Town, the
❻ **Bazaar del Mundo,** a shopping and dining enclave built to represent a colonial Mexican square. The central courtyard is always in blossom, with magenta bougainvillea, scarlet hibiscus, and irises, poppies, and petunias in season. Ballet Folklorico and flamenco dancers perform in the outdoor gazebo on weekend afternoons, and the bazaar frequently holds arts-and-crafts exhibits and Mexican festivals in the courtyard. Colorful shops specializing in Latin American crafts and unusual gift items border the square, beyond a shield of thick bushes and huge bird cages with cawing macaws and toucans. Although many of the shops here have high-quality wares, prices can be considerably higher than those at shops on the other side of Old Town plaza; it's a good idea to do some comparative shopping before you make any purchases.

Time Out The margarita is Old Town's premier drink, and **Casa de Pico** in the Bazaar del Mundo is one of Old Town's most popular spots to indulge in one. The excellent *antijitos,* or Mexican appetizers, including flavorful guacamole and nachos, are good accompaniments. Also in the bazaar, **La Panadería** bakery sells fresh, hot *churros*—long sticks of fried dough coated with cinnamon and sugar.

Old Town's boundaries and reputation as a historic attraction and shopping-dining center have spread in the past few years. Opened in late 1992 on San Diego Avenue beside the state park headquarters, **Dodson's Corner** is a modern retailer in a mid-19th-century setting; two of the shops in the complex, which sells everything from quilts and Western clothing to pottery and jewelry, are reconstructions of homes that stood on the spot in 1848. Farther away from the plaza, art galleries and expensive gift shops are interspersed with curio shops, restaurants, and open-air stands selling inexpensive Mexican pottery, jewelry, and blankets. San Diego Avenue continues as Old Town's main drag, with an ever-changing array of shopping plazas constructed in mock Mexican-plaza style. The best of these is the **Old Town Esplanade,** between Harney and Conde streets. Several shops display Mexican and South American folk art.

Historic sites punctuate the lineup of ice-cream and souvenir shops **7** on San Diego Avenue, including the **Thomas Whaley Museum,** built in 1856. This was southern California's first two-story brick structure, and it served as the county courthouse and government seat during the 1870s. An array of historical artifacts, including one of the six life masks that exist of Abraham Lincoln, is on display here. The place is most famed, however, for the ghost that is said to inhabit it; this is one of the few houses authenticated by the United States Department of Commerce as being haunted. The museum was expanded in 1993 to include the Darby-Pendleton House, a prefab residence built in Maine in 1850 and shipped here. *2482 San Diego Ave., tel. 619/298–2482. Admission: $5 adults, $4 senior citizens, $2.50 children 12–16, $1.50 children 5–11. Open daily 10–5. Closed national holidays.*

8 Farther down San Diego Avenue, **El Campo Santo,** an old adobe-walled cemetery established in 1849, was the burial place for many members of Old Town's founding families, as well as for a number of the gamblers and bandits who passed through town until 1880. Antonio Garra, a chief who led an uprising of the San Luis Rey Indians, was executed at El Campo Santo in front of the open grave he was forced to dig for himself. These days a peaceful spot for visitors to contemplate, the small cemetery was recently cleaned up, its monuments straightened, and wrought-iron gates reconstructed around some of the plots.

9 **Heritage Park,** up the Juan Street hill near Harney Street, is the site of several grand Victorian homes and the town's first synagogue, all moved by the Save Our Heritage Organization (SOHO) from other parts of San Diego and restored. Some of the ornate houses may seem surprisingly colorful, but they are accurate representations of the bright tones of the era. The homes are now used for offices, shops, restaurants, and, in one case, a bed-and-breakfast inn. The climb up to the park is a bit steep, but the view of the harbor is great.

10 The rolling hillsides of the 40-acre **Presidio Park,** overlooking Old Town from the north end of Taylor Street, are popular with picnickers, and many couples have taken their wedding vows on the park's long stretches of lawn, some of the greenest in San Diego. You may encounter enthusiasts of a new sport, grass skiing, gliding over the grass and down the hills on wheels. Unless you love to climb, drive to the top of Presidio Park and then wander around on foot. At the

⑪ north end, near Taylor Street, the **Junipero Serra Museum** is perched atop a 160-foot hill overlooking Mission Valley and the site of the original Spanish presidio and mission. The museum houses an interesting collection of artifacts from San Diego's presidio days (1769–1825). *Tel. 619/297–3258. Admission: $3 adults. Open Tues.– Sat. 10–4:30, Sun. noon–4:30.*

Tour 6: Mission Bay and Sea World

Numbers in the margin correspond to points of interest on the Tour 6: Mission Bay Area map.

San Diego's monument to sports and fitness, Mission Bay is a 4,600-acre aquatic park dedicated to action and leisure. Admission to its 27 miles of bayfront beaches and 17 miles of ocean frontage is free. All you need for a perfect day is a bathing suit, shorts, and the right selection of playthings. Above the lawns facing I–5, the sky is flooded with the bright colors of huge, intricately made kites.

When explorer Juan Rodríguez Cabrillo first spotted the bay in 1542, he called it Baja Falso (False Bay) because the ocean-facing inlet led to acres of swampland inhospitable to boats and inhabitants. In the 1960s the city planners decided to dredge the swamp and build a bay with acres of beaches and lawns for play. Only 25% of the land was permitted to be commercially developed, and, as a result, only a handful of resort hotels break up the striking natural landscape.

① The **Visitor Information Center,** at the East Mission Bay Drive exit from I–5, is an excellent tourist resource for the bay and all San Diego. The free *Mission Bay Guide* lists everything from places to rent bikes, boats, and diving equipment to local locksmiths and insurance companies; it also includes a good map of the area that notes where swimming, waterskiing, sailing, and other sports are permissible. The center is a gathering spot for the runners, walkers, and exercisers who take part in group activities. From the low hill outside the building, you can easily appreciate the bay's charms. *2688 E. Mission Bay Dr., tel. 619/276–8200. Open Mon.–Sat. 9–5 (until 6 or 7 in summer), Sun. 9:30–4:30 (until 5:30 in summer).*

A 5-mile-long pathway runs through this section of the bay from the trailer park and miniature golf course, south past the high-rise Hilton Hotel to Sea World Drive. Playgrounds and picnic areas abound on the beach and low grassy hills of the park. Group gatherings, company picnics, and birthday parties are common along this stretch, where huge parking lots seem to expand to serve the swelling crowds on sunny days. On weekday evenings, a steady stream of joggers, bikers, and skaters releasing the stress from a day at the office line the path. In the daytime, swimmers, water-skiers, fishers, and boaters—some in single-person kayaks, others in crowded powerboats—vie for space in the water. The San Diego Crew Classic, which takes place in April, fills this section of the bay with teams from all over the country and college reunions, complete with flying school colors and keg beer. Swimmers should note signs warning about water pollution; certain areas of the bay are chronically polluted, and bathing is strongly discouraged.

② **Fiesta Island,** off East Mission Bay Drive and Sea World Drive, is a smaller, man-made playground popular with jet- and water-skiers.

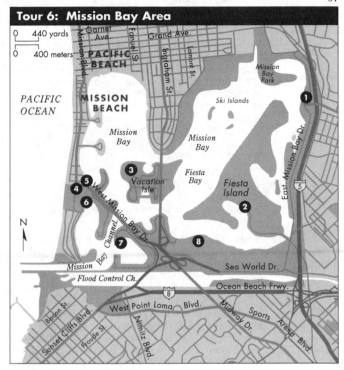

In July, the annual Over-the-Line Tournament, a competition involving a local variety of softball, attracts thousands of players and oglers, drawn by the teams' raunchy names and outrageous behavior.

Ingraham Street is another main drag through the bay, from the shores of Pacific Beach to Sea World Drive. The focal point of this part of the bay is **Vacation Isle.** You don't have to stay at the island's lavish Princess Resort to visit its lushly landscaped grounds, model yacht pond, and bayfront restaurants. Ducks are as common as tourists here, and Vacation Isle's village is a great family playground. Powerboats take off from Ski Beach, across Ingraham Street, which is also the site of the Taxaco Star Mart Cup hydroplane races, held in September. The noise from these boats is deafening, and the beach is packed from dawn till dark.

West Mission Bay Drive runs from the ocean beyond Mission Boulevard to Sea World Drive. The pathways along the Mission Beach side of the bay are lined with vacation homes, many of which can be rented by the month. Those who are fortunate enough to live here year-round have the bay as their front yards, with wide sandy beaches, volleyball courts, and—less of an advantage—an endless stream of sightseers on the sidewalk. **Belmont Park,** once an abandoned amusement park at the corner of Mission Boulevard and West Mission Bay Drive, is now a shopping, dining, and recreation area between the bay and the Mission Beach boardwalk. Twinkling lights outline the refurbished old Belmont Park roller coaster on which screaming thrill-seekers ride. Nearby, younger riders enjoy the antique carousel, as well as the fresh cotton candy sold at the stand just next to it. The Plunge, an indoor freshwater swimming pool, has also been renovated and is open to the public, making Belmont Park a focal point for the ocean beach area.

At the dock of the Bahia Hotel (998 W. Mission Bay Dr., tel. 619/488–0551), on the eastern shores of West Mission Bay Drive, you can
⑤ board the *Bahia Belle* for a sunset cruise of the bay. From September through November and from January through June, the restored paddle boat departs Friday and Saturday every hour on the half hour from 7:30 PM to 1:30 AM; in July and August, it sails Wednesday through Sunday on the same schedule. Owned and operated by the hotel, the boat is free for guests of the Bahia or its sister hotel, the Catamaran. All other adults pay $5 for unlimited cruising; children under 12 pay $3. Those who cruise at 9:30 PM or later must be at least 21.

⑥ **Ventura Cove,** opposite the Bahia, is a good, quiet picnic spot. The frontage road past the sport fishing marina leads to **Marina Village,** the only shopping center on the bay, with specialty shops and bayview restaurants.

⑦ **Hospitality Point,** at the end of the frontage road, is another pretty, secluded spot for a picnic with a view of sailboats and yachts entering the open sea. At the entrance to Hospitality Point, the Mission Bay Park Headquarters offers area maps and other recreational information. *2581 Quivira Ct., tel. 619/221–8900. Open weekdays 8–5.*

Time Out   The **Hyatt Islandia** (1441 Quivira Rd.) spreads out a copious brunch on Sunday for $19. **Sportsmen's Sea Foods** (1617 Quivira Rd.) serves good fish-and-chips and seafood salads to eat on the inelegant but scenic patio (by the marina, where sportfishing boats depart daily) or to take out to your chosen picnic spot. Many folks prefer to bring their own food: Picnics and barbecues are popular at the bay, where many picnic areas have stationary barbecue grills.

Spread over 100 tropically landscaped bayfront acres, where a cool
⑧ breeze always seems to rise from the water, **Sea World** is one of the world's largest marine-life amusement parks. A hospitality center to the right of the entrance reminds visitors that this popular attraction is owned by Anheuser-Busch: Adults can get two small free cups of beer in the building, which also houses a deli restaurant. Next door are stables for the huge Clydesdale horses that are hitched daily near the Penguin Encounter (*see below*).

The traditional favorite exhibit at Sea World is the Shamu show, with giant killer whales entertaining the crowds in a recently constructed stadium, but performing dolphins, sea lions, and otters at other shows also delight audiences with their antics. At another popular exhibit, the Penguin Encounter, a moving sidewalk passes through a glass-enclosed arctic environment, in which hundreds of emperor penguins slide over glaciers into icy waters (the penguins like it cold, so you may consider bringing a light sweater along for this one). Imaginative youngsters are especially fond of the Shark Encounter, which features a variety of species of the fierce-looking predators. The hands-on California Tide Pool exhibit gives visitors a chance to explore San Diego's indigenous marine life with a guide well versed in the habits of these creatures. At Forbidden Reef, you can feed bat rays and come nose to nose with creepy moray eels. The newest exhibit, Rocky Point Preserve, allows visitors to interact with bottlenose dolphins and houses Alaskan sea otters that were treated after the 1989 *Exxon-Valdez* oil spill.

Not all the exhibits are water oriented. Children are entranced by Cap'n Kids' World, an enclosed playground with trampolines, swinging wood bridges, towers for climbing, and giant tubs filled with plastic balls. The Wings of the World show features a large assemblage of free-flying exotic birds. Those who want to head aloft themselves may consider the park's Sky Tower, a glass elevator that ascends 265 feet; the views of San Diego County from the ocean to the mountains are especially pleasing in early morning and late evening. A six-minute sky-tram ride that leaves from the same spot travels between Sea World and the Atlantis Hotel across Mission Bay. Admission for the Sky Tower and the tram is $2 apiece, or $3 for both.

Sea World is filled with souvenir shops and refreshment stands; it's difficult to come away from here without spending a lot of money on top of the rather hefty entrance fee. Many hotels, especially those in the Mission Bay area, offer Sea World specials; some include price reductions, while others allow two days of entry for a single admission price—a good way to spread out what can otherwise be a very full day of activities. *Sea World Dr., at the west end of I–8, tel. 619/226–3901 for recorded information or 619/226–3815. Admission: $27.95 adults, $19.95 children 3–11; parking $5. 90-minute behind-the-scenes walking tours: $5 adults, $4 children 3–11. D, MC, V. Gates open 10–dusk; extended hours during summer. Call ahead to inquire about park hours for the day you intend to visit.*

Tour 7: La Jolla

Numbers in the margin correspond to points of interest on the Tour 7: La Jolla map.

La Jollans have long considered their village to be the Monte Carlo of California, and with good cause. Its coastline curves into natural coves backed by verdant hillsides and covered with lavish homes worth millions. Though La Jolla is considered part of San Diego, it has its own postal zone and a coveted sense of class; old-monied residents mingle here with visiting film stars and royalty who frequent established hotels and private clubs. If development and construction have radically altered the once-serene and private character of the village, it has gained a cosmopolitan air that makes it a popular vacation resort for the international set.

The Native Americans called the site La Hoya, meaning "the cave," referring to the grottos dotting the shoreline. The Spaniards changed the name to La Jolla, meaning "the jewel," and its residents have cherished the name and its allusions ever since.

To reach La Jolla from I–5, take the Ardath Road exit if you're traveling north and drive slowly down Prospect Street so you can appreciate the breathtaking view. If you're heading south, get off at the La Jolla Village Drive exit, which will lead into Torrey Pines Road. For those who enjoy meandering, the best way to approach La Jolla from the south is to drive through Mission and Pacific beaches on Mission Boulevard, past the crowds of roller skaters, bicyclists, and sunbathers. The clutter and congestion ease up as the street becomes La Jolla Boulevard, where quiet neighborhoods with winding streets lead down to some of the best surfing beaches in San Diego. The boulevard here is lined with expensive restaurants and cafes, as well as a few take-out spots.

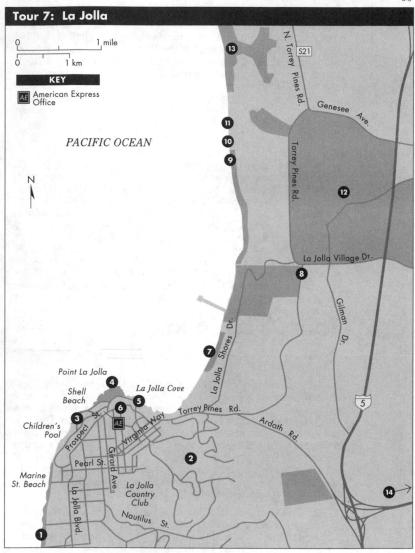

Tour 7: La Jolla

0 ——————— 1 mile
0 ——————— 1 km

KEY

AE American Express Office

PACIFIC OCEAN

N

Point La Jolla

Shell Beach

La Jolla Cove

Children's Pool

Marine St. Beach

Prospect St.

Virginia Way

Torrey Pines Rd.

Ardath Rd.

Pearl St.

Girard Ave.

La Jolla Blvd.

La Jolla Country Club

Nautilus St.

La Jolla Shores Dr.

La Jolla Village Dr.

Gilman Dr.

Torrey Pines Rd.

N. Torrey Pines Rd.

Genesee Ave.

S21

5

Ellen Browning Scripps Park, **4**
La Jolla Caves, **5**
La Jolla Shores, **7**
La Valencia Hotel, **6**
Mingei International Museum of World Folk Art, **14**
Mount Soledad, **2**
Salk Institute, **9**
San Diego Museum of Contemporary Art, **3**

Stephen Birch Aquarium–Museum, **8**
Torrey Pines City Park Beach, **11**
Torrey Pines Glider Port, **10**
Torrey Pines State Reserve, **13**
University of California at San Diego, **12**
Windansea Beach, **1**

1 At the intersection of La Jolla Boulevard and Nautilus Street, turn toward the sea to reach **Windansea Beach,** made famous by Tom Wolfe's *The Pump House Gang*, which pokes fun at the So-Cal surfing culture. The surfing here is said to be as good as that in Hawaii. As you head north, streets curve past other neighborhood beaches where local surfers jealously guard their watery turf. Road signs along La Jolla Boulevard and Camino de la Costa direct drivers and bicyclists past some of La Jolla's loveliest homes—many designed by such famous architects as Frank Lloyd Wright and Irving Gill—toward the village.

Time Out A breakfast of the excellent buttery croissants or brioches at **The French Pastry Shop** (5550 La Jolla Blvd.) will fortify you for some serious tanning at Windansea Beach. The health-conscious may want to stop in at **Windansea Natural Grocery** (6903 La Jolla Blvd.) and pick up a smoothie or hummus sandwich to bring along to the shore.

2 Nautilus Street east leads up to **Mount Soledad,** the highest spot in La Jolla. The cross on top of the mountain is an excellent vantage point from which to get a sense of San Diego's geography: Looking down from here, you can see the coast from the county's northern border to the south far beyond downtown—barring smog and haze. Sunrise services are held here on Easter Sunday.

As you approach the village, La Jolla Boulevard turns into Prospect Street, one of La Jolla's two main drags. The town's cultural center,
3 the **San Diego Museum of Contemporary Art** (700 Prospect St.), lies on the less trafficked southern end of Prospect. Housed in a remodeled Irving Gill home, the museum has a fine permanent collection of post-1950 art. The facility is currently undergoing expansion and renovation by architect Robert Venturi; it is not slated to reopen until early 1996. In the meantime, those interested in contemporary art must be content with visiting the much smaller downtown annex, opened in 1993 in the America Plaza complex (*see* Tour 1: Downtown and the Embarcadero, *above*).

Continue north on Prospect and turn west onto Coast Boulevard to
4 reach La Jolla's great natural coastal attraction, **Ellen Browning Scripps Park** at the **La Jolla Cove.** Towering palms line the sidewalk along Coast Boulevard, where strollers in evening dress are as common as Frisbee-throwers. The **Children's Pool,** at the south end of the park, is aptly named for its curving beach and shallow waters protected by a seawall from strong currents and waves. Each September the La Jolla Rough Water Swim takes place here, with hundreds of hardy swimmers plunging into the chilly waters and swimming a mile into the sea.

Smaller beaches appear and disappear with the tides, which carve small private coves in cliffs covered with ice plants. Some of these cliffs are unstable, but there are plenty of pathways leading down to the beaches. Just be sure to keep an eye on the tide to keep from getting trapped once the waves come in. A long layer of sandstone stretching out above the waves provides a perfect sunset-watching spot, with plenty of tiny tidal pools formed in eroded pockets in the rocks; starfish, sea anemones, and hermit crabs cluster here when the tide is in. Again, keep an eye on the waves because these rocks can get mighty slippery.

At the north end of La Jolla Cove, an underwater preserve makes the adjoining beach the most popular one in the area. On summer days, when the water visibility reaches 20 feet deep or so, the sea seems almost to disappear under the mass of bodies floating face down, snorkels poking up out of the water. The small beach is literally covered with blankets, towels, and umbrellas, and the lawns at the top of the stairs leading down to the cove are staked out by groups of scuba divers putting on wet suits and tanks. If you're not here by noon, forget about finding a parking spot or a small square of sand for your towel. But no matter what time you arrive, be sure to walk through the park, past the groves of twisted junipers to the cliff's edge. Perhaps one of the open-air shelters overlooking the sea will be free, and you can spread your picnic out on a table and watch the scene and the scenery.

Just past the far northern point of the cove, in front of the La Jolla **⑤** Cave and Shell Shop, a trail leads down to **La Jolla Caves**; it's some 133 steps down to the largest one, Sunny Jim Cave. For claustrophobic types, there are photos of the watery grottoes in the shop, along with a good selection of shells and coral jewelry. *1325 Coast Blvd., tel. 619/454–6080. Admission to caves: $1.25 adults, 50¢ children 3–11. Open Mon.–Sat. 10–5, Sun. 11–5, sometimes open later in summer.*

One block inland from the cove, Prospect Street is lined with toney restaurants and expensive boutiques; in recent years, a number of low-level office buildings and two-story shopping complexes have also cropped up here. At the intersection of Prospect and Girard **⑥** Avenue, La Jolla's other main drag, sits the pink Art Deco–style **La Valencia Hotel.** Operating as a luxury hotel since 1928, La Valencia has long been a gathering spot for Hollywood celebrities, who came down to escape from the Los Angeles bustle at this lovely hideaway; in the 1940s, Gregory Peck would invite friends to La Valencia's Whaling Bar to try to convince them to participate in one of his favorite projects, the La Jolla Theater. Today, the hotel's grand lobby with floor-to-ceiling windows overlooking the cove is a popular wedding spot, and the Whaling Bar is a still a favorite meeting place for La Jolla's power brokers.

Like Prospect Street, Girard Avenue is lined with expensive shops and office buildings; it also hosts La Jolla's only movie house, which tends to show nonmainstream films. The shopping and dining district has spread to Pearl and other side streets, where a steady parade of amblers and sightseers stroll about, chatting in many languages. Wall Street, a quiet tree-lined boulevard, was once the financial heart of La Jolla, but banks and investment houses can now be found throughout town. The La Jolla nightlife scene is an active one, with jazz clubs, piano bars, and watering holes for the elite younger set coming and going with the trends.

Time Out   **Alfonso's** (1251 Prospect St.) is La Jolla's original sidewalk cafe, with tables crowded together under a shady awning. The margaritas here are excellent, as are the chips, salsa, and huge carne asada burritos. Another favorite gathering spot is the **Pannikin** (7467 Girard Ave.), where locals chat over cups of steaming fresh coffee and flaky croissants. There are only a few tables on the front-porch patio, but you can get your coffee and wander around the shop while you wait for a spot.

If you continue north of the cove on La Jolla Shores Drive, you'll come to the La Jolla Beach and Tennis Club, host of many tennis tournaments. **La Jolla Shores'** beaches are some of the finest in San Diego, with long stretches allotted to surfers or swimmers. Just beyond the beaches is the campus of the Scripps Institute of Oceanography, formerly the site of the marine institute's aquarium.

The largest oceanographic exhibit in the United States, Scripps' **Stephen Birch Aquarium–Museum** reopened in late 1992 about 1½ miles northwest of its original site, on a signed drive leading off North Torrey Pines Road just south of La Jolla Village Drive. To those familiar with the old facility, the new $1 million marine museum may be a bit of a disappointment. It's considerably more expensive but not very much larger than the former facility, and a single artificial tidal pool at the back of the building is a poor substitute for the many natural seaside tidal pools outside the old aquarium. That said, there's a lot to enjoy here. More than 30 huge tanks are filled with colorful saltwater fish, and a spectacular 70,000-gallon tank simulates a La Jolla kelp forest. Next to the fish themselves, the most interesting attraction is the 12-minute simulated submarine ride (children under 3 not admitted); the ocean noises and marine-life visuals are realistic almost to the point of inducing seasickness. *2300 Expedition Way, tel. 619/534–3474. Admission: $6.50 adults, $5.50 senior citizens 60 and older, $4.50 children 13–17, military, and students with current ID, $3.50 children 4–12; parking $2.50. Open daily 9–5. Closed Thanksgiving and Christmas.*

As La Jolla Shores Drive goes north, it curves onto Torrey Pines Road, off which you'll soon glimpse the world-famous **Salk Institute,** designed by Louis Kahn. The same road that leads to the institute ends at the **Torrey Pines Glider Port.** On days when the winds are just right, gliders line the clifftops, waiting for the perfect gust to carry them into the sky. Seasoned hang gliders with a good command of the current can soar over the sea for hours, then ride the winds back to the cliffs. Less-experienced fliers sometimes land on the beach below, to the cheers and applause of the sunbathers who scoot out of their way. The view from atop the cliffs with the colorful gliders in the sky is spectacular.

The beach at the foot of the cliffs is officially named **Torrey Pines City Park Beach,** but locals call it Black's Beach. For many years, Black's was widely accepted as being clothing-optional; although nudity is now prohibited by law, it is practiced whenever the authorities are out of sight. This is one of the most beautiful and secluded beaches in San Diego, with long stretches of pale sand backed by steep cliffs whose colors change with the light from the sun. There are no rest rooms, showers, or snack shops, though some hardy entrepreneurs do lug ice chests filled with sodas and beer down the cliffs to sell to the unprepared. The paths leading down to the beach are steep, and the cliffs are very unstable. Cliff rescues are not uncommon, particularly when daring explorers ignore the safety signs and strike out on uncharted trails. Stick to the well-traveled paths.

At the intersection of Torrey Pines Road and Genessee Avenue is the northern entrance to the **University of California at San Diego.** The massive campus spreads over canyons and eucalyptus groves, where students and faculty jog, bike, and roller-skate to class. If you're interested in contemporary art, ask at one of the two information booths for a map of the Stuart Collection, a thought-provoking group of sculptures located at different points around campus; Nam June Paik and Jenny Holtzer are among the artists whose works are displayed. UCSD's Price Center features both an excellent two-level bookstore and a good coffeehouse, Roma. Look for the postmodern Central Library, which resembles a large spaceship.

(13) A bit farther north is **Torrey Pines State Reserve,** a 1,750-acre sanctuary for the United States' rarest pine tree, the *Pinus torreyana.* About 6,000 of these unusual trees, some as tall as 60 feet, grow on the clifftops above one of San Diego County's loveliest beaches. This park is one of only two places where the torrey pine can be found—the other is Santa Rosa Island, about 175 miles to the northwest. The reserve has several hiking trails leading to the cliffs, 300 feet above the ocean; trail maps are available at the park station. Picnic areas are scattered in pine groves, and wildflowers grow profusely in the spring. The beach below the reserve, called Torrey Pines State Beach, is another of the loveliest in the county. If you walk south past the lifeguard towers, you can find a secluded spot under the golden brown cliffs and feel as if there is no one on the beach but you. When the tide is out, it's possible to walk south all the way to Black's Beach through arches and over rocky promontories carved by the waves. *North Torrey Pines Rd. (also known as Old Hwy. 101), tel. 619/755–2063. From I–5, take Genessee Ave. west exit, then turn right (north) on Old Hwy. 101. Open daily 9–sunset. Parking: $4. There is a large parking lot by the beach and another up the hill by the park station.*

La Jolla's newest enclave is the Golden Triangle, spreading through the Sorrento Valley east of I–5. High-tech research-and-development companies, attracted to the area in part by the facilities of UCSD, Scripps, and Salk, have developed huge state-of-the-art compounds in areas that were populated solely by coyotes and jays not so long ago. The area along La Jolla Village Drive and Genessee Avenue has become an architectural wonderland full of futuristic buildings. The most striking are those in Michael Graves's Aventine complex, visible from I–5 at the La Jolla Village Drive exit. About half a mile south (just off the Nobel exit) and equally eye-catching, the huge, white Mormon Temple is reminiscent of a medieval castle; completed in 1993, it still startles drivers heading up the freeway.

The first major establishment in the Golden Triangle was University Towne Center, a huge shopping mall with an indoor ice-skating
(14) rink. The **Mingei International Museum of World Folk Art** is located here among the shops and restaurants. The museum has some wonderfully creative shows featuring pottery, textiles, costumes, and gadgets from all over the world. *4405 La Jolla Village Dr., tel. 619/453–5300. Admission: $3 adults, $1 children 5–12. Open Tues.–Sat. 11–5, Sun. 2–5.*

Sightseeing Checklists

Museums and Historic Sites

Children's Museum of San Diego. *See* Chapter 4, San Diego for Children.

Junipero Serra Museum. *See* Tour 5: Old Town, *above.*

Maritime Museum. *See* Tour 1: Downtown and the Embarcadero, *above.*

The Marston House. A classic example of the American Craftsman style, this 16-room residence was built in 1905 by Irving Gill and William S. Hebbard for a prominent San Diego businessman and is now maintained by the San Diego Historical Society. The lovely grounds are landscaped in the English Romantic tradition. *3525 7th Ave., tel. 619/298–3142. Admission: $3. Open Fri.–Sun. noon–4:30.*

Mingei International Museum of World Folk Art. *See* Tour 7: La Jolla, *above.*

Mission San Diego de Alcala. Established by Father Junipero Serra in 1769 on Presidio Hill, the mission moved to its present location in 1774. The Padre Luis Jayme Museum—named for California's first Catholic martyr, killed by Native Americans—features relics of early mission days. You can also visit the original mission chapel. *10818 San Diego Mission Rd., tel. 619/281–8449. Admission: $1 adults. Open daily 9–5. Closed Thanksgiving, Christmas, and New Year's Day.*

Mission San Luis Rey. Father Fermin Lasuen, a successor to Father Junipero Serra, established the "King of the Missions." The most extensive collection of old Spanish vestments in the United States is on display in the museum. *4050 Mission Ave., San Luis Rey, 4 mi east of I–5 in Oceanside, tel. 619/757–3651. Admission: $3 adults, $1 children under 12. Open Mon.–Sat. 10–4:30, Sun. noon–4:30.*

Museum of Man. *See* Tour 4: Balboa Park, *above.*

Museum of Photographic Arts. *See* Tour 4: Balboa Park, *above.*

Museum of San Diego History. *See* Tour 4: Balboa Park, *above.*

Reuben H. Fleet Space Theater and Science Center. *See* Tour 4: Balboa Park, *above.*

San Diego Aerospace Museum. *See* Tour 4: Balboa Park, *above.*

San Diego Automotive Museum. *See* Tour 4, Balboa Park, *above.*

San Diego Model Railroad Museum. *See* Tour 4, Balboa Park, *above.*

San Diego Museum of Art. *See* Tour 4: Balboa Park, *above.*

San Diego Museum of Contemporary Art. *See* Tour 1: Downtown, and Tour 7: La Jolla, *above.*

San Diego Natural History Museum. *See* Tour 4: Balboa Park, *above.*

San Diego Sports Museum Hall of Champions. *See* Tour 4: Balboa Park, *above.*

Timken Art Gallery. *See* Tour 4: Balboa Park, *above.*

Villa Montezuma. The Jesse Shepard House, built in 1887, is a fine example of Queen Anne Victorian architecture with a California flair. The house has stained-glass windows with portraits of Shakespeare, Beethoven, Mozart, and Goethe. Redwood paneling and massive fireplaces decorate the living quarters, which have been restored by the San Diego Historical Society. *1925 K St., tel. 619/239–2211. Admission: $3 adults. Open Sat. and Sun. noon–4:30 PM.*

Parks and Gardens

With its huge urban green spaces and vast expanses of wilderness, San Diego County is in many ways one big park. The flowers bloom year-round here, with red and white poinsettias popping up everywhere at Christmas and candy-colored pink and yellow flowered ice plants edging the roads year-round. The dry climate, which seems inhospitable to growing things, actually nurtures some amazing flora. The golden, bushy stalks of pampas grass grow in wild patches near Sea World. Birds of paradise poke up straight and tall, tropical testimonials to San Diego's temperate climate. Bougainvillea covers roofs and hillsides in La Jolla, spreading magenta blankets over whitewashed adobe walls. Towering palms and twisted junipers are far more common than maples or oaks, and fields of wild daisies and chamomile cover dry, dusty lots.

Citrus groves pop up in unlikely places, along the freeways and back roads. When the orange, lemon, and lime trees blossom in spring, the fragrance of their tiny white blossoms is nearly overpowering. Be sure to drive with your windows down—you'll be amazed at the sweet, hypnotic scent. Jasmine seems to be the city's flower, blooming on bushes and vines in front yards and parking lots.

Balboa Park is really a series of botanical gardens, with a verdant, tropical oasis in its midst at the San Diego Zoo. The animals are fascinating, for sure, but the zoo's real charm and fame come from its tradition of creating hospitable environments that replicate natural habitats as closely as possible. Botanists will particularly enjoy Tiger River, a $500,000 collection of endangered tropical plants.

Cultivated and wild gardens are an integral part of all Balboa Park, thanks to the "Mother of Balboa Park," Kate Sessions, who made sure both the park's developed and undeveloped acreage bloomed with the purple blossoms of the jacaranda tree and planted thousands of palms and other trees throughout the park. Left alone, Balboa Park would look like **Florida Canyon,** which lies between the main park and Morley Field, along Park Boulevard. Volunteers from the **San Diego Natural History Museum** give free guided nature walks throughout the county on weekends. For information on tours and special activities, call 619/232–3821.

The Rose Garden, along Park Boulevard overlooking Florida Canyon, has more than 2,000 rose plants. In the adjacent **Cactus Garden,** trails wind around prickly cacti and soft green succulents, many indigenous to the area. The **Spanish Alcazar Garden,** off El Prado across from the Museum of Man, blooms with colorful, seemingly perennial, flower beds. **Palm Canyon,** near the Organ Pavilion, has more than 60 varieties of palm trees along a shady bridge. East of the pavilion, the rocks and trees of the **Japanese Garden** are arranged to inspire contemplation. The redwood-lathed **Botanical Building,** built in 1915, houses a beautiful selection of tropical flowers and plants, with ceiling-high tree ferns shading tiny, fragile orchids and feathery bamboos.

Mission Bay Park is more of a playground than a botanical wonder, but its grassy lawns are a soothing sight for displaced East Coasters. **Old Town State Park,** though historic in focus, has some lovely small, grassy spots for resting and picnicking. The lawns between the historic district and Bazaar del Mundo, by the plaza, are particularly inviting and often hold arts-and-crafts shows. **Presidio Park** has a beautiful private canyon surrounded by palms at the bottom of the hill, off Taylor Street just before it intersects with I–8. At **Torrey Pines States Reserve,** north of La Jolla atop an oceanside cliff, beautiful trails wind amid the twisted pines.

Other Places of Interest

The **San Diego Wild Animal Park,** about 30 miles northeast of downtown San Diego, is an extension of the San Diego Zoo. The 2,200-acre preserve in the San Pasqual Valley is designed to protect endangered species of animals from around the world. Five exhibit areas have been carved out of the dry, dusty canyons and mesas to represent the animals' natural habitats in North Africa, South Africa, East Africa, Asian Swamps, and Asian Plains.

The best way to see these preserves is on the 50-minute, 5-mile Wgasa Bushline Monorail ride (included in the price of admission). As you pass in front of the large, naturally landscaped enclosures, you'll see animals bounding through prairies and mesas as they would in the wild. More than 3,000 animals from some 450 species roam or fly through the expansive grounds. Enemy species are separated from each other by deep moats, but only the truly predatory tigers, lions, and cheetahs are kept in isolation. Photographers with zoom lenses can get spectacular shots of zebras, gazelles, and rhinos (a seat on the right-hand side of the monorail is best for viewing the majority of the animals). The trip is especially enjoyable in the early evening when the heat has subsided and the animals are active and feeding. On summer nights, the monorail travels through the park after dark, when soft amber sodium-vapor lamps highlight the animals in action. The setting, seemingly far from civilization, with clear starry skies, is enthralling and nearly as exciting as the real thing.

The park is as much a botanical garden as a zoo, and botanists collect rare and endangered plants for preservation. The 5-foot-tall desert cypress found here is native to the Sahara; only six such trees are still in existence there.

The 1¼-mile-long Kilimanjaro Hiking Trail winds through some of the park's hilliest terrain in the East Africa section, with observation decks overlooking the elephants and lions. A 70-foot suspension bridge, made of Douglas fir poles, spans a steep ravine, leading to the final observation point and a panorama of the San Pasqual Valley and the Wild Animal Park.

The park's center is called Nairobi Village, where the sound of African drums provides a constant background of safari noise. The ticket booths are designed to resemble the tomb of an ancient king of Uganda, and dancers regularly perform complex African tribal dances in the center of the village. In the Petting Kraal, deer, sheep, and goats affectionately tolerate tugs and pats and are quite adept at posing for pictures with struggling toddlers on their backs. At the Congo River Fishing Village, 10,000 gallons of water pour each minute over a huge waterfall into a large lagoon. The park's latest (March 1993) addition, the Hidden Jungle, features creatures that creep, flutter, or just hang out in a tropical habitat: Gigantic cockroaches and bird-eating spiders share the turf with colorful butterflies and hummingbirds and oh-so-slow-moving two-toed sloths.

Ravens, vultures, hawks, and a great horned owl perform throughout the day at the Bird Show Amphitheater. All the park's animal shows are entertainingly educational. The gift shops have a wide assortment of African crafts and animal-oriented souvenirs, and free-loan cameras are available. Serious shutterbugs might consider joining one of the park's special photo caravans ($60–$85, including admission). *To reach the San Diego Wild Animal Park, take I–15 north to Via Rancho Pkwy. in Escondido, then follow the signs (6 mi) to the park, tel. 619/234–6541 or 619/480–0100. Admission: $17.45 adults, $15.70 senior citizens, $10.45 children 3–11. D, MC, V. (A combination pass—$22 adults, $11 children—affords entry, within 5 days of purchase, to both the San Diego Zoo and the San*

Diego Wild Animal Park.) Parking: $3. Gates open daily 9 AM, closing time (generally 4 PM in winter, 5 PM in summer) may be extended for special events; call ahead for information.

Scenic Drives

Unless you're on the freeway, it's hard *not* to find a scenic drive in San Diego, but an officially designated 52-mile **Scenic Drive** over much of central San Diego begins at the foot of Broadway. Road signs with a white sea gull on a yellow-and-blue background direct the way through the Embarcadero to Harbor and Shelter islands, Point Loma and Cabrillo Monument, Mission Bay, Old Town, Balboa Park, Soledad Mountain, and La Jolla. It's best to take this three-hour drive, outlined on some local maps, on the weekend, when the commuters are off the road.

San Diego for Free

San Diego's main attractions are its climate and natural beauty, which are accessible to all, free of charge. The 70 miles of beaches are free—no boardwalks with admission fees, no high-priced parking lots. You can easily while away a week or two just visiting a different beach community each day. (*See* Chapter 6, Beaches, *for more details.*) Nearly all San Diego's major attractions in our Exploring section are situated amid huge parks, gardens, and waterfronts, with plenty of natural wonders to keep you amused. See also the Parks and Gardens section, above, for some of the best spots to picnic or lounge with a book.

Balboa Park's museums offer free admission on Tuesdays on a rotating basis; call 619/239–0512 for a schedule. Free organ concerts take place in the Spreckels Organ Pavilion on Sunday afternoons, and a variety of choral groups and bands appear there on summer evenings, also for free. There is no charge to wander through the Botanical Building, an enclosed tropical paradise.

Seaport Village hosts a variety of free seasonal events throughout the year, often with fireworks displays. Both the **Embarcadero Marina Park South** and **Sea World** have fireworks on summer evenings that are visible from downtown, Mission Bay, and Ocean Beach.

Navy ships docked at the downtown Embarcadero are sometimes open for free tours. Walking tours through Old Town are free, and the tour guides are excellent history teachers.

Off the Beaten Track

Don't think you've finished seeing San Diego once you've hit all the main attractions. The real character of the place doesn't shine through until you've visited a few neighborhoods and mingled with the natives. Then you can say you've seen San Diego.

Mission Hills is an older neighborhood near downtown that has the charm and wealth of La Jolla and Point Loma without the crowds. The prettiest streets are above Presidio Park and Old Town, where huge mansions with rolling lawns resemble eastern estates; to see them, head up Fort Stockton Drive from the Presidio or Juan Street past Heritage Park in Old Town to Sunset Boulevard. Washington Street runs up a steep hill from I–8 through the center of Mission Hills. Palmier Bistro, at the corner of Washington Street and Goldfinch Street, has wonderful pâtés, pastries, and wines to enjoy there or take away. On Goldfinch, visit the Gathering, a neighborhood restaurant with great breakfasts and outdoor tables for reading the Sunday paper in the sun.

Hillcrest, farther up Washington Street beginning at 1st Avenue, is San Diego's Castro Street, the center for the gay community and artists of all types. University, 4th, and 5th avenues are filled with cafés, boutiques, and excellent bookstores. The Guild Theater and Hillcrest Cinemas, both on 5th Avenue, show first-run foreign films. The Blue Door, next to the Guild, is one of San Diego's best small bookstores. The '50s retro-style Corvette Diner, on 4th Avenue between University Avenue and Washington Street, features burgers and shakes and campy waitresses. Quel Fromage, a coffeehouse on University Avenue between 5th and 6th avenues, has long been the place to go to discuss philosophical or romantic matters over espresso.

Like most of San Diego, Hillcrest has been undergoing massive redevelopment. The largest project is the **Uptown District,** on University Avenue at 8th Avenue. This self-contained residential-commercial center was built to resemble an inner-city neighborhood, with shops and restaurants within easy walking distance of high-price town houses. Restaurants include Cane's, a trendy pasta cafe, and La Salsa, part of a chain of excellent Mexican take-out stands.

Washington Street eventually becomes Adams Avenue, San Diego's Antiques Row, with shops displaying an odd array of antiques and collectibles. Adams Avenue leads into **Kensington** and **Talmadge,** two lovely old neighborhoods overlooking Mission Valley. The Ken Cinema (4061 Adams Ave.) shows older cult movies and current art films.

Ocean Beach, the westernmost point of the continental United States, is a holdover from the radical days in the '60s and still considered something of a hippie haven. Of all the mainland beach towns, OB is the most self-contained, with a mixed populace of young families, longtime residents, and drifters. The OB Pier is the best spot for getting a real feel for the place, though you may find the crowd a bit unsavory. For the bikinied beauties on roller skates, visit the Mission Beach boardwalk, where the parade is never-ending.

San Diego's large Vietnamese, Cambodian, and Korean communities congregate in **Linda Vista** and **North Park.** There are wonderful neighborhood restaurants in these relatively nondescript areas. The Mexican-American community is centered in **Barrio Logan,** under the Coronado Bridge. Chicano Park, just under the bridge supports, has huge murals depicting Mexican history, painted by artists from all over California.

4 San Diego for Children

By Lori Chamberlain

Lori Chamberlain is a native San Diegan. Her two small children, Sophie and Ryder, were her research assistants for this chapter.

It's hard to overstate San Diego's qualifications as a kid-friendly place to visit. For starters, it has an abundance of some of the best natural playgrounds for children of all ages: beaches. But if the weather is not cooperative or you've always found beaches to be just too filled with sand, San Diego also boasts one of the world's great zoos; a splashy marine park; an excellent group of museums covering everything from ancient civilization to outer space; train rides; ships; indoor fun zones; and the famous Palomar Observatory.

Because of the relaxed southern California culture, San Diego is an easy place to be with kids in general. Few restaurants, for example, make children unwelcome—and some are specifically designed for those traveling with children at the restaurant-unfriendly age. In addition, intense competition by hotels for the lucrative family market means low rates or special programs for youngsters at many places. There are also plenty of sources in town for kiddie supplies, including some great stores for books, toys, or clothing, as well as a number of arts venues specifically geared toward children.

Exploring

The well-known sights in San Diego live up to their reputations and shouldn't be missed. But consider, too, some of the lower-key attractions, which may prove less crowded and equally well suited to your children's interests.

The Major Sights

The San Diego Zoological Society maintains two excellent zoos in the San Diego area. If you have time, visit both; otherwise, you'll have to make a tough choice. The **San Diego Zoo** (*see* Tour 4 in Chapter 3, Exploring San Diego) has an extensive Children's Zoo, with exhibits at kid-height and a petting area with well-behaved goats, sheep, and pot-bellied pigs. The 50-minute monorail ride through Africa and Asia at the **Wild Animal Park** (*see* Other Places of Interest in Chapter 3, Exploring San Diego), about 45 minutes from town, is best for kids old enough to sit for that period of time. Younger ones should enjoy stroking the exotic hoofed animals in the Petting Kraal or feeding the ducks and other waterfowl in the lagoon surrounding Nairobi Village, near the entrance to the park.

Sea World (*see* Tour 6 in Chapter 3, Exploring San Diego) is another popular place for kids, although at the price of entrance, you'll want to be sure your children are old enough (at least 3) to enjoy it. Not to be missed here are the Shamu show (sit up front if you *want* to get very wet), the dolphin exhibit (they'll eat little fish tidbits right out of your hand), the bat ray exhibit (you can pet them as they swim by), and the Penguin Encounter (no touching, but these guys are endlessly amusing). Cap'n Kids' World, an imaginative, no-holds-barred playground, will captivate youngsters and focus their energy for hours. The play equipment is designed for a variety of ages—the younger ones like tumbling in huge pools of plastic balls, while older children enjoy racing all over the rope swings and balconies.

The **Stephen Birch Aquarium-Museum** (*see* Tour 7 in Chapter 3, Exploring San Diego) offers another marine experience. Kids 5 and older should enjoy the simulated submarine ride (the cutoff age is 3, but the experience may be a bit scary for little ones), and a tidal pool gives younger children a chance to hold and pet starfish and sea anemones.

Tidal pools in their natural setting may be seen at **Cabrillo National Monument** (*see* Tour 2 in Chapter 3), where kids can also climb up into an old lighthouse and, outside the visitor center, look through viewers at the surrounding cityscape and naval installations.

You may follow a visit to the San Diego Maritime Museum (*see below*) with a **harbor excursion** or, for a real bargain, a **ferry trip to Coronado** (*see* Staying in San Diego in Chapter 1, Essential Information, for both).

At **Seaport Village** (*see* Tour 1 in Chapter 3, Exploring San Diego), the Flying Horses Carousel should temporarily divert kids who are less keen on shopping than their parents.

Museums

Many of Balboa Park's museums (*see* Tour 4 in Chapter 3, Exploring San Diego) are geared toward, or have exhibits designed for, children. The Omnimax theater at the **Reuben H. Fleet Space Theater and Science Center,** for example, screens first-rate nature and science films, and the science center offers a wide variety of imaginative hands-on exhibits illustrating the laws of physics in ways you'll wish you'd learned in school. The **Natural History Museum** has a solid collection that includes a large dinosaur skeleton, as well as excellent seasonal shows: Recent displays starred robotic dinosaurs and—a kid's dream—a huge array of robotic insects. The **Model Railroad Museum,** also a winner, houses one of the world's largest collections of minigauge trains. For artistically oriented children, the **San Diego Museum of Art** offers special programs.

At the **San Diego Maritime Museum** (*see* Tour 1 in Chapter 3, Exploring San Diego), you can climb aboard the 1863 clipper ship *Star of India*, as well as an 1898 ferryboat and a World War I vintage steam yacht.

The **Mingei International Museum** (*see* Tour 7 in Chapter 3, Exploring San Diego) has colorful folk art exhibits from all parts of the world—often more interesting to kids than "high art."

The **Children's Museum of San Diego** reopened in 1993 in the downtown area, near the Convention Center. The new facility has approximately 26,000 square feet of space devoted to interactive, experiental environments for kids. Included are an art zone, where children can work on group projects or their own projects to take home, and a toddler area. One special exhibit in 1994 featured giant robotic dinosaurs; another highlighted interactive projects by local artists—for example, a low-rider car in which children could take a simulated cruise through the streets of Tijuana. *200 W. Island St., tel. 619/233–5437. Admission: $4 adults and children 2 and older, $2 senior citizens. Open Tues.–Sat. 10–4:30, Sun. noon–4:30.*

Fire-fighting artifacts of all sorts fill the **Firehouse Museum:** motorized, and horse- and hand-drawn fire engines, extinguishers, an extensive collection of helmets, and other memorabilia. *1572 Columbia St., tel. 619/232–3473. Admission free. Open Thurs. and Fri. 10–2, Sat. and Sun. 10–4.*

Fun Parks

The jewel in the crown of Belmont Park (*see* Tour 6 in Chapter 1, Essential Information) is the classic **Giant Dipper Roller Coaster,** with more than 2,600 feet of tracks and 13 hills. Riders must be taller than 4'2". *Tel. 619/488–1549. Admission: $2.50. Open Sun.–Thurs. 11–6, Fri. and Sat. 11–10.*

Also in Belmont Park, **Pirate's Hideaway** is a fantastic maze of brightly colored tunnels, slides, an obstacle course, and more for kids 12 months to 12 years. Teenagers 13 to 17 are welcome if accompanied by an adult *and* a child under 13. Socks are required. *Tel. 619/539–7529. Admission: children, $4.50 weekdays, $6.50 weekends; adults, $2.50 daily. Open Mon.–Thurs. 11–8, Fri. 11–9, Sat. 10–9, Sun. 10–7, extended hours on holidays.*

In North County, the **Discovery Zone** has similar facilities, also for kids from 1 to 12 years. *459 College Blvd., Oceanside, tel. 619/630–1100. Admission: $4.99 per person for unlimited time. Open Mon.–Sat. 10–9, Sun. 10–7.*

The **Family Fun Center** has three miniature-golf courses, batting cages, boats, go-carts, tank tag, and video-game rooms. *6999 Claremont Mesa Blvd., tel. 619/560–4211. Admission free. Open Mon.–Thurs. and Sun. 9 AM–midnight, Fri.–Sat. 9 AM–2 AM; outside attractions may close earlier.*

Marshal Scotty's offers 15 rides, ponies, go-carts that make their circuits on River Canyon raceway, and picnic grounds. *I–8 at Lack Jennings Park Rd. exit, tel. 619/443–0236. Admission: $5.95 adults, $7.95 children 3–12. Open Sat. and Sun. 10–5. River Canyon Raceway open Tues.–Thurs. 3–10, Fri. 3–midnight, Sat. noon–midnight, Sun. noon–10.*

Off the Beaten Track

You can pet bat rays at the low-key **Chula Vista Nature Interpretive Center,** a wetland preserve about 15 minutes south of downtown. Hands-on exhibits focus on marine life as well as other animal life typical of salt marshes. Take I–5 south to E Street and park in the lot at E Street and Bay Boulevard; a shuttle will take you across the salt marsh to the museum. *1000 Gunpowder Point Dr., tel. 619/422–2481. Admission: $3.50 adults, $2.50 senior citizens, $1 children 6–17 (admission includes round-trip shuttle). Open Tues.–Sun. 10–5; feedings at 10:30 AM and 4 PM.*

Under the aegis of the **San Diego Railroad Museum,** the Campo Depot, built in 1915, operates a scenic 1½-hour train trip through the San Diego backcountry on weekends. Plan to get here in time to take the guided walking tours of the museum's approximately 90 pieces of vintage railroad equipment. *50 mi east of San Diego (take I–8 east, exit at Buckman Springs Rd., and follow the signs), tel. 619/595–3030 for general information or 619/478–9937 for Campo depot. Depot admission free; train ride $10 adults, $8 senior citizens, $3 children 6–12. Open weekends 10–4; trains depart at 12:01 PM and 2:30 PM; 45-min tours of the restoration area are given at around 11 AM and 1:30 PM; additional 4 PM tours are sometimes offered in the summer.*

For a well-rounded day trip with children, consider heading out to the **Palomar Observatory,** an hour or so outside San Diego. You can't actually look through the 200-inch Hale telescope, but there are lots of exhibits here on stars and the universe. Then visit the **Palomar Mountain State Park** or the **Cuyamaca Rancho State Park,** where you can hike and picnic. Top this off with a drive through the mountains to the old mining town of **Julian** to visit a gold mine and get some excellent apple pie. For details on all these attractions, see the

Inland North County section of Chapter 12, Excursions from San Diego.

If you're in San Diego in June or early July, don't miss the **Del Mar Fair** (*see* The San Diego North Coast in Chapter 12, Excursions from San Diego), a *big* exposition with lots of rides, livestock, hundreds of exhibits, food, entertainment, and contests.

Shopping

If you've brought the wrong clothes for your kids or find yourself without enough toys or other amusements, no problem: San Diego is an easy place to get any supplies that you may need—or that your children decide they have to have.

Books

In La Jolla, **The White Rabbit** has a good selection of reading material for children (*see* Bookstores in Chapter 5, Shopping). Among the many places to pick up comics are **Amazing Comix** (1800 Rosecrans, near the Sports Arena, tel. 619/225–0279; other locations) and **The Comic Gallery** (4224 Balboa Ave., Claremont Mesa, tel. 619/483–4853; other locations).

Clothing

The Gap Kids, in Horton Plaza, University Town Centre, and La Jolla (7835 Girard Ave., tel. 619/454–2052), is probably the best bet for children's togs. **Nordstrom,** also located in several of the area shopping malls, carries good-quality lines of kids clothing. For slightly less pricey attire, try **Mervyn's** in Horton Plaza. **Gymboree,** in the Horton Plaza and the Fashion Valley malls, is good for baby gear. (*See* Chapter 5, Shopping, for mall locations.)

Toys and Gadgets

In addition to the toy stores listed in Chapter 5, **Whistle Stop Model Trains** (3834 4th Ave., downtown, tel. 619/295–7340) carries books on trains and railroads, in addition to model trains. **Brad Burt's Magic Shop** (4688 Convoy, Claremont Mesa, tel. 619/571–4749) offers a good selection of tricks and clown supplies. If you want to join the fun at Mission Beach, you can pick up a kite at **Kite Country** in Horton Plaza (tel. 619/233–9495), **Top of the Line Kites** (3015 Saint Charles, Point Loma, tel. 619/224–8505; closed on weekends), and **Homer's** (4871 Newport Ave., Ocean Beach, tel. 619/222–5834). **The Nature Company** (7840 Girard Ave., La Jolla, tel. 619/459–0871; branches in Horton Plaza and Fashion Valley) carries books and gizmos of interest to kids and also sponsors nature programs for children.

Beaches, Parks, and Playgrounds

San Diego itself is a huge outdoor playground, its beaches and parks unrivaled in quantity and quality by any other U.S. city. Specially designated children's play areas, many with excellent equipment, just add to the town's myriad outdoor kiddie options.

Beaches

A number of the San Diego beaches described in Chapter 6 are pa. ticularly attractive for children. Try the **Children's Pool** in La Jolla and **La Jolla Cove,** which also features tidal pools and a large grassy area for picnicking. Wide and well-guarded **La Jolla Shores** beach is nicely suited for families. Other good bets include **Silver Strand State Beach** in Coronado, with its light action on the waves, and **Del Mar Beach,** a guarded spread of sand near a playground, shops, and restaurants.

If you're visiting in July, you may want to visit the Imperial Beach Pier to admire the sand castles built during Sand Castle Days (*see* Festivals and Seasonal Events in Chapter 1, Essential Information).

Parks

Balboa Park is a must-see for those traveling with children of any age (*see* Tour 4 in Chapter 3, Exploring San Diego). In addition to the San Diego Zoo and museums, noted above, the park has a restored wooden carousel, a miniature train ride, a somewhat old-fashioned playground, *plenty* of grass, and, on weekends, an interesting variety of street performers.

Mission Bay Park (*see* Tour 6 in Chapter 3, Exploring San Diego) is another sure thing for those toting tots and older kids. The east side of the park has a series of well-equipped playgrounds and good space for flying kites. For those with slightly older children, the sidewalks around the bay are perfect for roller-blading. Belmont Park, which borders Mission Bay Park on the west, has both a restored giant roller coaster (*see* Fun Parks, *above*) and the city's most beautiful swimming pool. (Don't venture here on a sunny Saturday, however, unless you're willing to fight the crowds for a parking spot.) In addition to the sand, there's plenty of grass for lounging and picnicking. And, of course, there's the water.

Playgrounds

The high price of real estate in San Diego means not everyone has a house with a huge backyard; in addition, as in most other places, parents here use playgrounds as a guilt-free way to socialize with other parents. There are a number of well-equipped, well-maintained playgrounds in town; the **City Parks and Recreation Department** (tel. 619/525–8285) can tell you which one is nearest your hotel.

Though there are some playgrounds in the downtown area, better ones can be found close by on the west side of Mission Bay. Doyle Community Park, near University Towne Center on Regents Road at Berino Court, has an impressive collection of new and progressive playground equipment. The playground at Kate O. Sessions Memorial Park (Pacific Beach, on Soledad Road and Loring Street) is small, but there's lots of grass for flying kites and beautiful views of the city and bay. In La Jolla, the La Jolla Recreation Center (615 Prospect St.) has both new and traditional playground equipment within smelling distance of the ocean. In Del Mar, you can push your child on the swings and watch the waves breaking down below at a small playground at the foot of 15th Street, across the street from the Amtrak depot; adjacent to the park is a grassy area suitable for picnicking.

Dining

In the relaxed atmosphere for which San Diego is famous, kids are almost always welcome in restaurants, and most places make at least some accommodation for them: child-size portions; seats for children; or, at a minimum, friendliness. Generally, the only places you may wish to avoid are upscale restaurants listed in Chapter 8 in the $$$ and $$$$ price ranges.

Restaurants

Of the places reviewed in Chapter 8, the bustling **Piatti's, California Café, The Fish Market, Hob Nob Hill, The Hard Rock Café, Old Town Mexico Cafe,** and **El Indio** are particularly suited for families; your children's din will blend right in. **SamSons** (tel. 616/455–1461), suitable for children anytime, hosts Kid's Night Out on Sunday evenings, with live entertainment by Nels, a very good singer, and KC the clown. (Junior critics have been known to like this free show better than the expensive Raffi concert they saw the week before.) Call ahead for seating times and for reservations.

Other non-fast-food options for families include **Baja Grill** (1342 Camino Del Mar, Del Mar, tel. 619/792–6551), where a fish pond will entertain your kids while you finish eating your seafood dinner; **Pizza Nova** (Costa Verde Shopping Center, on Genessee across from University Towne Center, tel. 619/458–9525); and **The Old Spaghetti Factory** (275 5th Ave., downtown, tel. 619/233–4323). If your children are not restaurant-trained, or if you want takeout for a nice picnic, try the terrific chicken at **Saffron** (3731 India St., downtown, tel. 619/574–0177).

Fast-Food Outlets

Chuck E Cheese (9840 Hibert, tel. 619/578–5860 in Mira Mesa, other locations in La Mesa, Escondido, Oceanside, and National City) offers mediocre food in an environment given over to kids, including toys, games, and those big ball enclosures. In Del Mar, **McDonald's** (2705 Via de la Valle, tel. 619/481–8595) and **Burger King** (12847 El Camino Real, tel. 619/792–4011) both have playgrounds on the premises.

Sweets and Treats

There are plenty of good ice-cream parlors in town, but for the full-on experience, try **Farrell's** (136 Fashion Valley, tel. 619/291–1887), a loud, lively, and very popular sit-down place with more ice cream delights than you can eat comfortably.

Lodging

Virtually all tourist-oriented sections of San Diego have lodgings suited to a family pocketbook and/or recreational needs. The top area for all-around child appeal, however, would have to be Mission Bay, near beaches; parks; the Belmont roller coaster; and, of course, Sea World (many Mission Bay hotels offer Sea World packages or discounts). Conversely, although downtown has attractions for all ages, it's still generally desolate at night; accommodations in the lively Embarcadero section are the only ones that can be recommended.

Some of the more expensive hotels and resorts in San Diego have special activity programs and camps to keep their guests' offspring occupied; many places offer excellent family discounts, and a number of lodgings are well-suited to those traveling with children because they have kitchen and laundry facilities. Unless otherwise indicated, full reviews of the following hotels are found in Chapter 9, Lodging.

Children's Programs

Loew's Coronado Bay Resort has year-round day and evening programs for children ages 4–14. Programs depend on the age of the children enrolled and include arts and crafts as well as a variety of outdoor activities. Prices are $17 per child for half-day programs, $12 for evening programs, and $30 for a full day of events. There is a discount for the second child enrolled.

During the summer, the **Hotel del Coronado** offers activities, such as sand-castle-building and educational bike rides; egg hunts are organized at spring break. There's a youth tennis program for ages 5–15 during the summer, and the regular behind-the-scenes tour of the hotel includes visits to haunted rooms.

From Memorial Day through Labor Day, **San Diego Hilton Beach and Tennis Resort** organizes daytime and evening activities, such as pool games, parties, and movies, for children 5 and older; the program is free, but parents must stay on the property. There's also a small playground on the premises.

On Fridays and Saturdays from Memorial Day through Labor Day, children ages 3 through 15 can take part in an evening (5–10 PM) program at the **Hyatt Islandia;** the cost for supervised activities, such as games, videos, and arts and crafts, is $5 per child per hour, $2.50 for the second child in the same family. Parents must stay on the hotel property.

The **San Diego Princess Resort** runs a Kid Camp from June through August and organizes activities for children during spring break. The rates are $10 per day for children 5–12; lunch is $2 extra.

Rancho Bernardo Inn (*see* the Inland North County section in Chapter 12, Excursions from San Diego) also has a children's camp during spring break and the month of August.

Family Rates

Many hotels and motels run family specials or allow children to stay free in the same room with their parents, with nominal charges for cribs and $5–$10 charges for extra beds; inquire when making reservations. For example, at the sister **Catamaran** and **Bahia** hotels in Mission Bay, there's no charge for children 12 and under; at the **Hotel del Coronado,** children 15 and under stay in their parents' room gratis. Some of the **Days Inn** hotels (tel. 800/325–2525; six locations in San Diego) charge only a small fee for children under 18; all allow children 12 and under to stay in their parents' room at no extra charge. Children of any age stay free with their parents at the **San Diego Mission Valley Hilton.** There's no charge for food for children under 12 at **Holiday Inn on the Bay** in the Embarcadero area. The **Kona Kai Resort** in Shelter Island often runs family specials: one held in 1994 had rates of $62 for four in a room with two queen-size beds.

Facilities

Although cooking and doing laundry don't play a large part in most parents' dream vacations, many like to know that the option for those activities is there—if only to ignore it. The **La Jolla Cove Motel** has kitchenettes and laundry facilities, as well as lower room rates than most hotels in the La Jolla Cove area. Farther north, **La Jolla Palms Inn** has even lower rates and offers many remarkably large rooms with huge closets; some rooms have kitchenettes, and three suites feature separate eat-in kitchens.

Embassy Suites San Diego Bay, in the Embarcadero area, has in-room refrigerators, microwaves, and separate sleeping areas. At the **Best Western Shelter Island Marina Inn,** you can book reasonably priced two-bedroom suites with eat-in kitchens. Full or partial kitchens are also available at the **Bahia** and **Catamaran** hotels in Mission Beach, and the **Outrigger Motel,** near Shelter Island, offers large rooms with eat-in kitchens at economical rates. In the Embarcadero section, **Holiday Inn on the Bay** has laundry facilities.

Baby-sitting

Agencies Many of the concierges at San Diego's best hotels recommend **Marion's Child Care** (tel. 619/582–5029) and **Reliable Baby Sitter Agency** (tel. 619/296–0856) for baby-sitting services.

The Arts

San Diego offers a nice range of cultural entertainment for all types of kids, whether your child is a budding violinist or thinks Yo Yo Ma is a type of string toy.

Theater

San Diego Junior Theatre (Casa del Prado, Balboa Park, tel. 619/239–1311) puts on six productions each year, featuring student actors ages 8–18, under the direction of theater professionals.

San Diego Children's Theatre (tel. 619/675–0463) stages a few musicals each year at the Poway Center for the Performing Arts (15500 Espola Rd. [approximately 20 min north of downtown San Diego on I–15], Poway, tel. 619/748–0505), starring children 4 years of age and up.

Christian Youth Theater (tel. 619/696–1929 or 619/588–0206 for camp information), a nondenominational theater program, presents 15 productions by and for youths in various locations around San Diego County. Performances in 1994 included *Aladdin, Cinderella, Wizard of Oz, Wind in the Willows,* and *Tom Sawyer.* It also runs classes and camps for children ages 6–18.

The **San Diego Actors Theatre** (tel. 619/268–4494) sponsors the Children's Classics series of fairy tales and children's stories adapted for the stage at two locations: the Better Worlde Galeria (4010 Goldfinch St., Mission Hills, tel. 619/260–8007) and L'Auberge Del Mar Garden Amphitheater (1540 Camino Del Mar, tel. 619/259–1515). Performances of such stories as the Mad Hatter's Tea Party, Little Red Riding Hood, and Rapunzel are held on various Saturday mornings throughout the year (call ahead for schedules); child volunteers perform with the group.

For the younger set, the San Diego Guild of Puppetry operates a **Puppetry Hotline** (tel. 619/685–5045). Many of the performances are staged at the Marie Hitchcock Puppet Theater (Palisades Building, Balboa Park), which is celebrating 30 years of puppetry.

The oldest theater in San Diego, located in the heart of downtown, the **Spreckles Theater** (*see* Theater in Chapter 10, The Arts) has a Children's Series that includes major productions by the National Theatre for Children, the San Diego Children's Theatre, and the American Ballet Ensemble.

Dance

San Diego Civic Youth Ballet (Casa del Prado Theatre, Balboa Park, tel. 619/233–3060) stages ballets in spring and at Christmas featuring dancers ages 5–19.

Music

At Copley Symphony Hall (*see* Concerts in Chapter 10, The Arts), **The San Diego Symphony** has young people's concerts on weekday mornings October–May; call 619/699–4200 for information. During the summer, the symphony sponsors outdoor Pops concerts near Seaport Village that the whole family can enjoy.

Budding musicians will enjoy the Discovery series for rising stars put on at 3 PM on selected Sundays by the **La Jolla Chamber Music Society** (tel. 619/459–3728); concerts are held at the Sherwood Auditorium (*see* Concerts in Chapter 10, The Arts) from September through May.

Art

If your kids are at least 2½ years old, you can drop them off at **Artworks** (437 S. Hwy. 101, Suite 121, Solana Beach, tel. 619/481–2738) and let them do their thing in a variety of different art media ($10 per hour). The center also features such classes as printmaking, sculpture, drawing, painting, and woodworking; fees vary. One Friday night per month from 5 to 9 PM the center hosts the Verry Merry Unbirthday, a program for children ages 4–10 that includes art, pizza, and juice ($20).

5 Shopping

By Marael
Johnson
Revised by Jon
and Noonie
Corn

Most San Diego shops are open daily 10–6; department stores and shops within the larger malls stay open until 9 PM on weekdays. Sales are advertised in the daily *San Diego Union–Tribune* and in the *Reader,* a free weekly that comes out on Thursday.

Shopping Districts

San Diego's shopping areas are a mélange of self-contained mega-malls, historic districts, quaint villages, funky neighborhoods, and chic suburbs.

Coronado Across the bay, Coronado is accessible by car or ferry. **Orange Avenue,** in the center of town, has six blocks of ritzy boutiques and galleries. The elegant Hotel del Coronado, also on Orange Avenue, houses exclusive (and costly) specialty shops. **Old Ferry Landing,** where the San Diego ferry lands, is a waterfront center similar to Seaport Village.

Downtown **Horton Plaza,** in the heart of center city, is a shopper's Disneyland—visually exciting, multilevel department stores; one-of-a-kind shops; fast-food counters; classy restaurants; a farmers' market; live theater; and cinemas. Surrounding Horton Plaza is the 16-block Gaslamp Quarter, a redevelopment area that features art galleries, antiques, and specialty shops housed in Victorian buildings and renovated warehouses.

The Paladion, just across 1st Avenue from Horton Plaza, is San Diego's answer to Rodeo Drive. This posh complex, opened in 1992, houses a collection of upscale boutiques—including Cartier, Tiffany, Gucci, Alfred Dunhill, Gianni Versace, and Salvatore Ferragamo.

Hotel Circle The Hotel Circle area, northeast of downtown near I–8 and Freeway 163, has two major shopping centers. **Fashion Valley** and **Mission Valley Center** contain hundreds of shops, as well as restaurants, cinemas, and branches of almost every San Diego department store.

Kensington/ These are two of San Diego's older, established neighborhoods, situ-
Hillcrest ated several miles north and east of downtown. **Adams Avenue,** in Kensington, is Antiques Row. More than 20 dealers sell everything from postcards and kitchen utensils to cut glass and porcelain. **Park Boulevard,** in Hillcrest, is the city's center for nostalgia. Small shops, on either side of University Avenue, stock clothing, accessories, furnishings, and bric-a-brac of the 1920s–60s. **Uptown District,** a shopping center on University Avenue, has the neighborhood's massive Ralph's grocery store, as well as several specialty shops.

La Jolla/ La Jolla, about 15 miles northwest of downtown on the coast, is an
Golden ultra-chic, ultra-exclusive resort community. High-end and trendy
Triangle boutiques line Girard Avenue and Prospect Street. Coast Walk, nestled along the cliffside of Prospect Street, offers several levels of sophisticated shops, galleries, and restaurants, as well as a spectacular ocean view. The Golden Triangle area, several miles east of coastal La Jolla, is served by **University Towne Centre,** between I–5 and Highway 805. This megamall features the usual range of department stores, specialty shops, sportswear chains, restaurants, and cinemas. Nearby **Costa Verde Centre,** on the corner of Genessee and La Jolla Village Drive, is an enormous strip mall of convenience stores and inexpensive eateries.

North County This rapidly expanding area boasts an array of high-range shopping districts. One of the most attractive retail centers in the area, **Del Mar Plaza** (15th St. and Camino Del Mar) boasts a spectacular view of the Pacific and many excellent restaurants, boutiques, and spe-

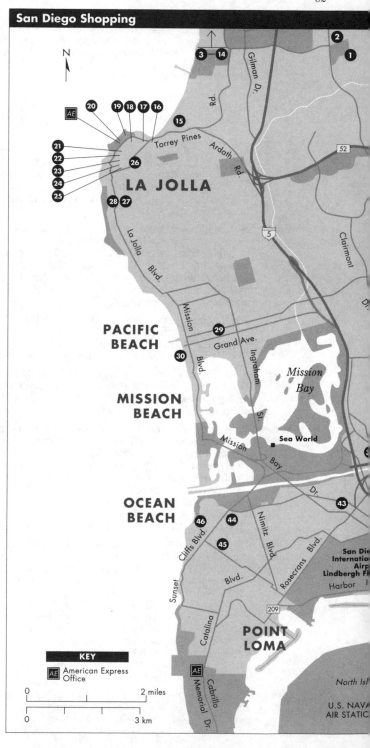

San Diego Shopping

KEY

AE American Express
Office

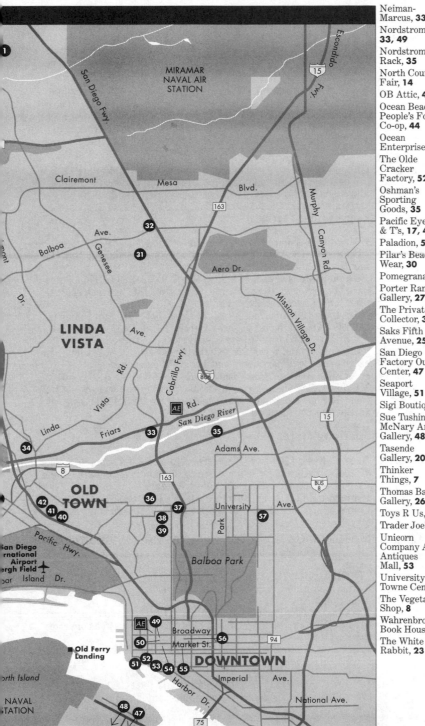

cialty stores. Farther north in Encinitas is the **Lumberyard** (1st St. and Old Hwy. 1), an upscale strip mall where one can find everything from yogurt shops and stationary to sportswear and sushi. Inland from Del Mar in Escondido, one of the area's newest enclosed malls, **North County Fair** (Via Rancho Parkway, east of Hwy. 15), is anchored by Nordstrom, Robinson-May, and the Broadway.

Old Town North of downtown, off I–5, this popular historic district is reminiscent of a colorful Mexican marketplace. Adobe architecture, flower-filled plazas, fountains, and courtyards highlight the shopping areas of **Bazaar del Mundo, La Esplanade,** and **Old Town Mercado,** where you will find international goods, toys, souvenirs, and arts and crafts.

Seaport Village On the waterfront, a few minutes from downtown, **Seaport Village** offers quaint theme shops, restaurants, arts-and-crafts galleries, and commanding views of Coronado, the bridge, and passing ships.

Department Stores

I. Magnin (Fashion Valley, tel. 619/297–2100). This upscale retailer stocks exclusive, traditional fashions, accessories, and gift items for men and women.

Neiman-Marcus (Fashion Valley, tel. 619/692–9100). This Texas-based department store is world-famous for fine apparel, couture, furs, jewels, accessories, and gifts.

Nordstrom (Fashion Valley, tel. 619/295–4441; Horton Plaza, tel. 619/239–1700; University Towne Centre, tel. 619/457–4575). Up-to-the-minute, moderate-to-expensive clothing and accessories for men, women, and teens are found at these stores, noted for their extensive shoe departments and customized service.

Saks Fifth Avenue (7600 Girard Ave., La Jolla, tel. 619/459–4123; Mission Valley Center, tel. 619/260–0030). Contemporary sportswear for men and women of all ages, designer apparel, lingerie, and accessories are featured.

Specialty Stores

Accessories **Bags, Belts and Beyond** (7886 Girard Ave., La Jolla, tel. 619/459–3536). Here there are discounted designer handbags, belts, costume jewelry, accessories, and collectible gift items.
Pomegranate (1152 Prospect Ave., La Jolla, tel. 619/459–0629). Come to this store for fine accessories and exceptional antique jewelry.

Antiques **Maidhof Bros.** (1891 San Diego Ave., Old Town, tel. 619/574–1891) is one of California's oldest and largest dealers in nautical and brass items.
The OB Attic (4921 Newport Ave., Ocean Beach, tel. 619/223–5048) features an assortment of antique and used furniture along with collectible items.
The Olde Cracker Factory (448 W. Market St., Gaslamp Quarter, tel. 619/233–1669) houses three floors of specialty shops in a converted brick warehouse.
The **Private Collector** (800 W. Washington St., Mission Hills, tel. 619/296–5553) has an extensive variety of antiques, both large and small.
Unicorn Company Arts & Antiques Mall (704 J St., Gaslamp Quarter, tel. 619/232–1696) is the largest antiques complex in San Diego.

Art Galleries **Africa and Beyond** (1250 Prospect Ave., La Jolla, tel. 619/454–9983) has a splendid collection of ethnic art, crafts, masks, jewelry, and beads.

Porter Randall Gallery (5624 La Jolla Blvd., La Jolla, tel. 619/551–8884) has become a major venue for contemporary art. The gallery also hosts literary events and poetry readings.

Sue Tushingham McNary Art Gallery (Hotel del Coronado Arcade, Coronado, tel. 619/435–1819) displays paintings, lithographs, etchings, miniatures, and prints of San Diego scenes.

Tasende Gallery (820 Prospect St., La Jolla, tel. 619/454–3691) specializes in modern European painting and sculpture.

Thomas Babeor (7470 Girard Ave., La Jolla, tel. 619/454–0345) carries the work of nationally recognized modern European and American artists.

Bargains **The Garment Center** (1911 San Diego Ave., Old Town, tel. 619/597–0788 or 619/453–6814). This is the place for manufacturers' end-of-season merchandise, discounted up to 60%.

Nordstrom Rack (Mission Valley Center, tel. 619/296–0143). Top-of-the-line, end-of-season collections from Nordstrom Department Store, at about 50% off, are featured here.

San Diego Factory Outlet Center (Camino de la Plaza, San Ysidro, last exit off I–5 before the Mexican border, tel. 619/690–2999). There are more than 25 discount factory outlets here, including Nike, Mikasa, Levi Strauss, and Eddie Bauer.

Beachwear **Hansen's** (1105 1st St., Encinitas, tel. 619/753–6595), one of San Diego's oldest surfboard manufacturers, now also features a full line of recreational clothing and casual wear.

La Jolla Surf Systems (2132 Avenida de la Playa, La Jolla, tel. 619/456-2777) carries swimsuits and other resort wear.

Pilar's Beach Wear (3745 Mission Blvd., Mission Beach, tel. 619/488–3056) has one of California's largest selections of imported and American major-label swimsuits, offering mix-and-match as well as split sizes.

Bookstores **Blue Door** (3823 5th Ave., Hillcrest, tel. 619/298–8610) has an extensive selection of hard-to-find literary paperbacks, poetry, and magazines.

Esmeralda Book Shop (1555 Camino Del Mar, Del Mar, tel. 619/755–2707), which carries hard-to-find and unusual selections along with best-sellers, has a cappuccino bar and patio.

John Cole's Book Shop (780 Prospect St., La Jolla, tel. 619/454–4766), in a 1904 cottage with loads of character, offers a fascinating selection of books on art and architecture.

Wahrenbrock's Book House (726 Broadway, San Diego, tel. 619/232–0132) is one of San Diego's oldest and largest used-book stores.

The White Rabbit (7755 Girard Ave., La Jolla, tel. 619/454–3518) features books for prereaders through junior high school age.

Boutiques for Men **Custom Shirts of La Jolla** (7643 Girard Ave., La Jolla, tel. 619/459–6147) stocks fine slacks, jackets, and sportswear. Shirts are made to order from more than 300 fabrics.

Durante's (1412 Camino Del Mar, Del Mar, tel. 619/755–0116) offers a good selection of sportswear and beach attire.

Gentleman's Quarter (1224 Prospect St., La Jolla, tel. 619/459–3351; Flower Hill Mall, 2710 Via de La Valle, Del Mar, tel. 619/481–7124) specializes in European designer suits, shirts, and sportswear.

International Male (3964 5th St., San Diego, tel. 619/294–8600) sells contemporary men's fashions at reasonable prices.

Boutiques for Women **Capriccio** (6919 La Jolla Blvd., La Jolla, tel. 619/459–4189) is a *Women's Wear Daily* recommendation for high-end European and designer ensembles and elegant evening wear.

Chico's (Del Mar Plaza, Del Mar, tel. 619/792–7080), like its Santa Fe counterpart, specializes in brightly colored, natural-fiber clothing with a southwestern accent.

Jigsaw (1418 Camino Del Mar, Del Mar, tel. 619/259–7175) offers an eclectic mix of funky New York and chic LA style, including wonderful bathing suits and hard-to-find accessories.

Sigi Boutique (788 Girard Ave., La Jolla, tel. 619/454–7244) displays a range of European clothing and accessories.

Crafts Galleries **Brushworks Gallery** (425 Market St., downtown, tel. 619/238–4381) features contemporary crafts.

International Gallery (643 G St., Gaslamp Quarter, tel. 619/235–8255) carries fine gifts; crafts; and folk, primitive, and native art from around the world.

Food **Greentree Grocers** (3560 Mt. Acacia Blvd., San Diego, tel. 619/560–1975) features excellent organic produce, meats, and health supplies.

Horton Plaza Farmers Market (Horton Plaza, tel. 619/696–7766) has spectacular displays of gourmet foods, including cheeses, meats, produce, and deli specialties.

Ocean Beach People's Food Co-op (4765 Voltaire St., Ocean Beach, tel. 619/224–1387) is where you'll find San Diego's largest selection of organic grains, beans, and produce.

Trader Joe's (1211 Garnet Ave., Pacific Beach, tel. 619/272–7235; 8657 Villa La Jolla Dr., La Jolla, tel. 619/546–8629), part of a California chain, stocks an affordable and eclectic selection of gourmet foods from around the world.

The Vegetable Shop (6123 Calzada del Bosque, Rancho Santa Fe, tel. 619/756–3184) is one of San Diego's greatest culinary assets. The premium fruits and vegetables picked daily make their way into such famed eateries as Berkeley's Chez Panisse and Los Angeles's Spago, as well as into many of San Diego's finer restaurants.

Jewelry **Ben Bridge Jeweler** (Horton Plaza, tel. 619/696–8911; Mission Valley Center, tel. 619/294–2808; University Towne Centre, tel. 619/453–9996) offers fine watches, diamonds, repairs, and custom work.

The Collector (1274 Prospect St., La Jolla, tel. 619/454–9763) is a world-renowned source for colored gemstones and contemporary pieces designed by international jewelers and resident goldsmiths.

Gary Gilmore Goldsmith (4919 Newport Ave., Ocean Beach, tel. 619/225–1137) carries elegant, simple jewelry crafted by the owner; you may want to buy that engagement ring here.

J. Jessop & Sons (Horton Plaza, tel. 619/239–9311) has been in business for nearly a century, specializing in diamonds, gems, and fine watches.

Luggage **John's Fifth Avenue Luggage** (3833 4th Ave., Hillcrest, tel. 619/298–0993; Fashion Valley, tel. 619/574–0086) has a large selection of luggage, attaché cases, and travel accessories.

Le Travel Store (Horton Plaza, tel. 619/544–0005) stocks luggage, totes, travel packs, luggage carts, and travel accessories.

Perfume **The House of Versailles** (Hotel del Coronado Arcade, Coronado, tel. 619/435–1010) is a world-famous perfumery offering custom blending and pH and fragrance compatibility analysis.

Seashells **La Jolla Cave and Shell Shop** (1325 Coast Blvd., La Jolla, tel. 619/454–6080) stocks specimen and decorative shells, coral, and nautical gifts.

Seaport Village Shell Company (817-D W. Harbor Dr., tel. 619/234–1004) has a unique collection of shells, coral, and jewelry.

Sporting Goods **Fit for Sports** (1735 University Ave., Hillcrest, tel. 619/299–9644) carries a large assortment of well-priced running shoes, clothing, and accessories.

Ocean Enterprises (7710 Balboa Ave., Claremont, tel. 619/565–6054) stocks high-quality wet suits, dry suits, and skin- and scuba-diving equipment.

Oshman's Sporting Goods (Mission Valley Center, tel. 619/299–0701) has all types of athletic and camping equipment, including athletic shoes and sportswear.

Swap Meets Bargain shoppers spend their weekend mornings at **Kobey's Swap Meet** (3500 Sports Arena Blvd., near Midway and Rosecrans, tel. 619/226–0650). The open-air market seems to expand every week, with sellers displaying everything from futons to fresh strawberries from the farming communities. The back section with secondhand goods is a bargain-hunter's delight. Admission to the swap meet, open Thursday–Sunday 7 AM–3 PM, is $1.

Toys **Imaginarium** (322 Horton Plaza, tel. 619/237–0122; University Towne Centre, tel. 619/755/4488) offers an excellent supply of international toys, dolls, and educational materials.

Thinker Things (2670 Via de la Valle, Del Mar, tel. 619/755–4488) carries an extensive collection of dolls and puppets in addition to its toys, crafts, and games.

Toys R Us (1240 W. Morena Blvd., Mission Bay area, tel. 619/276–7094) is a supermarket of toys, stuffed animals, and games for all ages.

T-shirts **Pacific Eyes & T's** (1241 Prospect St., La Jolla, tel. 619/454–7532; 2461 San Diego Ave., Old Town, tel. 619/692–0059) has T-shirts in every price category.

6 Beaches

By Kevin
Brass

Revised by Jon
and Noonie
Corn

San Diego's beaches are one of its greatest natural attractions. In some places, the shorefront is wide and sandy; in others, it's narrow and rocky or backed by impressive sandstone cliffs. You'll find beaches teeming with activities and deserted spots for romantic sunset walks. San Diego is a prime destination for surfers; the variety of breaks and their exposure to ocean swells make the surf off this portion of the Pacific coast remarkably consistent and fun. For a surf and weather report, call 619/221–8884.

Overnight camping is not allowed on any San Diego city beaches, but there are campgrounds at some state beaches throughout the county; call 800/444–7275 for state beach camping reservations. Lifeguards are stationed at city beaches (from Sunset Cliffs to Black's Beach) in the summertime, but coverage in winter is provided by roving patrols only. Dogs are not permitted at most beaches in San Diego, and tickets for breaking the law can be very expensive. However, it is rarely a problem to bring your pet to isolated beaches during the winter.

Pay attention to all signs listing illegal activities; undercover police often patrol the beaches, carrying their ticket books in coolers. Glass is prohibited on all beaches, and fires are allowed only in fire rings or barbecues. Alcoholic beverages—including beer—are completely banned on some city beaches; others allow you to partake between 8 AM and 8 PM only. Check out the signs posted at the parking lots and lifeguard towers before you hit the shore with a six pack or some wine coolers. Imbibing in beach parking lots, on boardwalks, and in landscaped areas is always illegal; where drinking is permitted, stay on the sand. For more information on the beach-booze ban, call Pacific Beach Community Relations (tel. 619/581–9920) or Ocean Beach Community Relations (tel. 619/531–1540). For a general beach and weather report, phone 619/289–1212.

Beaches are listed from south to north. For information on Mission Bay, *see* Tour 6: Mission Bay and Sea World in Chapter 3, Exploring San Diego.

South Bay

Border Field State Beach. The southernmost San Diego beach is different from the majority of California beaches. Located just north of the Mexican border, it is a marshy area with wide chaparrals and wildflowers, a favorite among horse riders and hikers. However, frequent sewage contamination from Tijuana makes the water dangerous for swimming. For this reason, the beach is often closed. There is ample parking, and there are rest rooms and fire rings. *Exit I–5 at Dairy Mart Rd. and head west along Monument Rd.*

South Beach. One of the few beaches where dogs are free to romp, this is a good spot for long, isolated walks. The often-contaminated water and rocky beach tend to discourage crowds. The downside: There are few facilities, such as rest rooms, and sewage contamination from Tijuana can create a health hazard at times. *Located at the end of Seacoast Dr. Take I–5 to Coronado Ave. and head west on Imperial Beach Ave. Turn left onto Seacoast Dr.*

Imperial Beach. This classic southern California beach, where surfers and swimmers congregate to enjoy the water and waves, provides a pleasant backdrop for the Frisbee games of the predominantly young crowd. There are lifeguards on duty during the summer, parking lots, food vendors nearby, and rest rooms. Note: Although the surf here can be excellent, this is another spot at which

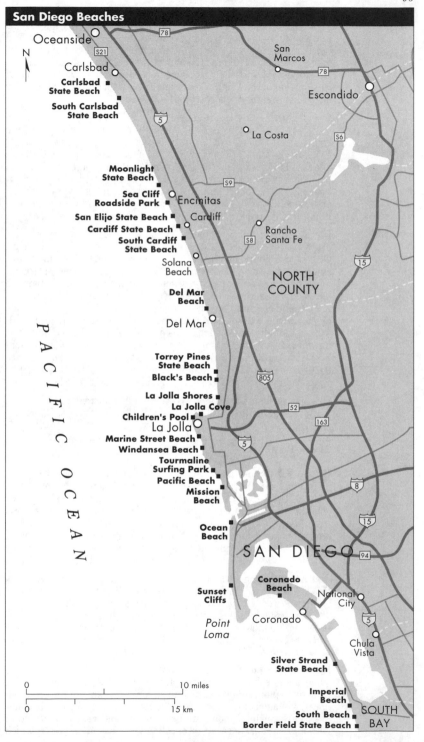

San Diego Beaches

N

Oceanside

S21

Carlsbad

**Carlsbad
State Beach**

**South Carlsbad
State Beach**

78

San
Marcos

78

Escondido

S6

La Costa

S9

**Moonlight
State Beach**

**Sea Cliff
Roadside Park** Encinitas

San Elijo State Beach Cardiff

Cardiff State Beach

**South Cardiff
State Beach**

Solana
Beach

S8

Rancho
Santa Fe

NORTH
COUNTY

15

**Del Mar
Beach**

Del Mar

P A C I F I C

**Torrey Pines
State Beach**

Black's Beach

La Jolla Shores

La Jolla Cove

Children's Pool

La Jolla

Marine Street Beach

Windansea Beach

**Tourmaline
Surfing Park**

Pacific Beach

**Mission
Beach**

805

52

163

5

O C E A N

**Ocean
Beach**

8

15

SAN DIEGO 94

**Coronado
Beach**

National
City

5

**Sunset
Cliffs**

*Point
Loma*

Coronado

Chula
Vista

**Silver Strand
State Beach**

0   10 miles

0   15 km

**Imperial
Beach**

South Beach

Border Field State Beach

SOUTH
BAY

to be careful of sewage contamination. *Take Palm Ave. west from I–5 until it hits water.*

Coronado

Silver Strand State Beach. Farther north on the isthmus of Coronado (commonly mislabeled an island), Silver Strand was set aside as a state beach in 1932. The name is derived from the tiny silver seashells found in abundance near the water. The water is relatively calm, making this beach ideal for families. Four parking lots provide room for more than 1,500 cars. Parking is free from Labor Day through February; the rest of the year the cost is $4 per car. There is also an RV campground (cost: $14 per night) and a wide array of facilities but no hook-ups; spots are available on a first-come, first-served basis. *Tel. 619/435–5184. Take the Palm Ave. exit from I–5 west to Hwy. 75; turn right and follow the signs.*

Coronado Beach. With the famous Hotel Del Coronado as a backdrop, this wide stretch of sandy beach is one of the largest and most picturesque in the county. It is surprisingly uncrowded on most days, since the locals go to the less touristy areas in the south or north. It's perfect for sunbathing or games of Frisbee and Smash Ball (played with paddles and a small ball). Parking can be a little difficult on the busiest days, but there are plenty of rest rooms and service facilities, as well as fire rings. The view (even for a brief moment) as you drive over the Coronado Bridge makes it a worthwhile excursion. *From the bridge, turn left on Orange Ave. and follow the signs.*

Point Loma

Sunset Cliffs. Beneath the jagged cliffs on the west side of the Point Loma peninsula is one of the more secluded beaches in the area, popular primarily with surfers and locals. The tide goes out each day to reveal tidal pools teeming with life at the south end of the peninsula, near Cabrillo Point. Farther north, the often-large waves attract surfers and the lonely coves attract sunbathers. Stairs are available at the foot of Bermuda and Santa Cruz avenues, but much of the access is limited to treacherous cliff trails. There are no facilities. Your visit here will be much more enjoyable at low tide; check the local newspaper for tide schedules. *Take I–8 west to Sunset Cliffs Blvd. and head south.*

San Diego

Ocean Beach. The north end of this beach, past the second jetty, is known as Dog Beach because it's the only one within the San Diego city limits that allows canines to romp around without a leash. The south end of Ocean Beach, near the pier, is a hangout for surfers and transients. Much of the area, though, is a haven for local volleyball players, sunbathers, and swimmers. You'll find food vendors and fire rings here; limited parking is available. *Take I–8 west to Sunset Cliffs Blvd. and head south. Turn right on Voltaire St., West Point Loma Blvd., or Newport Ave.*

Mission Beach. The boardwalk stretching along Mission Beach is popular with strollers, roller skaters, and bicyclists. Surfers, swimmers, and volleyball players congregate at the south end, which tends to get extremely crowded, especially on hot summer days. Toward the north end, near the Belmont Park roller coaster, the beach narrows and the water grows rougher—and the crowd gets even thicker. The refurbished Belmont Park is now a shopping and dining complex. Parking can be a challenge, but there are plenty of rest rooms and restaurants in the area. *Exit I–5 at Garnet Ave. and head west to Mission Blvd. Turn south and look for parking.*

Pacific Beach. The boardwalk turns into a sidewalk here, but there are still bike paths and picnic tables running along the beachfront. The beach is a favorite for families, teens, and surfers alike. Parking can be a problem, although there is a small lot at the foot of Ventura Place. *Exit I–5 at Garnet Ave. and head west to Mission Blvd. Turn north and look for parking.*

La Jolla

The beaches of La Jolla combine unusual beauty with good fishing, exciting scuba diving, and excellent surf. On the down side, they are very crowded and have limited parking facilities. Don't even think about bringing your pet—dogs are not even allowed on the sidewalks above some La Jolla beaches.

Tourmaline Surfing Park and **Windansea Beach.** These La Jolla beaches are two of the top surfing spots in the area. Tourmaline has the better parking area of the two and is more hospitable to tourists. The surf at Windansea is world-class, but the local crowd can be "gnarly." *Take Mission Blvd. north (it turns into La Jolla Blvd.) and turn west on Tourmaline St. (for the surfing park) or Nautilus St. (for Windansea Beach).*

Marine Street Beach. This is a classic stretch of sand for sunbathing and Frisbee games. *Accessible from Marine St. off La Jolla Blvd.*

Children's Pool. For the tykes, a shallow lagoon with small waves and no riptide provides a safe, if crowded, haven. *Follow La Jolla Blvd. north. When it forks, take the left, Coast Blvd.*

Shell Beach. Just north of the Children's Pool is a small cove, accessible by stairs, with a relatively secluded and beautiful beach. The exposed rocks just off the coast here have been designated a protected habitat for seals; you can watch them sun themselves and frolick in the water. *Continue along Coast Blvd. north from the Children's Pool.*

La Jolla Cove. Just north of Shell Beach is La Jolla Cove, one of the prettiest spots in the world. A beautiful, palm-tree-lined park sits on top of cliffs formed by the incessant pounding of the waves. At low tide the tidal pools and cliff caves provide an exciting destination for explorers. Divers explore the underwater delights of the San Diego–La Jolla Underwater Park, an ecological reserve. The cove is also a favorite of rough-water swimmers, for whom buoys mark distances. The beach below the cove is beautiful and great for kids over 8 years old. *Follow Coast Blvd. north to the signs, or take the La Jolla Village Dr. exit from I–5, head west to Torrey Pines Rd., turn left and drive down the hill to Girard Ave. Turn right and follow the signs.*

La Jolla Shores. This is one of the most popular and overcrowded beaches in the county. On holidays, such as Memorial Day, all access routes are usually closed. The lures are a wide sandy beach; fun surf for boogie-boarders, body-surfers, and regular surfers alike; and a concrete boardwalk paralleling the beach. There is also a wide variety of facilities, from posh restaurants to snack shops, within walking distance. Go early to get a parking spot. *From I–5 take La Jolla*

Village Dr. west and turn left onto La Jolla Shores Dr. Head west to Camino del Oro or Vallecitos St. Turn right and look for parking.

Black's Beach. At one time, this was the only legal nude beach in the country. But the late 1970s prohibition against public nudity doesn't stop people from braving the treacherous cliff trails for a chance to take off their clothes. Above the beach, hang-gliders and sail-plane enthusiasts launch from the Torrey Pines Glider Port. Because of the difficult access, the beach is always relatively uncrowded. The waves here are excellent for surfers, but the shorebreak can be powerful. Only experienced swimmers should take the plunge. *Take Genessee Ave. west from I–5 and follow the signs to the glider port; easier access, via a paved path, is available on La Jolla Farms Rd., but parking there is limited to 2 hrs.*

Del Mar

Torrey Pines State Beach. This is one of the easiest and most comfortable beaches to visit in the area. The large parking lot (admission: $4) is rarely full. There is year-round lifeguard service, and fire rings are available for beach parties. Torrey Pines tends to get crowded during the summer, but more isolated spots under the cliffs are within a short walk in either direction. Exotic trails up into the hillside park offer lovely hikes. *Tel. 619/653–6995. Take the Carmel Valley Rd. exit west from I–5. Open daily 9–sunset.*

Del Mar Beach. The numbered streets of Del Mar, from 15th to 29th, end at a wide, sandy beach, popular with volleyball players, surfers, and sunbathers. Although parking can be a problem on nice summer days, access is relatively easy, and the beach and water are both extremely comfortable. The portions of Del Mar south of 15th Street are lined with beautiful cliffs and are rarely crowded. Leashed dogs are permitted on most sections of Del Mar Beach year-round; between October and May, dogs may run free at Rivermouth, Del Mar's northernmost beach. During the annual summer meeting of the Del Mar Thoroughbred Club, horse bettors can be seen sitting on the beach in the morning working on the *Daily Racing Form* before heading across the street to the track in the afternoon. *Take the Via de la Valle exit from I–5 west to Old Hwy. 101 (also known as Camino del Mar in Del Mar) and turn left.*

Solana Beach

Most of the beaches of this little city are tucked away under cliffs; access is limited to private stairways. But at the west end of Lomas Santa Fe Drive, at a beach area known to the locals as Pillbox because of the bunkerlike structures on top of the cliffs, you'll find a large parking lot, rest rooms, and easy access to a small cove beach. During low tide, it's an easy walk to the beaches under the cliffs. *From I–5 take Lomas Santa Fe Dr. west to its end.*

Cardiff

The area along Old Highway 101 north of Solana Beach is blessed with three state beaches. A small parking lot immediately to the north of the cliffs of Solana Beach marks **South Cardiff State Beach.** A reef break makes it extremely popular with surfers, which is also true of **Cardiff State Beach,** a mile to the north. A full campground with store and shower facilities can be found at **San Elijo State Beach,** a little farther to the north. Parking at state beaches is $4 per car. For camping reservations at San Elijo, call 800/444–7275.

From I–5, turn west on Lomas Santa Fe Dr. to Old Hwy. 101 and turn right.

Encinitas

Undoubtedly one of the most picturesque spots in the county is **Sea Cliff Roadside Park,** off Old Highway 101 on the south end of Encinitas. Palm trees and the golden domes of the nearby Self Realization Fellowship earned the beach its local nickname, Swami's. It is also considered to be one of the top surfing spots in the area. The only access to the beach is by a long stairway leading down from the clifftop park. *Follow Old Hwy. 101 north from Cardiff, or exit I–5 at Encinatas Blvd., go west to Old Hwy. 101, and turn left.*

Tucked into a break in the cliffs a mile to the north is **Moonlight State Beach,** with large parking areas and full facilities. *Take the Encinitas Blvd. exit from I–5 and head west until you hit the Moonlight parking lot.*

Carlsbad

Winter storms badly erode the southern Carlsbad beaches, leaving them somewhat rockier than most southern California beaches. This is particularly true of **South Carlsbad State Beach,** which has lost large amounts of sand over the years. Still, it's an excellent swimming spot, and there is overnight camping (tel. 800/444–7275). No overnight camping is allowed at **Carlsbad State Beach,** farther to the north, but there is a fishing area and a parking lot. In 1987, a boardwalk was built that runs below the cliffs a bit to the north and has eased access to the Carlsbad beaches. *Exit I–5 at La Costa Ave. and head west to Old Hwy. 101. Turn north and follow the coastline.*

Oceanside

Two miles of wide, sandy beaches are extremely popular with swimmers, surfers, and the marines from nearby Camp Pendleton. The surf is good around the Oceanside Pier at the foot of 6th Avenue and on either side of the two jetties. The exceptionally sandy beaches are ideal for almost all beach sports. *Take Vista Way west from I–5 to Hill St. (Old Hwy. 101) and turn right. Best access points are from Cassidy St. and the Oceanside Harbor area.*

7 Sports and the Outdoors

Participant Sports

*By Kevin
Brass*

*Revised by Jon
and Noonie
Corn*

At least one stereotype of San Diego is true—it is an active, out-doors-oriented community. People recreate more than spectate. It's hard not to, with such a wide variety of choices available.

Ballooning

Enjoy the views of the Pacific Ocean, the mountains, and the coast-line south to Mexico and north to San Clemente from a hot-air balloon at sunrise or sunset. The conditions are perfect: necessary winds and wide-open spaces. Ballooning companies operating in the San Diego area include **California Dreamin'** (2153 Woodland Heights Glen, Escondido, tel. 619/471–1393 or 800/794–7599), **Pacific Horizons** (16236 San Dieguito Rd., Rancho Santa Fe, tel. 619/756–1790 or 800/244–1790), and **Skysurfer Balloon Company** (1221 Camino Del Mar, Del Mar, tel. 619/481–6800 or 800/660–6809).

Bicycling

On any given summer day, Old Highway 101, from La Jolla to Ocean-side, looks like a freeway for cyclists. Never straying more than a quarter-mile from the beach, it is easily the most popular and scenic bike route around. Although the roads are narrow and winding, experienced cyclists like to follow Lomas Santa Fe Drive in Solana Beach east into beautiful Rancho Santa Fe, perhaps even continuing east on Del Dios Highway, past Lake Hodges, to Escondido. For more leisurely rides, Mission Bay, San Diego Harbor, and the Mission Beach boardwalk are all flat and scenic. For those who like to race on a track, San Diego even has a velodrome in Balboa Park. Call the Velodrome Office (tel. 619/296–3345) for more information. San Diego County also offers challenging mountain-bike trails. Local bookstores and camping stores sell trail guides.

Bikes can be rented at any number of places, including **Bicycle Barn** in Pacific Beach (746 Emerald St., tel. 619/581–3665) and **Hamel's Action Sports Center** in Mission Beach (704 Ventura Pl, tel. 619/488–5050). **Performance Bicycle Shop** (3619 Midway Dr., tel. 619/223–5415), known for its catalogue business, has an impressive supply of bicycles and bicycling accessories at its San Diego location. A free comprehensive map of all county bike paths is available from the local office of the **California Department of Transportation** (tel. 619/688–6699).

Bocce Ball

The popular Italian version of lawn bowling is played on Monday, Wednesday, and Friday, from 1 to 5 PM, on courts in the Morley Field section of Balboa Park. The games are open to the public, and there are usually bocce balls at the courts. Call 619/692–4919 for more information.

Diving

Enthusiasts from all over the world flock to San Diego to skin-dive and scuba-dive in the areas off La Jolla and Point Loma that are rich in ocean creatures and flora. At La Jolla Cove, you'll find the **San Diego–La Jolla Underwater Park,** an ecological preserve. Farther north, off the south end of Black's Beach, the rim of **Scripps Canyon** lies in about 60 feet of water. The canyon plummets to more than 900 feet in some sections. Another popular diving spot is Sunset Cliffs in Point Loma, where a wide variety of sea life is relatively close to shore. Strong rip currents make it an area best enjoyed by experienced divers.

Diving equipment and boat trips can be arranged through **San Diego Divers** (tel. 619/224–3439), **Ocean Enterprises** (tel. 619/565–6054), **Del Mar Ocean Sports** (tel. 619/792–1903) or at the several **Diving Locker** locations throughout the area. It is illegal to take any wildlife from the ecological preserves in La Jolla or near Cabrillo Point. Spearfishing requires a license (available at most dive stores), and it is illegal to take out-of-season lobster and game fish out of the water. For general diving information, contact the San Diego City Lifeguards' Office (tel. 619/221–8884).

Fishing

Variety is the key. The Pacific Ocean is full of corbina, croaker, and halibut just itching to be your dinner. No license is required to fish from a public pier, such as the Ocean Beach pier. A fishing license from the state Department of Fish and Game (tel. 619/525–4215), available at most bait-and-tackle stores, is required for fishing from the shoreline, although children under 15 won't need one.

There is also a wealth of well-stocked freshwater lakes in the area. Lake Jennings and Lake San Vicente in the East County are popular spots for catching trout and bass. Lakes Morena and Jennings offer both fishing and camping facilities. For general information on lakes, call 619/465–3474. Three freshwater lakes—Dixon, Hodges, and Wohlford—surround the North County city of Escondido. Camping is allowed at Wohlford at the Oakvale Lodge (tel. 619/749–2895) and at Lyle's at Dixon Lake (tel. 619/741–3328; Dixon Lake ranger station, tel. 619/741–4680). Boats can be rented at all the above-mentioned lakes; a state fishing license is required.

Several companies offer half-day, day, or multiday fishing expeditions in search of marlin, tuna, albacore, and other deep-water fish. **Fisherman's Landing** (tel. 619/221–8500), **H & M Landing** (tel. 619/222–1144), and **Seaforth Boat Rentals** (tel. 619/223–7584) are among the companies operating from San Diego. **Helgren's Sportfishing** (tel. 619/722–2133) offers trips from Oceanside Harbor.

Fitness

Several hotels offer full health clubs, at least with weight machines, stationary bicycles, and spas. These include, in the downtown area, the **Doubletree San Diego** (910 Broadway Circle, tel. 619/239–2200) and the **Pan Pacific** (402 W. Broadway, tel. 619/239–4500). Other hotels with health clubs are the **Hotel del Coronado** (1500 Orange Ave., Coronado, tel. 619/435–6611); **La Costa Resort and Spa** (Costa del Mar Rd., Carlsbad, tel. 619/438–9111); **Le Meridien** (2000 2nd St., Coronado, tel. 619/435–3000); the **San Diego Hilton Beach and Tennis Resort** (1775 E. Mission Bay Dr., Mission Bay, tel. 619/276–4010); and the **Sheratons on Harbor Island** (1590 Harbor Island Dr., Harbor Island, tel. 619/291–6400).

Guests of the **Hanalei Hotel** (2770 Hotel Circle, tel. 619/297–1101) have access to the tennis and racquetball courts, weight room, saunas, and other facilities of the nearby **Mission Valley Health Club** (901 Hotel Circle S, tel. 619/298–9321). Guests of the **Hyatt Regency** in La Jolla (3777 La Jolla Village Dr., tel. 619/552–1234) can use the splendid facilities at the **Sporting Club at Aventine** (8930 University Center La., tel. 619/552–8000). The dozen **Family Fitness Centers** in the area (including centers in Mission Valley, tel. 619/281–5543; Sports Arena/Point Loma area, tel. 619/224–2902; and Golden Triangle/UTC, tel. 619/457–3930) allow nonmembers to use the facilities for a small fee. Both **Gold's Gym** (249 Garnet Ave., tel. 619/272–3400) in Mission Beach and the downtown **Bodyworks Health & Fitness** (1130 7th Ave., tel. 619/232–5500) allow nonmembers to use the facilities for a small fee. If you just want a good aerobics workout, try **The Body Workshop** in Pacific Beach (926 Turquoise St., tel. 619/488–5060).

Frisbee Golf

This is just like golf, except it's played with Frisbees. A course, laid out at Morley Field in Balboa Park, is open seven days a week from dawn to dusk, and there is no charge to play. Rules are posted. Directions to the field are available from the always-genial Balboa Park Information Center (tel. 619/239–0512).

Golf

It would be difficult to find a better place to play golf year-round than San Diego. The climate—generally sunny, without a lot of wind—is perfect for the sport, and there are courses in the area to suit every level of expertise. Experienced golfers can play the same greens as PGA-tournament participants, while beginners or rusty players can book a week at a golf resort and benefit from expert instruction. You'd also be hard-pressed to find a locale that has more scenic courses, offering everything from sweeping views of the ocean to lovely, verdant hills inland.

As you may expect, these advantages make San Diego very popular with golfers; during busy vacation seasons, it can be difficult to get a good tee-off time. Call in advance to see if it's possible to make a reservation. You don't necessarily have to stay at a resort to play its course; check if the one you're interested in is open to nonguests. Most public courses in the area offer an inexpensive current list of fees and charges for all San Diego courses. The **Southern California Golf Association** (tel. 818/980–3630 or 213/877–0901) publishes an annual directory with detailed and valuable information on all member clubs. Another good resource for golfers is the **Southern California Public Links Information Service** (tel. 714/994–4747). The following is not intended to be a comprehensive list but offers suggestions on some of the best places to play in the area.

Public Courses
Carmel Mountain Ranch Country Club (14050 Carmel Ridge Rd., San Diego, tel. 619/487–9224): 18 holes, driving range, equipment rentals. A challenging course with many difficult holes, Carmel Mountain Ranch is not particularly scenic: It's in a suburban area and runs through a housing development.

Coronado Golf Course (2000 Visalia Row, Coronado, tel. 619/435–3121): 18 holes, driving range, equipment rentals, clubhouse. Views of San Diego Bay and the Coronado Bridge from the back nine holes on this good walking course make it very popular—and rather difficult to get on.

Eastlake Country Club (2375 Clubhouse Dr., Chula Vista, tel. 619/482–5757): 18 holes, driving range, equipment rental, snack bar. This new facility is a fun course for golfers of almost all levels of expertise; it's not overly difficult, and features such as water hazards provide a challenge.

Four Seasons Resort–Aviara (7447 Batiquitos Dr., Carlsbad, tel. 619/929–0077): 18 holes, driving range, equipment rental. The resort that Aviara was supposed to anchor has not yet materialized, but this well-maintained Arnold Palmer–designed course was ranked by *Golf Digest* as one of the five best new resort golf courses for 1992.

Mission Bay Golf Course (2702 N. Mission Bay Dr., San Diego, tel. 619/490–3370): 18 holes, driving range, equipment rentals. A not-very-challenging executive (par 3 and 4) course, Mission Bay is lit for night play.

Mt. Woodson Country Club (16422 North Woodson, Ramona, tel. 619/788–3555): 18 holes, equipment rentals, golf shop, snack bar. This heavily wooded course in the mountains outside San Diego offers scenic views and interesting wooden cart bridges.

Rancho San Diego Golf Course (3121 Willow Glen Rd., El Cajon, tel. 619/442–9891): 36 holes, driving range, equipment rentals. A good walking course, Rancho San Diego has nice putting greens and lots of cottonwood trees.

Redhawk Golf Course (45100 Redhawk Pkwy., Temecula, tel. 909/695–1424 or 800/451–HAWK in CA): 18 holes, driving range, golf shop, snack bar. The extremely difficult design of this course will prove frustrating to those who are not experienced golfers, but experts should enjoy Redhawk.

Steele Canyon Golf Course (3199 Stonefield Dr., Jamul, tel. 619/441–6900): 27 holes, driving range, golf shop, and snack bar. Carts are a necessity at this very hilly, Gary Player–designed course with lovely views.

Torrey Pines Municipal Golf Course (11480 N. Torrey Pines Rd., La Jolla, tel. 619/452–3226): 36 holes, driving range, equipment rentals. One of the best public golf courses in the United States, Torrey Pines offers stunning views of the Pacific from every hole and is sufficiently challenging to host the Buick Invitational in February. It's not easy to get a good tee time at this justly popular course, but every golfer visiting the area should try to play it at least once.

Resorts **Carlton Oaks Lodge and Country Club** (9200 Inwood Dr., Santee, tel. 619/448–4242): 18 holes, driving range, equipment rentals, clubhouse. Many local qualifying tournaments are held at this very difficult, Pete Dye–designed course, with lots of trees and water hazards.

Carmel Highland Doubletree Golf and Tennis Resort (14455 Penasquitos Dr., San Diego, tel. 619/672-9100): 18 holes, driving range, equipment rental, clubhouse. This fairly hilly, well-maintained resort course is just across I–15 from the Carmel Mountain Ranch public course (*see above*).

Handlery Hotel & Country Club (950 Hotel Circle, San Diego, tel. 619/298–0511): 27 holes, driving range, equipment rentals. Offering an excellent staff of professional instructors, Handlery resort also features nice putting greens on its challenging course. It's perfect for golfers who want a vacation with lessons.

La Costa Resort and Spa (Costa del Mar Rd., Carlsbad, tel. 619/438–9111 or 800/854–5000): 36 holes, driving range, clubhouse, equipment rental, pro shop. One of the premier golf resorts in southern

California, La Costa hosts the annual PGA and Senior PGA Tournament of Champions in January. You'll find every golf amenity on the premises: a nice driving range, an excellent golf school, and a fabulous pro shop. All this doesn't come cheap, but, then again, how many courses will send a limo to pick you up at the airport?

Pala Mesa Resort (2001 Old Hwy. 395, Fallbrook, tel. 619/728–5881): 18 holes, driving range, equipment rentals. Narrow fairways help make this a very challenging course, but it's well maintained and offers nice views of the inland mountains.

Rancho Bernardo Inn and Country Club (17550 Bernardo Oaks Dr., Rancho Bernardo, tel. 800/542–6096): 18 holes, driving range, equipment rentals. The golf's fine here, and Rancho Bernardo Inn lays out one of the best Sunday brunches in the county.

Singing Hills Country Club (3007 Dehesa Rd., El Cajon, tel. 619/442–3425): 54 holes, driving range, equipment rentals. Set in a canyon surrounded by small mountains, this lush, green course has lots of water hazards. One of *Golf Digest*'s favorites, Singing Hills comes very highly recommended by everyone who's played it. Hackers will love the executive par-3 course; seasoned golfers can play the championship courses.

Temecula Creek Inn Golf Resort (44501 Rainbow Canyon Rd., Temecula, tel. 909/694-1000): 27 holes, golf shop. Not only does it have a picturesque, wooded course, but Temecula Creek also features one of the best restaurants in the county and is near a number of wineries.

Whispering Palms Country Club (5690 Concah del Golf, Rancho Santa Fe, tel. 619/756–2471): 27 holes, driving range, equipment rental, pro shop. The well-maintained Whispering Palms, a nice walking course in a pretty area near polo grounds and stables, is one of the more popular places to play in the San Diego area.

Hang Gliding

The **Torrey Pines Glider Port,** perched on the cliffs overlooking the ocean just north of La Jolla, is one of the most spectacular—and easiest—spots to hang glide in the world. However, it is definitely for experienced pilots only. Hang-gliding lessons are available from **Hang Gliding Center** (tel. 619/450–9008) and **Ultimate High Aviation** (tel. 619/748–1739), among others. For general information about the gliderport, contact the Torrey Pines Hang Gliders Association (tel. 619/457–9093).

Horseback Riding

Expensive insurance has severely cut the number of stables that offer horses for rent in San Diego County. The businesses that remain have a wide variety of organized excursions. **Holidays on Horseback** (tel. 619/445–3997), in the East County town of Descanso, leads rides ranging from a few hours to a few days in the Cuyamaca Mountains. It rents special, easy-to-ride fox trotters to beginners. **Bright Valley Farm** (11990 Campo Rd., Spring Valley, tel. 619/670–1861) is a wonderful place to ride. South of Imperial Beach, near the Mexican border, **Sandi's Rental Stables** (tel. 619/424–3124) leads rides through Border Field State Park.

Jet-skiing

Waveless Mission Bay and the small Snug Harbor Marina (tel. 619/434–3089), just east of the intersection of Tamarack Avenue and I–5 in Carlsbad, are favorite spots for this exhilarating sport. **California Water Sports** (tel. 619/434–3089) has information about equipment rentals and purchases. Jet-Skis can be launched from most beaches, although they need to be ridden beyond surf lines, and some beaches have special regulations governing their use. **Seaforth Boat Rentals** (tel. 619/223–1681) rents Jet-Skis for use in the South Bay Marina, and they are also available at Snug Harbor in Carlsbad.

Jogging

There is no truth to the rumor that San Diego was created to be one big jogging track, but it often seems that way. From downtown, the most popular run is along the Embarcadero, which stretches around the bay. There are nice, uncongested sidewalks through most of the area. The alternative for downtown visitors is to head east to Balboa Park, where a labyrinth of trails snake through the canyons. Mission Bay, renowned for its wide sidewalks and basically flat landscape, may be the most popular jogging spot in San Diego. Trails head west around Fiesta Island from Mission Bay, providing distance as well as a scenic route. Del Mar has the finest running trails along the bluff; park your car near 15th Street and run south along the cliffs for a gorgeous view of the ocean. There are organized runs almost every weekend. For more information, call *Competitor* magazine (tel. 619/793–2711) or the **San Diego Track Club** (tel. 619/452–7382). **The Tinley Store** (1229 Camino Del Mar, tel. 619/755–8015) has all the supplies and information you'll need for running in San Diego. Some tips: Don't run in bike lanes, and check the local newspaper's tide charts before heading to the beach.

Off-Road Driving

The 40,000-acre Ocotillo Wells State Vehicular Recreation Area (tel. 619/767–5391) provides plenty of room to ride around in dune buggies and on motorcycles and three-wheel vehicles. It can be reached by following Highway 78 east from Julian.

Roller-Blading

The sidewalks at Mission Bay are perfect for roller-blading; you can admire the sailboats and kites while you get some exercise. You can rent Roller-blades at **Hamel's Action Sports Center** in Mission Beach (tel. 619/488–5050) and at the **Bicycle Barn** in Pacific Beach (tel. 619/581–3665).

Sailing

The city that is hosting the 1995 America's Cup Races is perfect for sailing. The winds are consistent, especially during the winter. If you're bringing your boat to San Diego, there are several marinas that rent slips to the public, including the **Best Western Shelter Island Marina Inn** (2051 Shelter Island Dr., tel. 619/223–0301); the **Dana Inn and Marina** (1710 W. Mission Bay Dr., tel. 619/222–6440); **Hyatt Islandia** (1441 Quivira Rd., tel. 619/224–1234); the **Kona Kai Club** (1551 Shelter Island Dr., tel. 619/222–1191); the **San Diego Marriott** (333 W. Harbor Dr., tel. 619/234–1500); and the **Sunroad Resort Marina** (955 Harbor Island Dr., tel. 619/574–0736). Both the

San Diego Yacht Club (1011 Anchorage La., tel. 619/222–1103) and
the **Southwestern Yacht Club** (2702 Qualtrough St., tel. 619/222–
0438) have reciprocal arrangements with other yacht clubs.

If you left your boat at home, vessels of various sizes and shapes,
from small paddleboats to sleek 12-meters, can be rented from the
Bahia Resort Hotel (998 W. Mission Bay Dr., tel. 619/488–0551); the
Catamaran Resort Hotel (3999 Mission Blvd., tel. 619/488–1081);
Harbor Sailboats (2040 Harbor Island Dr., tel. 619/291–9570); the
Hotel Del Coronado (1500 Orange Ave., Coronado, tel. 619/435–
6611); the **Hyatt Islandia** (1441 Quivira Rd., tel. 619/224–1234); the
Mission Bay Sports Center (1010 Santa Clara Pl., tel. 619/488–1004);
and **Seaforth Boat Rental** (1641 Quivira Rd., tel. 619/223–1681).

If you'd rather leave the sailing to others, charters with full crews
can be arranged through **The Charter Connection** (7045 Charmant
Dr., No. 2, tel. 619/224–8585); **Fraser Charters, Inc.** (2353 Shelter
Island Dr., tel. 619/225–0588); **Hornblower Dining Yachts** (2825 5th
Ave., tel. 619/238–1686); and **Interpac Yachts** (1050 Anchorage La.,
tel. 619/222–0327). **Harbor Sailboats** (2040 Harbor Island Dr., Suite
104, tel. 619/291–9570) and the **Mission Bay Sports Center** (1010
Santa Clara Pl., tel. 619/488–1004) offer lessons. For general infor-
mation, including tips on overnight anchoring, contact the Harbor
Police (tel. 619/291–3900).

Skiing

Have breakfast on the beach and ski in the afternoon. Several ski
resorts are within a two- to four-hour drive. In the Big Bear Lake
area, in the San Bernardino Mountains east of Los Angeles, **Bear
Mountain Ski Resort** (tel. 909/585–2517), **Snow Summit** (tel.
909/866-5766), and **Snow Valley** (tel. 909/867–2751) usually have
good snow December–April. All are accessible by following I–15
north to I–10 east. Farther to the north, about an eight-hour drive
away, **Mammoth Mountain** earns its name—it's one of the largest
facilities in the west. Bus trips and junkets are constantly being
organized to make the drive easier. Check with any of the local sport-
ing-goods stores, most of which will also offer equipment for rent.

Surfing

In San Diego, surfing is a year-round sport (thanks to wet suits in
the winter) for people of all ages, many of whom are addicted to this
way of life. Beginners should paddle out at Mission, Pacific, Tourmaline, La Jolla Shores, Del Mar, or Oceanside beaches. Experienced surfers should hit Sunset Cliffs, the La Jolla reef breaks,
Black's Beach, or Swami's (Sea Cliff Roadside Park) in Encinitas
(*see* Chapter 6, Beaches, *for directions*). Most public beaches have
separate areas for surfers. Those interested in devoting some time
to learning how to surf may consider the seven-day sessions at the
Paskowitz Surfing Summer Camps in San Onofre; call (tel. 310/276-
5754) or write (Box 522, San Clemente 92674) for a brochure. For a
shorter commitment, consider **Kahuna Bob's Surf School** (1058
Hermes Ave., Encinitas, tel. 619/943–7009), for sessions seven days
a week; a two-hour lesson costs $30, and all equipment is supplied.

Many local surf shops rent boards, including **Star Surfing Company**
(tel. 619/273–7827) in Pacific Beach and **La Jolla Surf Systems** (tel.
619/456–2777) and **Hansen's** (tel. 619/753–6595) in Encinitas.

Swimming

If the ocean is too cold and salty, there are several public pools open for those interested in getting in a few laps. The most spectacular pool in town is the **Mission Beach Plunge** (3115 Ocean Front Walk, tel. 619/488–3110), in Belmont Park, where the public can swim weekdays 6–8 AM, noon–1, and 3:30–8, weekends 8–4. Admission is $2.25. The **Copley Family YMCA** (3901 Landis St., tel. 619/283–2251) and the **Downtown YMCA** (500 W. Broadway Ave., tel. 619/232–7451) are both centrally located. The **Magdalena Ecke YMCA** (200 Saxony Rd., Encinitas, tel. 619/942–9622) is convenient for visitors to North County.

Tennis

Most of the more than 1,300 courts spread around the county are in private clubs, but there are a few public facilities. **Morley Field** (tel. 619/295–9278), in Balboa Park, has 25 courts, 19 of which are lighted. Nonmembers can make reservations after paying a nominal fee for the use of the courts; if you're lucky, a court may be available when you come in to pay the fee. The **La Jolla Recreation Center** (tel. 619/552–1658) offers nine free public courts near downtown La Jolla, five of them lighted. There are 12 lighted courts at **Robb Field** (tel. 619/531–1563) in Ocean Beach, with a small day-use fee.

The list of hotel complexes with tennis facilities includes the **Bahia Resort Hotel** (tel. 619/488–0551); **Hilton San Diego** (tel. 619/276–4010); the **Hotel del Coronado** (tel. 619/435–6611); the **Kona Kai Beach and Tennis Resort** (tel. 619/222–1191); the **LaCosta Resort and Spa** (tel. 619/438–9111); and the **Rancho Bernardo Inn and Country Club** (tel. 619/487–1611). Intense tennis instruction is available at **Rancho Bernardo Inn Tennis College** (tel. 619/487–2413) in Rancho Bernardo.

Volleyball

Ocean Beach, South Mission Beach, Del Mar, and Moonlight Beach are the most popular congregating points for beach-volleyball enthusiasts. A warning: The competition can be fierce. Some of the best players in the world can show up on any given day.

Waterskiing

Mission Bay is one of the most popular waterskiing areas in southern California. It is best to get out early when the water is smooth and the crowds are thin. Boats and equipment can be rented from **Seaforth Boat Rentals** (1641 Quivira Rd., near Mission Bay, tel. 619/223–1681). The private **San Diego and Mission Bay Boat and Ski Club** (2606 N. Mission Bay Dr., tel. 619/276–0830) operates a slalom course and ski jump in Mission Bay's Hidden Anchorage. Permission from the club or the Mission Bay Harbor Patrol (tel. 619/291–3900) must be obtained to use the course and jump.

Windsurfing

Also known as sailboarding, windsurfing is a sport best practiced on smooth waters, such as Mission Bay or the Snug Harbor Marina at the intersection of I–5 and Tamarack Avenue in Carlsbad. It's a tricky sport to learn, but it can be a lot of fun for novices as well as experts. Rentals and instruction are available at the **Bahia Resort**

Hotel (998 W. Mission Bay Dr., tel. 619/488–0551); the **Catamaran Resort Hotel** (3999 Mission Blvd., tel. 619/488–1081); **Mission Bay Sportcenter** (1010 Santa Clara Pl., tel. 619/488–1004); the **San Diego Sailing Center** (1010 Santa Clara Pl., tel. 619/488–0651); and **Windsport** (844 W. Mission Bay Dr., tel. 619/488–4642), all in the Mission Bay area. The **Snug Harbor Marina** (4215 Harrison St., Carlsbad, tel. 619/434–3089) also offers rentals and instruction. More experienced windsurfers will enjoy taking a board out on the ocean. Wave jumping is especially popular at the Tourmaline Surfing Park in La Jolla and in the Del Mar area.

Spectator Sports

Ever since the Clippers left for Los Angeles, San Diego hasn't had a professional basketball franchise. But it does have just about every other type of sporting team and event, including a few that are exclusive to the area. For information on tickets to any event, contact **Teleseat** (tel. 619/452–7328). **San Diego Jack Murphy Stadium** is at the intersection of I–8 and I–805.

Baseball

From April through September, the **San Diego Padres** (tel. 619/283–4494) slug it out for bragging rights in the National League West. Matches with such rivals as the hated Los Angeles Dodgers and San Francisco Giants are usually the highlights of the home season at San Diego Jack Murphy Stadium.

Tickets range from $5 to $11 and are usually readily available, unless the Padres are in the thick of the pennant race.

Basketball

There's no pro team, but the **San Diego State University Aztecs** (tel. 619/283–7378) are gaining national prominence. The Aztecs, competing in the Western Athletic Conference with such powers as Utah State and Brigham Young University, play at the Peterson Gym at the San Diego State campus (tel. 619/594–6947) December–March. Tickets are a bargain at $5 for adults, $3 for children.

The **University of San Diego** (tel. 619/260–4600), vying for points in the West Coast Athletic Conference with such schools as Pepperdine, the University of San Francisco, and the University of California at Santa Barbara, competes with the top teams in the country.

Dog Racing

In Tijuana, anorexic-looking greyhounds chase the electric bunny around the Agua Caliente track nightly, except Tuesday. *See* Spectator Sports in Chapter 13 *for details.*

Football

After almost a decade of less-than-stellar seasons, the **San Diego Chargers** (tel. 619/280–2111) have enjoyed a spectacular resurgence. The Chargers were one of the original AFL franchises, originally based in Los Angeles. They fill San Diego Jack Murphy Stadium August through December. Games with AFC West rivals Los Angeles Raiders and Denver Broncos are always particularly intense.

The San Diego State University Aztecs compete in the exciting Western Athletic Conference. The biggest game of the year is always a showdown with Brigham Young University. The winner of the WAC plays in the **Holiday Bowl** (tel. 619/283–5808), always known as one of the most exhilarating bowl games, and renowned for its exciting finishes. The big bowl game is played near the end of December in San Diego Jack Murphy Stadium, which is where the Aztecs play home games.

Golf

The La Costa Resort and Spa (tel. 619/438–9111) hosts the prestigious **Tournament of Champions** in January, featuring the winners of the previous year's tournaments. The **Buick Invitational** brings the pros to the Torrey Pines Municipal Golf Course in February (tel. 619/452–3226). In spring, **Ladies Professional Golf Association** is held at the Stoneridge Country Club (tel. 619/487–2117).

Horse Racing

Begun in the 1930s by Bing Crosby, Pat O'Brien, and their Hollywood cronies, the annual summer meeting of the **Del Mar Thoroughbred Club** (tel. 619/755–1141) on the Del Mar Fairgrounds—"Where the Turf Meets the Surf"—attracts hordes of Beautiful People, along with the best horses and jockeys in the country. The meeting begins in July and continues through early September, every day except Tuesday. But that isn't the end of horse-racing action in Del Mar. The Del Mar Fairgrounds also serves as a satellite-wagering facility (tel. 619/755–1167) with TV coverage of betting on races from tracks throughout California. Take I–5 north to the Via de la Valle Road exit.

Ice Hockey

The **San Diego Gulls** (tel. 619/688–1800), competing in and dominating the International Hockey League, bring an exciting game of hockey to this area. Games are played October–April at the San Diego Sports Arena (tel. 619/224–4171), with ticket prices ranging from $6 to $15.50.

Jai Alai

You can place bets on this vigorous sport, often called the world's fastest game, in Tijuana's Fronton Palacio. *See* Spectator Sports in Chapter 13.

Over-the-Line

As much a giant beach party as a sport, this game is a form of beach softball played with three-person teams. Every July, the world championships are held on Fiesta Island, with two weekends of wild beer drinking and partying. Some good athletes take part in the games, too. Admission is free, but parking is impossible and traffic around Mission Bay can become unbearable. Call the Old Mission Beach Athletic Club (tel. 619/688–0817) for more information.

Soccer

The most successful professional franchise in town is the **San Diego Sockers** (tel. 619/224–4625) indoor soccer team. The team has dominated the game, winning championships in the defunct North American Soccer League and the Major Indoor Soccer League, as well as in the current Continental Indoor Soccer League. Games are raucous, since San Diegans love to support their Sockers. The season runs October–May at the San Diego Sports Arena (tel. 619/224–4171). Take the Rosecrans exit from I–5 west to Sports Arena Boulevard and turn right.

8 Dining

By Kathryn Shevelow

When she's not busy tracking down interesting new restaurants, Kathryn Shevelow teaches in the Literature Department of the University of California at San Diego.

In spite of its ranking as the second-largest city in California, San Diego was, until recently, a rather slow-paced, provincial place. The fine weather and splendid beaches that contribute so much to the city's beauty also fostered an open-air, daytime-oriented culture that did little to encourage a sophisticated nightlife. San Diegans seemed to prefer suburban quietude to urban activity; after dark, downtown was given over to sailors, bars, and sex shops.

The restaurant scene was dominated by fast food, overcooked fish, and upper-class stodge. "Good food," with few exceptions, was the quasi-Continental fare served at the kind of indeterminate Chamber of Commerce restaurant humorist Calvin Trillin calls "La Maison de la Casa House." If the one bright light was always the abundance of authentic Mexican restaurants, even these did not often venture far beyond the standard fare of tacos, beans, and burritos.

But all that has begun to change in the past few years. Redevelopment of the downtown area has created a substantial nightlife scene, with a proliferation of clubs and good restaurants—especially on 4th and 5th avenues—that is nothing short of astonishing. Other areas have shared in the new sense of energy. It wasn't long ago that the streets of sleepy La Jolla turned in for the night at sunset (especially in the winter) and the uptown area (Hillcrest, Mission Hills, Normal Heights) was a semi-urban landscape of dreary streets punctuated by an occasional bar. Now night crawlers can party hearty in both sections of town after dark.

All this bodes well for residents and visitors who like to eat. True, for all the efforts it may make in that direction, San Diego is not Los Angeles or San Francisco, and perhaps will never be: There has not yet developed among San Diegans the kind of exacting culinary standards one finds in the demanding and vociferous residents of a truly great food city. Still, one can eat very well these days in San Diego.

Adding to the current proliferation of good restaurants specializing in California cuisine and European (especially Italian) cooking, various immigrant groups have recently arrived in San Diego, bringing their culinary traditions with them. The city now boasts a rich selection of Latin American, Middle Eastern, and Asian cuisines. The many Vietnamese restaurants throughout the city are especially noteworthy. Influenced by Chinese and French cooking styles, Vietnamese food retains its own character: Typically it is inexpensive, fresh, healthy, and very tasty. Particularly recommended are the noodle soups called "pho," the beef grilled in grape leaves, and the many dishes served to be wrapped at the table in lettuce and rice paper. Excellent Vietnamese restaurants, along with their equally good Chinese, Korean, and Japanese counterparts, can be found along Convoy Street and Linda Vista Road in Kearny Mesa; **My Ca'nh** (3904 Convoy St., tel. 619/268–4584) and **Phuong Trang** (4170 Convoy St., tel. 619/ 565–6750) are outstanding among them.

San Diego is an informal city. The advised attire at most of the restaurants listed below falls into three categories: "really casual," "casual," and "dressy casual." "Really casual" means you can come in directly from the beach and eat here if you throw on a shirt and flip flops. "Casual" indicates shorts are not a very good idea (except at lunch), and it's best if your jeans are clean and all in one piece. To the "casual" outfit add a sports jacket, stylish shirt, makeup, or some jewelry (or any combination thereof, depending on your inclination), and voilá—"dressy casual," appropriate for the majority of even the most expensive restaurants at dinnertime. Only one of the restaurants listed below requires men to wear ties.

Restaurants are grouped first by location and then by type of cuisine. Highly recommended restaurants are indicated by a star ★.

Category	Cost*
$$$$	over $50
$$$	$30–$50
$$	$20–$30
$	under $20

per person, without tax (7.75%), service, or drinks

Downtown

American **California Café.** On the top level of Horton Plaza, this stylish dining room with lots of windows and potted palms serves stylish California cuisine to match. The imaginative menu, which changes daily, may include smoked duck ravioli with basil and goat cheese, soba noodle salad with lemon wasabi dressing and wild mushrooms, or New Mexican chili fettuccine with shrimp and smoked corn. The crusty Italian bread is baked daily on the premises. *Upper Level, Horton Plaza, tel. 619/238-5440. Reservations suggested. Dress: casual to dressy casual. AE, D, DC, MC, V. $$*

Croce's. A tribute to the late singer-songwriter Jim Croce run by his widow, Ingrid, the popular Croce's used to be known more for its nightly jazz and pleasant, clublike ambience than for its cuisine. But with a new chef in the kitchen, Croce's now complements its high-quality music with high-quality food. The menu offers good salads and a range of appealing entrées; try the swordfish in grape leaves or the chicken cakes. Even those who are not jazz aficionados will find this restaurant a good bet for late-night dining, since Croce's kitchen doesn't close until midnight. *802 5th Ave., tel. 619/233-4355. Reservations accepted. Dress: casual. AE, D, DC, MC, V. $*

Pacifica Grill and Rotisserie. The local chain of Pacifica restaurants has been a mainstay of San Diego's dining renaissance. The downtown link, housed in a creatively refurbished former warehouse and featuring fresh, innovative, and reasonably priced cuisine, has developed a large group of loyal patrons. The crab cakes and the green-lip mussels appetizers are wonderful, and you can't go wrong with any of the fish dishes—say, the seared ahi with shiitake mushrooms—or the meats and poultry prepared on the rotisserie. If possible, save room for the justifiably famous crème brûlée. The selection of California wines is excellent. *1202 Kettner Blvd., tel. 619/696-9226. Reservations advised. Dress: dressy casual. AE, D, DC, MC, V. No lunch weekends. $$*

★ **Rainwater's.** Located directly above the Pacifica Grill, this tony restaurant is as well known around town for the size of its portions as for the high quality of its cuisine. The menu includes a number of meat and fish dishes, but this is really the place to come if you crave a perfectly done, thick and tender steak. All the entrées are accompanied by such tasty side dishes as shoestring potatoes, onion rings, and creamed corn. The food is pricey, but the satisfaction level is high. *1202 Kettner Blvd. (second floor), tel. 619/233-5757. Reservations advised. Dress: dressy casual to jacket and tie. AE, DC, MC, V. No lunch weekends. $$$*

Anthony's Star of the Sea Room, **27**

Athens Market, **37**

Bayou Bar and Grill, **36**

The Belgian Lion, **13**

Bella Luna, **33**

Berta's Latin American Restaurant, **14**

Cafe Japengo, **9**

Café Pacifica, **15**

California Café, **30**

California Cuisine, **24**

Calliope's Greek Cuisine, **22**

Canes California Bistro, **23**

Choices, **8**

Croce's, **31**

Dobson's, **28**

El Indio Shop, **18**

Fio's, **34**

The Fish Market, **38**

George's at the Cove, **1**

Hard Rock Café, **5**

Hob Nob Hill, **20**

Karinya Thai, **11**

Old Town Mexican Café, **16**

Pacifica Grill and Rotisserie, **25**

Palenque, **10**

Panda Inn, **29**

Panevino, **32**

Pannikin Brockton Villa, **3**

Rainwater's, **26**

Ristorante Piatti, **6**

SamSon's, **7**

Star of India, **4**

Thai Chada, **21**

Thai Saffron, **19**

Top O' the Cove, **2**

Tosca's, **12**

Trattoria la Strada, **35**

Triangles, **17**

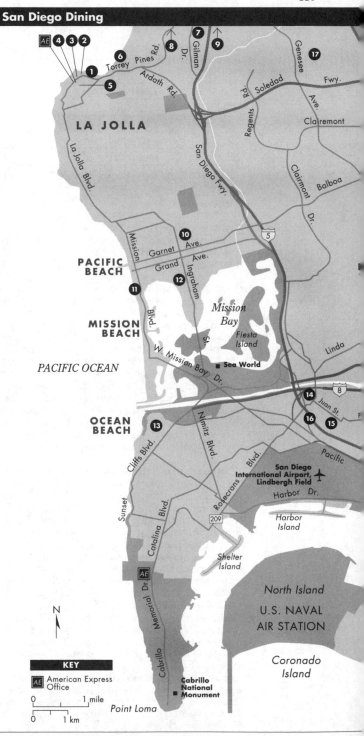

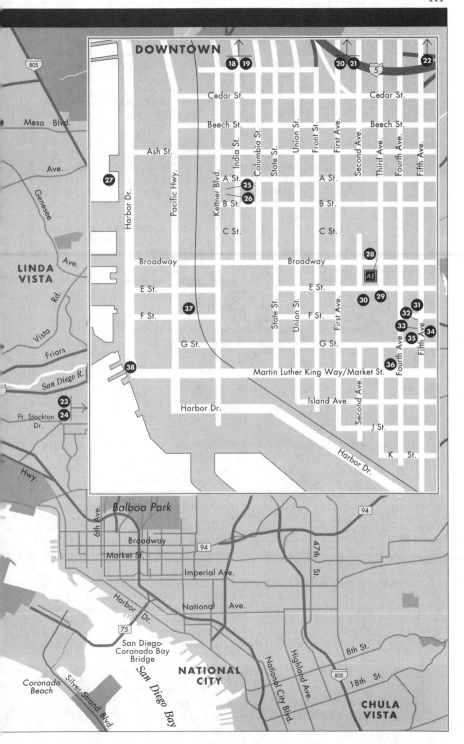

Cajun and Creole ★ **Bayou Bar and Grill.** The ceiling fans revolving lazily over this attractive room, with dark-green wainscoting and light-pink walls, help create a New Orleans atmosphere for the spicy Cajun and Creole specialties served here. You may start with a bowl of superb seafood gumbo and then move on to the sausage, red beans, and rice, the duck esplanade, or any of the fresh Louisiana Gulf seafood dishes. A tempting selection of rich Louisiana desserts includes bread pudding, praline cheesecake, and Creole pecan pie. *329 Market St., tel. 619/696–8747. Dinner reservations suggested. Dress: casual. AE, D, DC, MC, V. Dinner only. $–$$*

Chinese ★ **Panda Inn.** Even if you're allergic to shopping, the Panda Inn is reason enough to come to Horton Plaza. Arguably the best Chinese restaurant in town, this dining room at the top of the Plaza serves subtly seasoned and attractively presented Mandarin and Szechuan dishes in an elegant setting that feels far removed from the rush of commerce below. The fresh seafood dishes are noteworthy, as are the Peking duck, spicy Szechuan green beans, and "burnt" pork. Indeed, it's hard to find anything on this menu that's not outstanding. *506 Horton Plaza, tel. 619/233–7800. Reservations advised. Dress: casual. AE, D, DC, MC, V. $–$$*

Continental ★ **Dobson's.** At lunchtime, local politicos and media types rub elbows at the long, polished bar of this highly regarded restaurant; the show biz contingent arrives in the evening in stretch limos. Although the small two-tier building is suggestive of an earlier era—the lower level looks like a men's club and the upper level sports a wrought-iron balcony, elegant woodwork, and gilt cornices—there's nothing outdated about the cuisine. Among the range of carefully prepared entrées, which change daily, you may find roasted quail with fig sauce or chicken risotto. The tasty house salad is laced with fennel and goat cheese, and Dobson's signature dish, a superb mussel bisque, comes topped with a crown of puff pastry. The wine list is excellent. *956 Broadway Circle, tel 619/231–6771. Reservations advised. Dress: dressy casual. AE, DC, MC, V. No lunch Sat.; closed Sun. $$$*

Greek **Athens Market.** This cheerful eatery, decorated with Aegaean island scenes, bustles with downtown office workers and members of San Diego's small but active Greek community. As in many Greek restaurants, the appetizers here—such as *taramasalata* (fish roe dip) and stuffed grape leaves—can be superior to the somewhat heavy traditional beef and lamb entrées. Greek music, folk dancing, and belly dancers add to the festive atmosphere on weekend evenings. The adjacent Victorian-style coffeehouse, under the same ownership, keeps late hours for night owls in search of a caffeine fix. *109 W. F St., tel. 619/234–1955. Reservations suggested. Dress: casual. AE, D, DC, MC, V. $*

Italian **Bella Luna.** A recent, welcome addition to the "Italianization" of 5th Avenue, this small, stylish restaurant, whose owner hails from the island of Capri, more than holds its own against its longer-established neighbors. Paintings of "beautiful moons" in many shapes and sizes adorn the walls, and the service is gracious and attentive. The menu features dishes from all over Italy: Try the stuffed mozzarella appetizer or the calamari in tomato sauce. Pastas are particularly recommended, especially the linguine *alle vongole verace* (with clams in their shells), the fettuccini with salmon, and the black squid-ink linguine served with a spicy seafood sauce; if you still have room for an entrée, consider the rack of lamb. *748 5th Ave., tel. 619/239–3222. Dress: dressy casual. Reservations advised. AE, MC, V. No lunch Sun. $$–$$$*

Fio's. Glitzy young singles mingle with staid business-suit types in this lively, popular place, one of the earliest of the trendy Italian restaurants now proliferating in the Gaslamp District. Contemporary variations on traditional Italian cuisine are served in a high-ceilinged, brick-and-wood dining room overlooking the 5th Avenue street scene. The menu includes a range of imaginative pizzas baked in the wood-fired oven and the occasional hard-to-find classic Italian dish, such as the Emilian *ravioli di zucca*, ravioli stuffed with pumpkin and amaretto cookie crumbs, or the Tuscan *anitra in pignatto*, a casserole of preserved duck, sausage, and white beans. *801 5th Ave., tel. 619/234-3467. Reservations advised. Dress: dressy casual. AE, D, DC, MC, V. No lunch weekends. $$*

Panevino. This brick-walled Italian café is often crowded with diners who prefer its casual bistro atmosphere to the more trendy tone of neighboring restaurants. But the menu here is as *au courant* as any other in San Diego. Particularly recommended are the imaginative selection of pizzas and pastas: The spinach ravioli is always a good bet. You could easily make a meal of one of the excellent stuffed foccaccias and a salad or a plate of grilled vegetables, although a range of tasty and sometimes ambitious entrées is also offered; if it's available, try the quail cooked in balsamic vinegar. Panevino is one of the few good downtown restaurants outside of Horton Plaza that's open for lunch on weekends. *722 5th Ave., tel. 619/595-7959. Dress: casual to dressy casual. Reservations advised. AE, D, DC, MC, V. $$*

★ **Trattoria La Strada.** La Strada specializes in Tuscan cuisine prepared so well that your taste buds will be convinced they've died and gone to Italy. Try the *antipasto di mare*, with tender shrimp and shellfish, or the salad La Strada, with wild mushrooms, walnuts, and delectable shaved parmesan. The pastas, particularly the *pappardelle all'anitra* (wide noodles with a duck sauce), are excellent. The noise level can be high in the two high-ceilinged dining rooms; if you don't feel like raising your voice, you can always check out the fashions worn by the stylish young diners. *702 5th Ave., tel. 619/239-3400. Reservations advised. Dress: dressy casual. AE, D, DC, MC, V. No lunch weekends. $$-$$$*

Seafood **Anthony's Star of the Sea Room.** The Anthony's chain of local seafood restaurants, one of the oldest in San Diego, has long been serving up adequately prepared seafood dishes to tourists and residents alike. The flagship of the Anthony's fleet, the Star of the Sea Room, is much more formal and expensive than the others. The menu offers an enormous selection of fresh fish from around the world, and if the recipes are less exciting than those at other seafood restaurants, the magnificent harbor views go far in the way of compensation. Many of the dishes are prepared at the table. *1360 N. Harbor Dr., tel. 619/232-7408. Reservations strongly advised. Jacket and tie required. AE, D, DC, MC, V. Dinner only. $$$*

The Fish Market. This bustling, informal restaurant offers diners a choice from a large variety of extremely fresh fish, mesquite grilled and served with lemon and tartar sauce. Also good are shellfish dishes, such as steamed clams or mussels. Most of what is served here has lived in the water, but even dedicated fish-avoiders may think it worth their while to trade selection for the stunning view: Enormous plate-glass windows look directly out onto the harbor, and if you're lucky enough to get a windowside table, you can practically taste the salt spray. This is one of the rare places where families with young children can feel comfortable without sacrificing their taste buds. A more formal and expensive upstairs restaurant, The Top of the Market, offers a good Sunday brunch. *750 N. Harbor*

Dr., tel. 619/232–3474 for the Fish Market or 619/234–4867 for the Top of the Market; also in Del Mar, at 640 Via de la Valle, tel. 619/755–2277. Reservations accepted upstairs and for 8 or more downstairs, and at Del Mar. Dress: casual downstairs and at Del Mar, dressy casual upstairs. AE, D, DC, MC, V. $–$$$

Coronado

Home of beautiful beaches, an elegant old resort hotel, and one of the country's major naval stations, Coronado unfortunately does not abound in good restaurants. And those that are not bad tend to be overpriced. If you wish to eat in Coronado, here are some of your best bets, listed in descending order from very expensive to moderate: **Marius,** in the Le Meridien Hotel (tel. 619/435–3000); **Peohe's** (1201 1st St., tel. 619/437–4474); **Chez Loma** (1132 Loma Ave., tel. 619/435–0661); **Primavera Ristorante** (932 Orange Ave., tel. 619/435–0454); and the **Crown Room** and the **Prince of Wales Room** in the Hotel Del Coronado (tel. 619/435–6611).

Uptown

American **Hob Nob Hill.** The type of place where regulars arrive on the same day of the week at the same time and order the same meal they've been having for the past 20 years, this comforting restaurant is still under the same ownership and management as it was when it started in 1944; with its dark wood booths and patterned carpets, Hob Nob Hill seems suspended in the 1950s. But you don't need to be a nostalgia buff to appreciate the bargain-priced American home cooking—dishes such as pot roast, fried chicken, and corned beef like your mother never really made. Reservations are particularly suggested on Sundays, when everyone comes for the copious breakfasts. *2271 1st Ave., tel. 619/239–8176. Reservations accepted. Dress: casual. AE, D, MC, V. $*

California **California Cuisine.** Across the street from the Uptown district, this ★ minimalist chic dining room—gray carpet, stark white walls, and black-and-white photographs of urban landscapes—offers a suitably innovative menu. Daily selections may include grilled fresh venison served with wild mushrooms and mashed potatoes; the tasty warm chicken salad entrée is a regular feature. You can count on whatever you order to be carefully prepared and elegantly presented. Service is knowledgeable and attentive, the wine list is good, and the desserts are seriously tempting. Heat lamps make the back patio a romantic year-round option. *1027 University Ave., tel. 619/543–0790. Reservations advised. Dress: dressy casual. AE, D, DC, MC, V. No lunch weekends; closed Mon. $$*

Canes California Bistro. A light-filled neighborhood bistro, whose walls are decked, appropriately enough, with canes of all kinds, Canes attracts a diverse group of diners, from senior citizens to families to Uptown trendies. They come for food that is similarly diverse—everything from meat loaf and mashed potatoes to hamburgers with sun-dried tomato *aioli* (garlic mayonnaise) to pastas with roasted garlic and gorgonzola—and consistently good. The weekend buffet brunch features excellent breakfast breads, French beef stew, and yellow corn pancakes with sour cream and golden caviar. *Vermont St. (at University), tel. 619/299–3551. Reservations advised. Dress: casual. AE, D, DC, MC, V. $–$$*

Greek **Calliope's Greek Cuisine.** One of the best Greek restaurants in town, Calliope moves beyond the standard Hellenic fare to offer tasty variations on traditional dishes. Included on the menu, along with a good moussaka and lamb souvlaki, are fettuccine Aegean, topped with shrimp, fresh fish, and mushrooms in a tomato wine sauce, and artichokes Athenian, served over linguine in a tomato-herb sauce. Fans of Greek wines will see not only the usual retsinas, but also a selection of harder-to-find regional bottles. The white-walled dining room is light and airy. *3958 5th Ave., tel. 619/291–5588. Dress: casual. Reservations suggested. AE, D, DC, MC, V. No lunch weekends. $–$$*

Mexican **El Indio Shop.** El Indio has been serving some of the city's best Mexican fast food since 1940. The menu is extensive; try the large burritos, the *tacquitos* (fried rolled tacos) with guacamole, or the giant quesadillas. You can eat at one of the indoor tables or on the patio across the street; El Indio is also perfect for beach-bound take-out. *3695 India St., tel. 619/299–0333; 4120 Mission Blvd., tel. 619/272–8226; 409 F St., tel. 619/239–8151; 115 W. Olive Dr., San Ysidro, tel. 619/690–1122. Dress: really casual. D, MC, V. F. St. and San Ysidro shops closed Sun. $*

Thai **Thai Chada.** Don't be put off by appearances. Although it's housed
★ in a corner building that looks like a hamburger joint, this is one of the best Thai restaurants in town; the large windows and comfortable booths provide a low-key setting for consistently excellent food. Try any of the noodle dishes, especially the *pad thai*, rice noodles fried with fresh shrimp, egg, bean sprouts, scallions, and ground peanuts; the Tom Ka Kai chicken soup, with coconut milk, lemon grass, lime juice, and scallions; or the roast duck curry. A sister restaurant, Thai Chada 2, has recently opened in Pacific Beach. *142 University Ave., tel. 619/297–9548; Thai Chada 2, 1749 Garnet Ave., tel. 619/270–1888. Reservations advised. Dress: casual. AE, D, DC, MC, V. Sat. lunch at Thai Chada 2 only; both restaurants closed Sun. lunch. $–$$*

Thai Saffron. In recent years, San Diego has seen an upsurge in the growth of take-out restaurants offering tasty, health-conscious food. Saffron is one of the earliest and best of the eateries that specialize in chicken spit-roasted over a wood fire, accompanied by an appealing selection of side dishes. The chicken is wonderfully moist and comes with a choice of sauces: Try the peanut or chili. Among the accompaniments, the Cambodian salad is particularly fresh and crunchy. There's limited outdoor seating, but this is an ideal place to pick up lunch or dinner to take to Mission Bay or the beach. *3731B India St., tel. 619/574–0177. No reservations. Dress: casual. MC, V. $*

Old Town

Latin **Berta's Latin American Restaurant.** A San Diego rarity—and par-
American ticularly surprising in a section of town where the food often leans toward the safe and touristy—Berta's features a wide selection of Latin American regional dishes and a nice list of Latin American wines. While the wines are largely Chilean, the food, which manages to be wonderfully tasty and health-conscious at the same time, ranges all over the map. Try the Brazilian seafood *vatapa*, shrimp, scallops, and fish served in a sauce flavored with ginger, coconut, and chilis, or the Peruvian *pollo a la huancaina*, chicken with chilis and a feta cheese sauce. Service is friendly and helpful. The simple dining room is small, but there's also a patio. *3928 Twiggs St., tel. 619/295–2343. Reservations suggested on weekends. Dress: casual. AE, MC, V. $–$$*

Mexican **Old Town Mexican Café.** Singles congregate at the bar and families crowd into the wooden booths of this boisterous San Diego favorite, decked out with plants and colorful piñatas; an enclosed patio takes the overflow from both groups. You'll find all the Mexican standards here, as well as specialties, such as *carnitas,* chunks of roast pork served with fresh tortillas and condiments. The enchiladas with spicy ranchero or green chili sauce are nice variations on an old theme. You can watch the corn tortillas being handmade on the premises and pick up a dozen to take home with you. *2489 San Diego Ave., tel. 619/297–4330. Reservations accepted for parties of 10 or more. Dress: casual. AE, D, MC, V. $*

Seafood   **Cafe Pacifica.** Like its sister restaurant, Pacifica Grill and Rotisserie, Cafe Pacifica offers a menu that changes daily and features an impressive array of imaginative appetizers, salads, pastas, and entrées; it also does a crème brûlée worth blowing any diet for. The emphasis here is on seafood, however, and this restaurant serves some of the best in town. You can't go wrong with any of the fresh fish preparations grilled over mesquite and served with an herb-butter sauce, a Mexican-inspired salsa, or a fruit chutney. Other good bets include the tasty pan-fried catfish; yummy, greaseless fish tacos; and superb crab cakes. *2414 San Diego Ave., tel. 619/291–6666. Reservations advised. Dress: dressy casual. AE, D, DC, MC, V. $$–$$$*

Beaches

Belgian   **Belgian Lion.** The lace curtains at the windows of a rather forbidding white building, partially enclosed by a high wall, are the only hints of the cozy dining room within, where hearty Belgian dishes have been served to discerning diners for years. Among the signature dishes is the cassoulet, a wonderful rich stew of white beans, lamb, pork, sausage, and duck that makes you feel protected from the elements (even in San Diego, where there aren't many elements to be protected from). Lighter meals include sea scallops with braised Belgian endive or steamed salmon with leeks. An impressive wine list was carefully designed to complement the food. *2265 Bacon St., Ocean Beach, tel. 619/223–2700. Reservations strongly advised. Dress: dressy casual. AE, D, DC, MC, V. Open Thurs.–Sat. only, dinner only. $$–$$$*

Italian   **Tosca's.** This popular Pacific Beach eatery is in some way typical of pizza restaurants everywhere, with its fluorescent lighting and red-checkered vinyl tablecloths. But you are, after all, in California, which means you can opt for wheat or semolina crusts for your individually sized pizzas or calzones; choose toppings or fillings from an array of exotic ingredients, including artichokes, pesto, and feta cheese; and wash it all down with a microbrew from Sierra Nevada (on tap, yet). The young servers are cheerful and helpful. *3780 Ingraham St., tel. 619/274–2408. Dress: casual. AE, D, DC, MC, V. $*

Mexican   **Palenque.** A welcome alternative to the standard Sonoran-style
★   café, this family-run restaurant in Pacific Beach serves a wonderful selection of regional Mexican dishes. Recommendations include the chicken with mole, served in the regular chocolate-based or green chili version and the mouth-watering *camarones en chipotle,* large shrimp cooked in a chili and tequila cream sauce (an old family recipe of the proprietor). Piñatas and paper birds dangle from the thatched ceiling, and seating is in comfortable round-backed leather chairs; a small deck in front is nice for warm-weather dining. Palenque is a bit hard to spot from the street and service is often slow, but the food is worth your vigilance and patience. *1653 Garnet Ave., Pacific Beach, tel. 619/272–7816. Reservations advised. Dress: casual. AE, D, DC, MC, V. $–$$*

Thai   **Karinya Thai.** This popular restaurant in Pacific ꞉ cellent Thai cuisine in a relaxed but pretty sett꞉ diners recline on colorful floor cushions at low tab꞉ wrong with any of the dishes on the extensive me.... coct a meal from appetizers alone: The stuffed chicken wings aɴᴅ spicy fish cakes are particularly recommended. Among the entrées, the scallops in three sauces, beef strips with broccoli, and pad thai noodles are all worth a try. *4475 Mission Blvd., tel. 619/270–5050. Reservations suggested. Dress: casual. No lunch Sat.–Mon. MC, V. $–$$*

La Jolla

American   **Choices.** Off the beaten path and rather low on atmosphere—it's in the Sports and Health Center at the north of the Scripps Clinic complex—this small cafeteria offers indoor and outdoor tables with an ocean view, and very tasty, low-fat, low-cholesterol food. There's an excellent all-you-can-eat salad bar and a daily selection of healthy sandwiches and entrées. Choices is open for breakfast and lunch during the week but closes at 7 PM Monday–Thursday; it shuts down at 3 PM on Friday but reopens at 6 PM for dinner and folk music. *10820 N. Torrey Pines Rd., tel. 619/554–3663. No reservations. Dress: casual. AE, MC, V. Closed weekends. $*

Hard Rock Café. If you've been to Hard Rock Cafés in other cities, you'll know what to expect here. This high-energy shrine to rock-and-roll and American food cranks its music up to ear- shattering decibels and hangs rock memorabilia on every available inch of wall space. This is not a place to come for intimate—or audible—conversation, but the burgers are fine and you can bring home a T-shirt to commemorate the occasion. You don't have to be accompanied by a teenager, although it helps. *909 Prospect St., tel. 619/454–5101. No reservations. Dress: casual. AE, D, MC, V. $*

Pannikin Brockton Villa. Connected with the local chain of trendy coffeehouses, this informal restaurant in a restored beach house overlooks La Jolla Cove and the ocean. Come here for good coffee, decent muffins and pastries, and stunning views. You'll have to fight the crowds on sunny weekends. The Pannikin opens for breakfast; call ahead for dinner hours (summer only). *1235 Coast Blvd., tel. 619/454–7393. No reservations. Dress: casual. AE, MC, V. Breakfast and lunch only Sept.–May. $*

Continental   **Top O' the Cove.** Although the reliable but rather stolid menu of this La Jolla institution has been surpassed by glitzier newcomers, year after year San Diego diners give high marks for romance to this cozy, intimate spot with a beautiful ocean view. The filet mignon and roasted rack of lamb are reliable choices; calorie-counters may opt for the boneless chicken breast sautéed with shrimp and shellfish or sliced duck breast with black-currant sauce. The service is attentive but not overbearing, and the award-winning wine list is enormous. *1216 Prospect St., tel. 619/454–7779. Reservations advised. Dress: jacket and tie suggested. AE, DC, MC, V. $$$*

Triangles. In an attractive if slightly stiff setting—clubby dark wood booths in a contemporary high-rise bank building—this bar and grill in the Golden Triangle area strives for variety. The menu, which changes daily, may include sautéed sweetbreads, potato knishes, ravioli stuffed with porcini mushrooms, or shrimp cassoulet. Along with rich dishes, you'll also find many lighter and vegetarian preparations—nice for the health-conscious diner or the overstuffed vacationer. A small patio, surrounded by lush landscaping, is pleasant at lunch. *4370 La Jolla Village Dr., in the Northern Trust Bldg., tel.*

619/453–6650. Reservations advised. Dress: dressy casual to jacket and tie. AE, D, MC, V. No lunch Sat.; closed Sun. $$–$$$

Deli **SamSon's.** As close as you'll come to a real Jewish deli in San Diego, SamSon's has dill pickles set out on the tables; the menu and portions are enormous. If you're having trouble deciding, go for one of the daily soup-and-sandwich specials, especially the whitefish when it's available. And you can't go wrong with a lox plate for breakfast (SamSon's opens at 7 AM) or a corned beef sandwich for lunch. The two ample dining rooms are decorated in corny show-biz style, with movie stills covering the walls. *8861 Villa La Jolla Dr., tel. 619/455–1462. Reservations accepted. Dress: really casual. AE, D, DC, MC, V. $*

Indian **Star of India.** Rather higher priced than most other local Indian restaurants, the Star of India offers the best Indian food in town in a soothing setting of bamboo and quiet pastels. Particularly recommended are the chicken *tikka masala,* prepared tandoori style in a cream and tomato curry, and *saag gosht,* lamb in a spinach curry. Seafood dishes are generally the least successful. The excellent nan bread, baked in the tandoor oven, comes either plain or stuffed with a variety of fillings. An all-you-can-eat buffet lunch, available daily, is a good way to satisfy your curiosity about a variety of different dishes. *1000 Prospect St., tel. 619/459–3355; 423 F St., tel. 554–9891; 927 1st St., tel. 619/632–1113. Reservations suggested, especially on weekends. Dress: casual to dressy casual. AE, D, DC, MC, V. $$*

Italian **Ristorante Piatti.** On weekends, this trattoria-style restaurant is filled to overflowing with a lively mix of trendy singles and local families, who keep returning for the excellent country-style Italian food. A wood-burning oven turns out excellent breads and pizzas, and imaginative pastas include the *pappardelle fantasia* (wide saffron noodles with shrimp, fresh tomatoes, and arugula) and a wonderfully garlicky spaghetti *alle vongole* (served with clams in the shell). Among the *secondi* are good versions of roast chicken and Italian sausage with polenta. A fountain splashes softly on the tree-shaded patio, where heat lamps allow diners to sit out even on chilly evenings. *2182 Av. de la Playa, tel. 619/454–1589. Reservations strongly advised. Dress: dressy casual. AE, MC, V. $$*

Pacific Rim **Cafe Japengo.** In one of the most stylish dining rooms in town, framed by elegant marbled walls, accented with leafy bamboo trees, and dotted with unusual black-iron sculptures, Cafe Japengo serves excellent Pacific Rim cuisine. The inspiration for this eclectic and imaginative menu is largely Asian, with many North and South American touches. There's a selection of grilled, wood-roasted, and wok-fried entrées for dinner; try the ten-ingredient fried rice, the shrimp and scallops with dragon noodles, or the grilled swordfish with wild mushrooms. The curry fried calamari and the Japengo potstickers appetizers are guaranteed to stimulate your taste buds. You can also order fine sushi from your table or from a seat at the sushi bar. Although it is located in the very trendy, postmodern Aventine center, Cafe Japengo largely escapes the frenzied, noisy singles scene characteristic of the other restaurants in the complex. Unfortunately, the quality of the service doesn't match that of the food. *8960 University Center La., tel. 619/450–3355. Reservations advised. Dress: dressy casual. AE, D, DC, MC, V. No lunch weekends. $$$*

Seafood **George's at the Cove.** At most restaurants you get either good food
★ or good views; at George's, you don't have to choose. The elegant main dining room, with a wall-length window overlooking La Jolla

Cove, is renowned for its daily fresh seafood specials; the menu also offers several good chicken and meat dishes. The delectable three-mushroom soup, accented with sherry and rosemary, or the salmon-and-shrimp sausage make fine starters. The charbroiled apple-smoked salmon entrée is highly recommended, as are any of the shellfish pastas. Desserts are uniformly excellent. For more informal dining, try the Cafe on the second floor. The outdoor Terrace, on the top floor, affords a sweeping view of the coast; wonderful for breakfast, lunch, or brunch on a fine day, the Terrace (like the Cafe) does not take reservations, so you may have a wait. *1250 Prospect St., tel. 619/454-4244. Reservations advised for the main dining room. Dress: Main room, dressy casual to jacket and tie; Cafe and Terrace, casual. AE, D, DC, MC, V. Main room, $$$; Cafe and Terrace, $$.*

9 Lodging

By Sharon K. Gillenwater

Revised by Edie Jarolim

There are accommodations in San Diego to satisfy every taste, ranging from grand luxury high rises to funky beach cottages. Because new hotels are continually under construction, the city has a surplus of rooms—which means lower prices for those who shop around. The older properties in Hotel Circle frequently offer special rates and free tickets to local attractions, while many luxury hotels promote lower-priced weekend packages to fill rooms after the week's convention and business customers have departed. When you call to make reservations, find out if the place you're interested in is running any specials. It's always a good idea to book well in advance, especially during the busy summer season.

San Diego is very spread out, so the first thing to consider when selecting lodgings here is location. The various neighborhoods are rather diverse: You can choose to stay in the middle of a bustling metropolitan center or to kick back in a serene beach getaway. If you select one of the many hotels with a waterfront location and extensive outdoor sports facilities, you need never leave the premises. If you plan to do a lot of sightseeing, however, you may take into account a hotel's proximity to the attractions you most want to visit. In general, price need not be a major factor in your decision: Even the most expensive areas offer some reasonably priced—albeit rather modest—rooms.

If you are planning an extended stay or if you need lodgings for four or more people, you may consider an apartment rental. **Oakwood Apartments** (Oakwood Mission Bay West, 3866 Ingraham St., 92109; Oakwood Mission Bay E, 3883 Ingraham St., 92109, tel. 619/490–2100 booking for both) offers comfortable, furnished apartments in the Mission Bay area with maid service and linens; there's a minimum 30-day stay. At **San Diego Vacation Rentals** (1565 Hotel Circle S, Suite 390, 92108, tel. 619/296–1000), you can rent a coastal home or condo at competitive weekly and monthly rates; brochures of rentals are available on request.

Those wishing to find bed-and-breakfast accommodations in town can contact the **Bed & Breakfast Guild of San Diego** (tel. 619/523–1300), which currently lists eight high-quality member inns.

Highly recommended hotels are indicated by a star ★.

Category	Cost*
$$$$	over $165
$$$	$110–$165
$$	$70–$110
$	under $70

for a double room in high (summer) season, excluding 9% San Diego room tax

Coronado

Although Coronado doesn't have as many lodging facilities as some areas, it has a number of outstanding properties, and staying here is a unique experience: This quiet, out-of-the-way place feels as though it exists in an earlier, more gracious era. The peninsula, home to many wealthy retirees and naval personnel from the North Island Naval Air station, is connected to the mainland by the Silver Strand isthmus, but most tourists come here via the Coronado Bay Bridge or the ferry that leaves from San Diego's Embarcadero.

Boutiques and restaurants line Orange Avenue, the main street, and the beaches are fine, but if you plan to see many of San Diego's attractions, you'll probably spend a lot of time commuting across the bridge or riding the ferry.

$$$$ **Le Meridien.** Flamingos greet you at the entrance of this French-
★ owned resort, and other exotic wildlife roam the 16 acres of lushly landscaped grounds. This is a modern, $90 million complex, but it doesn't shout "I'm new and expensive": Instead, the low-slung, Cape Cod–style buildings perfectly capture Coronado's understated old-money ambience. The large rooms and suites are done in a cheerful California–country French fashion, with rattan chairs, blue-and-white-striped cushions, and lots of colorful Impressionist art; all rooms have separate showers and tubs. The glamorous spa facilities are excellent—sauna; steam; and facials, massages, and wraps—and the fitness schedule includes yoga and power walks, along with aerobics and step classes. *2000 2nd St., 92118, tel. 619/435–3000 or 800/543–4300, fax 619/435–3032. 300 rooms. Facilities: 2 restaurants, 3 pools, 2 whirlpools, spa, exercise room, aerobics, 6 lighted tennis courts, marina, shops. AE, D, DC, MC, V.*

Loews Coronado Bay Resort. You can park your boat at the 80-slip marina of this resort, set on a 15-acre private peninsula on the Silver Strand. Didn't bring it along this time? Never mind. You can rent one here. Rooms are somewhat formally but tastefully decorated, with pale yellows, pinks, and greens, and flowered bedspreads; all have furnished balconies with views of water—either bay, ocean, or marina. The Commodore Kids Club offers a nice variety of programs for children ages 4–12, and there's nightly entertainment in the hotel lounge. *4000 Coronado Bay Rd., 92118, tel. 619/424–4000, fax 619/424–4400. 450 rooms, 31 suites. Facilities: 3 restaurants, deli, fitness center, marina, 5 lighted tennis courts, 3 pools, 2 spas, bicycle rentals, boat, Windsurfer and Jet-Ski rentals, shops. AE, D, DC, MC, V.*

$$$–$$$$ **Hotel del Coronado.** Built in 1888, "the Del" is a historic and social landmark (*see* Chapter 3, Tour 2, *for details*). The rooms and suites in the original ornate Victorian building are charmingly quirky. Some have sleeping areas that seem smaller than the baths, while others are downright palatial; two are even said to come with a resident ghost. The public areas are grand, if perhaps a bit dark for modern tastes; a lower-level shopping arcade lined with historic photographs is fascinating, but tear yourself away to stroll around the hotel's lovely manicured grounds. More standardized accommodations are available in the newer high rise. *1500 Orange Ave., 92118, tel. 619/435–6611 or 800/468–3533, fax 619/522–8238. 691 rooms. Facilities: 3 restaurants, deli, pool, Jacuzzi, steamroom, sauna, croquet, bicycles, 6 lighted tennis courts, beach, shopping arcade. AE, D, DC, MC, V.*

$$–$$$ **Glorietta Bay Inn.** The main building of this property—located across the street from the Hotel Del, adjacent to the Coronado harbor, and near many restaurants and shops—was built in 1908 for sugar baron John D. Spreckels, who once owned most of downtown San Diego. Rooms here and in the newer motel-style buildings are attractively furnished, with flowered bedspreads and green rugs; all have refrigerators. Tours of the island's historical buildings depart from the inn's lobby three mornings a week (cost: $5). *1630 Glorietta Blvd., 92118, tel. 619/435–3101 or 800/283–9383, fax 619/435–6182. 98 rooms. Facilities: pool, bicycle rentals. AE, D, DC, MC, V.*

Downtown

Downtown San Diego is still reaping the benefits of a redevelopment effort that began in the early 1980s and attracted many new hotels to the area. There is much to see within walking distance of downtown accommodations—Seaport Village, the Embarcadero, the historic Gaslamp Quarter, a variety of theaters and night spots, and the spectacular Horton Plaza shopping center. The zoo and Balboa Park are also nearby. In addition, a number of good restaurants have opened in this part of town in the past few years. For nonstop shopping, nightlife, and entertainment, downtown can't be beat. Visitors should be aware, however, that the neighborhood is still rather transitional; many streets are rather deserted at night, and street hustlers and homeless people mingle with the crowds of tourists and office workers during the daytime.

$$$$ **Doubletree San Diego Hotel.** Although it is fronted by a startling lighted blue obelisk, this 1987 high rise is all understated marble, brass, and glass inside. The rooms are similarly elegant and low-key, with muted sea-green and coral color schemes. The lobby lounge is packed every night with local financiers and weary shoppers from the adjacent Horton Plaza; a piano player tinkles the ivories there on weekends. *910 Broadway Circle, 92101, tel. 619/239–2200 or 800/528–0444, fax 619/239–0509. 450 rooms. Facilities: restaurant, lobby lounge, sports bar, 2 lighted tennis courts, sauna, spa, pool, health club. AE, D, DC, MC, V.*

Hyatt Regency San Diego. Opened in late 1992 adjacent to Seaport Village, this high rise successfully combines Old World opulence with California airiness and space. Palm trees pose next to ornate tapestry couches in the high-ceiling, light-filled lobby, and all of the masculine, British Regency–style guest rooms have views of the water. Although its proximity to the convention center attracts a large business trade, this hotel also offers well-heeled leisure travelers an excellent location and fine facilities. *One Market Place, tel. 619/232–1234 or 800/233–1234, fax 619/233–6464. 875 rooms. Facilities: 2 restaurants, health club with weight room, steam, sauna, classes, spa, massage, 4 tennis courts, marina, piano lounge, shops. AE, D, DC, MC, V.*

The Pan Pacific Hotel. The excellent office and conference facilities at this striking pink hotel, built in 1991, draw business travelers, but the Pan Pacific is also fine for vacationers who want to be near all the downtown sights and restaurants; many of the upper-floor accommodations offer panoramic views of the city. The green prismlike sculpture that hangs from the 100-foot central atrium is a bit overwhelming, and the rather bland, beige-dominated standard rooms are not overly large, but this hotel has a very good health club and such extras as a complimentary airport shuttle. *400 W. Broadway, 92101, tel. 619/239–4500 or 800/626–3988, fax 619/239–3274. 436 rooms. Facilities: 2 restaurants, lounge; heated pool, spa, sun deck; fitness club with lap pool, massage, tanning, sauna, steam room, weight room, and classes; business center; shops. AE, D, DC, MC, V.*

$$$–$$$$ **Westgate Hotel.** A nondescript modern high rise hides what must
★ be the most opulent hotel in town: The lobby, modeled after the anteroom at Versailles, has hand-cut Baccarat chandeliers; rooms are furnished with antiques and Italian marble counters; and bath fixtures have 14-karat-gold overlays. There are breathtaking views of the harbor and the city from the ninth floor up, and afternoon high tea is served in the lobby to the accompaniment of harp music. All

Bahia Resort
Hotel, **21**

Balboa Park
Inn, **56**

Bay Club Hotel
& Marina, **29**

The Bed &
Breakfast Inn at
La Jolla, **3**

Best Western
Hacienda Hotel
Old Town, **35**

Best Western
Inn By the Sea, **2**

Best Western
Posada Inn, **31**

Best Western
Shelter Island
Marina Inn, **27**

Catamaran
Resort Hotel, **16**

Colonial Inn, **5**

Crystal Pier
Motel, **14**

Dana Inn &
Marina, **24**

Days Inn Hotel
Circle, **57**

Doubletree San
Diego Hotel, **49**

Embassy Suites
San Diego
Bay, **50**

Gaslamp Plaza
Suites, **51**

Glorietta Bay
Inn, **42**

Hanalei
Hotel, **38**

Harbor Hill
Guest House, **55**

Heritage Park
Bed & Breakfast
Inn, **36**

Holiday Inn on
the Bay, **46**

Horton Grand
Hotel, **47**

Hotel del
Coronado, **43**

Humphrey's Half
Moon Inn, **28**

Hyatt
Islandia, **23**

Hyatt Regency
La Jolla, **13**

Hyatt Regency
San Diego, **45**

Kona Kai Beach
and Tennis
Resort, **26**

La Jolla Cove
Motel, **8**

La Jolla Palms
Inn, **1**

La Pensione, **53**

La Valencia, **7**

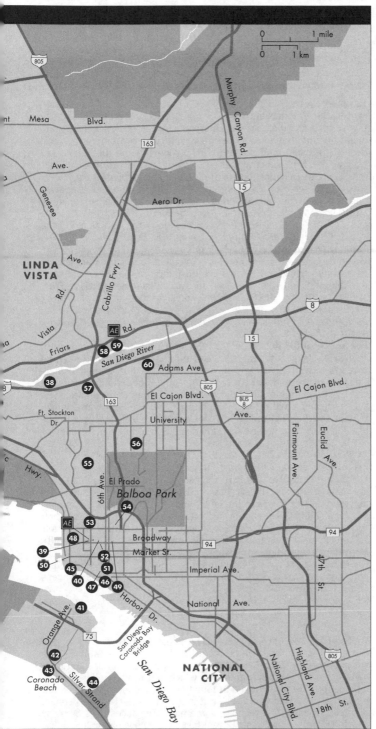

Le Meridien, **41**

Loews Coronado Bay Resort, **44**

Mission Bay Motel, **17**

Ocean Manor Apartment Hotel, **25**

Outrigger Motel, **30**

Pacific Shores Inn, **15**

Padre Trail Inn, **37**

Pan Pacific Hotel, **52**

Prospect Park Inn, **6**

Ramada Inn Old Town, **34**

Red Lion, **58**

Rodeway Inn, **54**

San Diego Hilton Beach and Tennis Resort, **20**

San Diego Marriott Mission Valley, **59**

San Diego Mission Valley Hilton, **60**

San Diego Princess Resort, **22**

Santa Clara Beach and Bay Motel, **19**

Scripps Inn, **4**

Sea Lodge, **9**

Sheraton Grande Torrey Pines, **12**

Sheratons on Harbor Island , **33**

Summer House Inn, **10**

Super 8 Bayview, **48**

Surfer Motor Lodge, **18**

Torrey Pines Inn, **11**

TraveLodge Point Loma, **32**

U.S. Grant Hotel, **40**

Westgate Hotel, **39**

this doesn't come cheap, but rates are lower than such luxury would seem to warrant. For a change of venue, the trolley can take you to Tijuana right from the hotel, and complimentary transportation is available within the downtown area. *1055 2nd Ave., 92101, tel. 619/238–1818, 800/221–3802, or 800/522–1564 in CA; fax 619/557-3737. 223 rooms. Facilities: 3 restaurants, lounge, exercise room, beauty salon, barber. AE, D, DC, MC, V.*

$$$ **Embassy Suites San Diego Bay.** It's a short walk to the convention center, the Embarcadero, and Seaport Village from one of downtown's most popular hotels. The front door of each spacious suite opens out onto the hotel's 12-story atrium. The contemporary-style decor is pleasant, and the views from rooms facing the harbor are spectacular. Business travelers will find it easy to set up shop here, and families can make good use of the in-room refrigerators, microwaves, and separate sleeping areas. A cooked-to-order breakfast and afternoon cocktails are complimentary, as are airport transfers. *601 Pacific Hwy., 92101, tel. 619/239–2400 or 800/362–2779, fax 619/239–1520. 337 suites. Facilities: restaurant, sports bar, pool, Jacuzzi, sauna, exercise room, gift shop. AE, D, DC, MC, V.*

Holiday Inn on the Bay. On the Embarcadero and overlooking San Diego Bay, this high-rise hotel is convenient for vacationers as well as business travelers. Rooms are unsurprising but new and comfortable, and views from the balconies are hard to beat. *1355 N. Harbor Dr., 92101, tel. 619/232–3861 or 800/465–4329, fax 619/232–4914. 600 rooms, 17 suites. Facilities: restaurant, lounge, lobby bar, heated pool, Jacuzzi, laundry facilities, complimentary airport and Amtrak shuttle. AE, D, DC, MC, V.*

Horton Grand Hotel. A delightful Victorian confection opened in 1986 in the heart of the historic Gaslamp District, the Horton Grand comprises two 1880s hotels moved brick by brick from nearby locations. It features delightfully retro rooms, individually furnished with period antiques, ceiling fans, and gas-burning fireplaces. The choicest rooms are those overlooking a garden courtyard, which twinkles with miniature lights each night. There's high tea in the afternoon and jazz in the evening. The place is a charmer, but service can be a bit erratic. *311 Island Ave., 92101, tel. 619/544–1886, 800/542–1886, or 800/HERITAGE; fax 619/239–3823. 132 rooms. Facilities: restaurant, lounge, Chinatown museum. AE, D, DC, MC, V.*

U. S. Grant Hotel. Built in 1910 and reopened in 1985, this San Diego classic is just across the street from Horton Plaza. Crystal chandeliers and marble floors in the lobby and Queen Anne–style mahogany furnishings in the rooms hark back to a more gracious era when such dignitaries as Charles Lindbergh and Franklin D. Roosevelt stayed here (this was also an era when rooms were somewhat small). These days, high-power business types still gather at the hotel's Grant Grill. In early 1994, the hotel was bought by the same company that owns the Horton Grand; renovations of the public areas are in the works. *326 Broadway, 92101, tel. 619/232–3121, 800/237–5029, or 800/HERITAGE; fax 619/232–3626. 280 rooms. Facilities: restaurant, piano lounge, exercise room, dress shop. AE, D, DC, MC, V.*

$$–$$$ **Balboa Park Inn.** Directly across the street from Balboa Park, this charming European-style bed-and-breakfast inn was built in 1915 and restored in 1982. Prices are reasonable for the one- and two-bedroom suites with kitchenettes, which can accommodate two to four people; they're housed in four two-story buildings connected by courtyards. Each suite has a different flavor—Italian, French, Spanish, or early Californian; some have fireplaces, wet bars, or whirlpool tubs. Continental breakfast and a newspaper are deliv-

ered to guests every morning. *3402 Park Blvd., 92103, tel. 619/298–0823 or 800/938–8181, fax 619/294–8070. 26 suites with baths. Facilities: sun terrace, deck, outdoor bar. AE, D, DC, MC, V.*

$$ Harbor Hill Guest House. This B&B offers quaint, comfortable rooms in a three-story home, with an entryway and kitchenette on each level; a carriage house connected to the main house provides a romantic getaway. Continental breakfast is included, and families are welcome. *2330 Albatross St., 92101, tel. 619/233–0638. 5 rooms with bath. MC, V.*

$–$$ Gaslamp Plaza Suites. Built in 1913 as San Diego's first "sky-
★ scraper," this 11-story structure in the Gaslamp district is only a block from Horton Plaza. It's listed on the National Register of Historic Places; elegant public areas boast lovely old marble, brass, and mosaic. Accommodations—either petite- or one-bedroom suites— are done in shades of burgundy and pink in attractive European style, with contemporary dark wood furniture. Guests can enjoy the view and a complimentary Continental breakfast and newspaper on the rooftop terrace. Many of the rooms rent as time shares; book ahead if you're visiting in high season. *520 E St., 92101, tel. 619/232–9500 or 800/443–8012, fax 619/238–9945. 63 suites. Facilities: restaurant, complimentary airport and Amtrak shuttle. AE, MC, D, DC, V.*
Rodeway Inn. Situated on one of the better streets downtown, this property is clean, comfortable, and nicely decorated. *833 Ash St., 92101, tel. 619/239–2285, 800/228–2000, or 800/522–1528 in CA, fax 619/235–6951. 45 rooms. Facilities: spa, sauna. AE, D, DC, MC, V.*

$ La Pensione. At long last, a decent budget hotel downtown, with
★ daily, weekly, and monthly rates; it's convenient to the restaurants and cafés of the city's version of Little Italy. Rooms are modern, clean, and well designed, with good working areas and kitchenettes. Another location, with 106 units, has a pretty central courtyard and harbor views from some of the rooms. *1700 India St., 92101, tel. 619/236–8000, fax 619/263–8088. 86 rooms. 1546 2nd Ave., 92101, tel. 619/236–9292, fax 619/236–9988. 106 rooms. Reservations tel. 800/232–HOTEL for both. 86 rooms. Facilities: kitchenettes, laundry facilities. AE, MC, V.*
Super 8 Bayview. There's nothing fancy about this motel, but the location is less noisy than those of other low-cost establishments. The accommodations are nondescript but clean, and there are rooms for nonsmokers, and some with VCRs and refrigerators. *1835 Columbia St., 92101, tel. 619/544–0164 or 800/537–9902, fax 619/237–9940. 101 rooms. Facilities: complimentary Continental breakfast, airport and Amtrak courtesy van, car rental agency, laundry facilities, free parking. AE, DC, MC, V.*

Harbor Island/Shelter Island/Point Loma

Two man-made peninsulas between downtown and the lovely community of Point Loma, Harbor Island and Shelter Island are both bordered by grassy parks, tree-lined paths, lavish hotels, and good restaurants. Harbor Island is closest to the downtown area and less than five minutes from the airport, while narrower Shelter Island is nearer to Point Loma. Both locations command breathtaking views of the bay and the downtown skyline. Not all the lodgings listed here are on the islands themselves, but all are in their vicinity.

$$$$ Sheratons on Harbor Island. Converted in 1992 into a single complex connected by a shuttle bus, former neighbors Sheraton Grand (now called the West Tower) and Sheraton Harbor Island East (the East Tower) are now legally married, but they retain their own personalities. The West Tower, which attracts business travelers, is the more luxurious of the two: Well-appointed rooms have large tables for paperwork and a separate area for entertaining. The East Tower, upgraded and expanded in a $32 million 1994 renovation, is more vacation oriented, with excellent sports facilities. Rooms in both towers afford sweeping views from the upper floors. *1380 Harbor Island Dr., 92101, tel. 619/291–2900 or 800/325–3535, fax 619/291–4847 (West), 619/543–0643 (East). 1,050 rooms. Facilities: 2 restaurants, bakery-deli, 2 lounges, 4 lighted tennis courts, sauna, spa, 3 pools, health club with fitness classes and massage, jogging trails, boat rentals, complimentary airport transfers. AE, D, DC, MC, V.*

$$$ **Bay Club Hotel & Marina.** Rooms in this appealing low-rise Shelter Island property are large, light, and attractively furnished with rattan tables and chairs and Polynesian tapestries; all have refrigerators and offer views of either the bay or the marina from outside terraces. A buffet breakfast and limo service to the airport or Amtrak are included in the room rate. *2131 Shelter Island Dr., 92106, tel. 619/224–8888 or 800/672–0800, 800/833–6565 in CA, fax 619/225–1604. 105 rooms. Facilities: restaurant, pool, spa, exercise room, gift shop, free underground parking. AE, D, DC, MC, V.*

$$–$$$ **Humphrey's Half Moon Inn.** This sprawling South Seas–style resort
★ has many grassy open areas with palm trees and tiki torches. The rooms are attractive, with rattan furnishings and nautical-style lamps; some have harbor or marina views. Locals throng to Humphrey's, the on-premises seafood restaurant, and to the jazz lounge; the hotel also hosts outdoor jazz concerts June–October. *2303 Shelter Island Dr., 92106, tel. 619/224–3411 or 800/542–7400 (Mon.–Fri. 8–5), 800/345–9995 (reservations), fax 619/224–3478. 182 rooms. Facilities: restaurant, lounge, putting green, pool, spa, bicycles, ping-pong, croquet, marina, gift shop, complimentary newspapers and airport/Amtrak transfers. AE, D, DC, MC, V.*

$$ **Best Western Posada Inn.** One of the more upscale members of the Best Western chain, the Posada Inn is not on Harbor Island but is located on one of the neighboring thoroughfares adjacent to Point Loma. Many of the rooms, which are clean, comfortable, and nicely furnished, have wonderful views of the harbor. A number of excellent seafood restaurants are within walking distance. *5005 N. Harbor Dr., 92106, tel. 619/224–3254 or 800/528–1234, fax 619/224–2186. 112 rooms. Facilities: restaurant, pool, spa, exercise room, lounge, complimentary airport transfers. AE, D, DC, MC, V.*

Best Western Shelter Island Marina Inn. This waterfront inn, with an airy, skylit lobby, is a good choice if you have a boat to dock; guest slips are available in the adjacent marina. Both harbor- and marina-view rooms are available. Standard accommodations are fairly small; if you're traveling with family or more than one friend, the two-bedroom suite with an eat-in kitchen is a good deal. *2051 Shelter Island Dr., 92106, tel. 619/222–0561 or 800/922–2336, fax 619/222–9760. 68 rooms, 29 suites. Facilities: restaurant, lounge, pool, spa, free parking. AE, D, DC, MC, V.*

Kona Kai Beach and Tennis Resort. Looking like a Polynesian ski lodge—thatched on the outside, with a fireplace and soaring roof indoors—the Kona Kai completed a needed sprucing up of its rooms and public areas in 1994. The hotel, which doubles as a members-only club for locals, has good sports facilities. *1551 Shelter Island Dr., 92106, tel. 619/222–1191, 800/KONA–KAI, fax 619/222–9738. 153 rooms. Facilities: 2 restaurants, lounge, health club, 2 lighted tennis* *courts, volleyball and racquetball, 2 pools, spa, private beach. AE, D, DC, MC, V.*

$ ★ **Outrigger Motel.** A good bet for those traveling as a family, this motel, adjacent to the two resort peninsulas, is less expensive than its offshore counterparts and offers large rooms with eat-in kitchens. Across the street from the Outrigger are fishing docks and the famous Point Loma Seafoods Market and Restaurant. It's a short, scenic walk along the bay from here to Harbor Island. *1370 Scott St., 92106, tel. 619/223-7105. 37 rooms with kitchens. Facilities: pool, laundry facilities. AE, D, DC, MC, V.*

TraveLodge Point Loma. For far less money, you'll get the same view here as at the higher-priced hotels. Of course, there are fewer amenities and the neighborhood (near the navy base) isn't as serene, but the rooms are adequate and clean. *5102 N. Harbor Dr., 92106, tel. 619/223-8171 or 800/525-9055. 45 rooms. Facilities: pool, sun deck, guest laundry, complimentary Continental breakfast. AE, D, DC, MC, V.*

Hotel Circle/Mission Valley/Old Town

Lining both sides of the stretch of I-8 that lies between Old Town and Mission Valley are a number of moderately priced accommodations that constitute the so-called Hotel Circle. A car is an absolute necessity here, since the only nearby road is the busiest freeway in San Diego. Although not particularly scenic or serene, this location is convenient to Balboa Park, the zoo, downtown, the beaches, the shops of Mission Valley, and Old Town. Mission Valley hotels, near movie theaters and restaurants as well as shops, are more upscale than those of Hotel Circle but generally less expensive than comparable properties at the beaches. Old Town itself has a few picturesque lodgings and is developing a crop of modestly priced chain hotels along nearby I-5; when you're making reservations, request a room that doesn't face the freeway.

$$$-$$$$ ★ **San Diego Marriott Mission Valley.** This high rise sits in the middle of the San Diego River valley, where the dry riverbed has been graded and transformed over the years into a commercial zone with sleek office towers and sprawling shopping malls. It has lots of facilities for business travelers but also caters to vacationers, with comfortable rooms, a friendly staff, a piano lounge, a disco, and free transportation to the malls. *8757 Rio San Diego Dr., 92108, tel. 619/692-3800 or 800/228-9290, fax 619/692-0769. 350 rooms. Facilities: restaurant, lounge, pool, tennis court, exercise room, sauna, whirlpool, disco, gift shop, free parking. AE, D, DC, MC, V.*

San Diego Mission Valley Hilton. Directly fronting I-8, this property has soundproofed rooms decorated in contemporary southwestern style. When you're indoors, the attractive modern accommodations, along with the stylish public areas and lush greenery in the back, make you forget this business-oriented hotel's proximity to the freeway. Children stay free, and small pets are accepted. *901 Camino del Rio S, 92108, tel. 619/543-9000, 800/733-2332, or 800/HILTONS, fax 619/296-9561. 350 rooms. Facilities: restaurant, sports bar-lounge, spa, pool, fitness center, complimentary parking and airport and shopping transfers. AE, D, DC, MC, V.*

$$$ **Best Western Hacienda Hotel Old Town.** This pretty white hotel, with balconies and Spanish tile roofs, is in a quiet part of Old Town, away from the freeway and the main retail bustle. The layout of this former shopping complex is a bit confusing, and accommodations are not really large enough to earn the "suite" label the hotel gives

them, but they're decorated in tasteful southwestern style and equipped with microwaves, coffee makers, minifridges, clock radios, and VCRs. *4041 Harney St., 92110, tel. and fax 619/298–4707 or 800/888–1991. 150 suites. Facilities: restaurant, pool, free indoor parking. AE, D, DC, MC, V.*

Hanalei Hotel. As its name suggests, the theme of this friendly Hotel Circle property is Hawaiian: Palm trees, waterfalls, koi ponds, and tiki torches abound here. A two-story complex offers poolside rooms, and a high-rise building surrounds a lovely Hawaiian-style garden. The rooms were refurbished in 1993–94 with tropical prints in rich colors; some have tile floors, and others have wall-to-wall carpeting. Guests have access to an adjacent golf course. *2270 Hotel Circle N, 92108, tel. 619/297–1101 or 800/882–0858, fax 619/297–6049. 412 rooms. Facilities: 2 restaurants, lounge, pool, spa, free parking and transport to Mission Valley. AE, D, DC, MC, V.*

Ramada Inn Old Town. The most established of the new hotels and motels springing up along I–5 at Old Town, the hacienda-style Ramada has Spanish colonial–style fountains, courtyards, and painted tiles, and southwest-style decor in the rooms. Popular with medium-size groups, the hotel lays on a very good Sunday brunch. *2435 Jefferson St., 92110, tel. 619/260–8500 or 800/272–6232, fax 619/297–2078. 152 rooms. Facilities: restaurant, heated pool, whirlpool, free breakfast and transfers to airport, bus, Amtrak. AE, D, DC, MC, V.*

Red Lion Hotel. Across from Fashion Valley Mall and adjacent to the Brickyard Hazard Center, which hosts a seven-plex cinema, four major restaurants, a food pavilion, and more than 20 shops, the Red Lion is also convenient to I–8. Public areas are light-filled and comfortable, well suited to this hotel's large business clientele. Rooms are spacious and decorated in attractive contemporary pastels, with light wood furniture. *7450 Hazard Center Dr., 92108, tel. 619/297–5466 or 800/547–8010, fax 619/688–4088. 300 rooms. Facilities: restaurant, nightclub, outdoor and indoor pools, hot tub, meeting rooms, shops, complimentary parking and airport shuttle. AE, D, DC, MC, V.*

$$–$$$ **Heritage Park Bed & Breakfast Inn.** One of the restored mansions of Heritage Park in Old Town, this romantic 1889 Queen Anne has eight quaint guest rooms and a suite decorated with period antiques. Breakfast and afternoon refreshments are included in the room rate. This appealing lodging has gone through a number of owners in the past few years. *2470 Heritage Park Row, 92110, tel. 619/295–7088 or 800/995–2470. 6 rooms with bath, 2 rooms with shared bath, 1 2-bedroom suite. AE, MC, V.*

$ **Days Inn Hotel Circle.** Rooms in this large complex are generally par for the chain-motel course but have the perk of a small refrigerator; some units also have stoves. *543 Hotel Circle S, 92108, tel. 619/297–8800 or 800/227–4743 (weekdays only), 800/325–2525 (reservations), fax 619/298–6029. 280 rooms. Facilities: restaurant, pool, spa, laundry, hair salon. AE, D, DC, MC, V.*

Padre Trail Inn. This standard, family-style motel is located slightly southwest of Mission Valley. Old Town, shopping, and dining are all within walking distance. *4200 Taylor St., 92110, tel. 619/297–3291 or 800/255-9988, fax 619/692–2080. 100 rooms. Facilities: restaurant, lounge, pool. AE, D, DC, MC, V.*

La Jolla

Million-dollar homes line the beaches and hillsides of La Jolla, one of the world's most beautiful, prestigious communities. The village—the heart of La Jolla—is chock-a-block with expensive boutiques, galleries, and restaurants. Don't despair, however, if you're not old money or even nouveau riche; this popular vacation spot has sufficient lodging choices for every pocket, even those on a budget.

$$$$ **Hyatt Regency La Jolla.** Designed by Michael Graves (who counts New York's Whitney Museum among his projects), the Hyatt is the cornerstone of the Aventine complex in La Jolla's Golden Triangle, about 10 minutes from the beach and the village. The postmodern mix of design elements of the striking lobby is carried out into the spacious, comfortable rooms, where warm cherry wood furnishings contrast with austere gray closets (their stainless-steel handles make them look rather like large wall safes). The hotel's four trendy restaurants include the excellent Japengo (*see* Dining, Chapter 8); you can work off some of the calories at one of the best health clubs in the city. Rates are lower on the weekends at this business-oriented hotel. *3777 La Jolla Village Dr., 92122, tel. 619/552–1234 or 800/233–1234, fax 619/552–6066. 400 rooms and suites. Facilities: 4 restaurants, lounge, outdoor pool and spa, 2 lighted tennis courts, health club with track and basketball court. AE, D,DC, MC, V.*

$$$–$$$$ **La Valencia.** A La Jolla landmark, this pink Art Deco confection
★ drew film stars down from Hollywood in the 1930s and '40s for its lovely setting and views of La Jolla Cove (*see* Chapter 3, Tour 1, *for details*). The clientele is a bit older and more staid these days, but the hotel is still in prime condition. Many of the individually decorated rooms have a genteel European look, with antique pieces and plush, richly colored rugs. The restaurants are excellent, the Whaling Bar is a popular gathering spot, and the hotel is ideally located near the shops and restaurants of La Jolla village and what is arguably the prettiest beach in San Diego. Prices are quite reasonable if you're willing to look out on the village, but on a clear, sunny day, the ocean views may be worth every extra penny. *1132 Prospect St., 92037, tel. 619/454–0771 or 800/451–0772, fax 619/456–3921. 100 rooms. Facilities: 3 restaurants, lounge, whirlpool, pool, exercise room, library. AE, MC, V.*

Sea Lodge. This low-lying compound, on the excellent La Jolla Shores beach, has a definite Spanish flavor to it, with its palm trees, fountains, red-tiled roofs, and Mexican tile work. The attractive rooms feature rattan furniture, nautical-design bedspreads, and terra-cotta lattice-board walls; all have hair dryers, coffee makers, and refrigerators, as well as wooden balconies that overlook lush landscaping and the sea. Early reservations are a must; families will find plenty of room and distractions for both kids and parents. *8110 Camino del Oro, 92037, tel. 619/459–8271 or 800/237–5211, fax 619/456–9346. 128 rooms, 19 with kitchenettes. Facilities: restaurant, lounge, heated pool, hot tub, sauna, beach, 2 tennis courts, pitch-and-putt golf course, ping-pong. AE, D, DC, MC, V.*

★ **Sheraton Grande Torrey Pines.** The view of the Pacific from this low-rise, high-class property atop the Torrey Pines cliffs is superb. The hotel blends into the clifftop, looking rather insignificant until you step inside the luxurious lounge and look out at the sea and the 18th hole of the lush green Torrey Pines golf course. Amenities include 24-hour concierge service, butler service, limousine service, a health club, a business center, and an excellent restaurant. The oversized rooms, decorated in off-white and pale pastels, are simple but elegant; all have balconies. *10950 N. Torrey Pines Rd., 92037, tel. 619/558–1500 or 800/325–3535, fax 619/450–4584. 400 rooms. Facilities: restaurant, lounge, pool, health club, 3 tennis courts, in-room*

*safes, complimentary transportation within 5 miles. AE, D, DC, MC,
V.*

$$$ **Colonial Inn.** A tastefully restored Victorian-era building, this is the
oldest hotel in La Jolla, offering turn-of-the-century elegance in its
public spaces; in keeping with the period, rooms are a bit formal and
staid. Ocean views cost more than village views. On one of La Jolla's
main thoroughfares but not in the thick of its busiest people traffic,
the Colonial Inn is near boutiques, restaurants, and the cove. *910
Prospect St., 92037, tel. 619/454–2181, 800/832–5525, or 800/826–1278
in CA; fax 619/454–5679. 75 rooms. Facilities: restaurant, lounge,
pool, complimentary Continental breakfast, morning newspaper,
and valet parking. AE, DC, MC, V.*
La Jolla Cove Motel. Offering studios and suites, some with spacious
oceanfront balconies, this motel overlooks the famous La Jolla Cove
beach. If it doesn't have the charm of some of the older properties
of this exclusive area, this motel gives its guests the same first-class
views at much lower rates. The free underground lot is also a bonus
in a section of town where a parking spot is a prime commodity. *1155
S. Coast Blvd., 92037, tel. 619/459–2621 or 800/248–2683. 110 rooms.
Facilities: solarium, sun deck, putting green, freshwater pool, spa,
kitchenettes available, laundry room, complimentary Continental
breakfast. AE, D, DC, MC, V.*
Scripps Inn. You'd be wise to make reservations well in advance for
this small, quiet inn tucked away on Coast Boulevard; its popularity
with repeat visitors ensures that it is booked year-round. Available
kitchen facilities and lower weekly and monthly rates (not available
in the summer season) make it particularly attractive to long-term
guests. All the rooms are individually decorated; many offer ocean
views and some have fireplaces or terraces. A lovely Continental
breakfast is served in the lobby each morning. *555 Coast Blvd. S, tel.
619/454–3391, fax 619/459–6758. 13 rooms. Facilities: kitchenettes.
AE, D, MC, V.*

$$–$$$$ **The Bed & Breakfast Inn at La Jolla.** Built in 1913 by Irving Gill,
this B&B is located in a quiet section of La Jolla just down the street
from the Museum of Contemporary Art. The individually decorated
rooms cover a wide range of sizes and styles—some are done in
Laura Ashley prints, others feature wicker or rattan furnishings—
but all are pretty and well tended and come with fresh fruit, sherry,
and terry robes. The lovely gardens in the back were planned by
Kate Sessions, who was instrumental in landscaping Balboa Park.
*7753 Draper Ave., 92037, tel. 619/456–2066. 16 rooms, 15 with private
baths. Facilities: gardens, sun deck, library, refrigerators and hair
dryers in some rooms. MC, V.*

$$–$$$ **Best Western Inn by the Sea.** In a quiet section of La Jolla Village,
within five blocks of the beach, the five-story Inn by the Sea has all
the modern amenities at reasonable rates for La Jolla. Rooms are
done in cheerful pastel tones and have private balconies with views
of either the sea or the village. Continental breakfast and newspaper
are included in the room rate. *7830 Fay Ave., 92037, tel. 619/459–4461
or 800/462–9732. 132 rooms. Facilities: pool, Jacuzzi, exercise room,
car rental desk, free parking. AE, D, DC, MC, V.*
Summer House Inn. Don't expect an idyllic hideaway: The Summer
House Inn stands at the intersection of two of the busiest roads in
La Jolla. Still, this pleasant, modern high rise is five minutes from
the village, a few blocks from the beach, and convenient to freeway
entrances. Rooms are done in a pleasant contemporary style; those
on the north side, away from Torrey Pines Road, are quietest, while
those on the highest floors have the best views (and are, accordingly,

more expensive). Locals come to Elario's restaurant, on the top floor, for its excellent live jazz. *7955 La Jolla Shores Dr., 92037, tel. 619/459–0261 or 800/666–0261, fax 619/459–7649. 90 rooms. Facilities: restaurant, jazz club, kitchenettes and suites available, pool, spa. AE, D, DC, MC, V.*

$$ **Prospect Park Inn.** This European-style inn rents a wide variety of
★ appealing rooms, many with sweeping ocean views from their balconies. Located in a prime spot in La Jolla village, it's near some of the best shops and restaurants in town and one block away from the beach. Continental breakfast is included in the very reasonable room rate, and parking is free. There is no smoking on the premises. *1110 Prospect St., 92037, tel. 619/454–0133 or 800/433–1609, fax 619/454–2056. 23 rooms. Facilities: kitchenettes, lounge. AE, D, DC, MC, V.*

★ **Torrey Pines Inn.** Located on a bluff between La Jolla and Del Mar, this hotel commands a view of miles and miles of coastline. It's adjacent to the public Torrey Pines Golf Course, one of the best in the county, and very close to scenic Torrey Pines State Beach and nature reserve; the village of La Jolla is a 10-minute drive away. Most of the rooms have been renovated with dark wood furnishings and Oriental fabrics; they're more attractive than the older, rather generic accommodations. This off-the-beaten-path inn is a very good value, especially for golfers. *11480 N. Torrey Pines Rd., 92037, tel. 619/453–4420, 800/995–4507, or 800/777–1700 for reservations, fax 619/453–0691. 74 rooms. Facilities: restaurant, coffee shop, 2 bars, pool, adjacent golf course. AE, D, DC, MC, V.*

$–$$ **La Jolla Palms Inn.** In the southern section of La Jolla, near some
★ excellent beaches, this modest motel is also near a wide variety of shops and restaurants. Many of the rooms are remarkably large, with huge closets; some have kitchenettes, and three suites offer separate eat-in kitchens. The rooms—done in pastel tones—are nothing to write home about, but this is an excellent value for families who want to stay in this tony area and still have a few dollars left over for shopping. *6705 La Jolla Blvd., 92037, tel. 619/454–7101 or 800/451–0358, fax 619/454–6957. 59 rooms. Facilities: heated pool, spa, pool table, guest laundry, complimentary Continental breakfast. AE, D, DC, MC, V.*

Mission Bay and Beaches

Staying near the water is a priority for most people who visit San Diego. Mission and Pacific beaches have the highest concentration of small hotels and motels. Both these areas have a casual atmosphere and a busy coastal thoroughfare offering endless shopping, dining, and nightlife possibilities. Mission Bay Park, with its beaches, bike trails, boat-launching ramps, golf course, and grassy parks, is also a hotel haven. You can't go wrong with any of these locations, as long as the frenzy of hundreds at play doesn't bother you.

$$$–$$$$ **Catamaran Resort Hotel.** If you check in at the right time, parrots
★ will herald your arrival at this appealing hotel, set between Mission Bay and Pacific Beach; the two resident birds are often poised on a perch in the lushly landscaped lobby, replete with a koi fish pond. The grounds are similarly tropical, and tiki torches light the way for guests staying at one of the six two-story buildings or the 14-story high rise (the view from the upper floors of the latter is spectacular). The popular Cannibal Bar hosts Top 40s and rock-and-roll groups, while a classical or jazz pianist tickles the ivories at the Moray Bar;

Catamaran guests can also take advantage of the entertainment facilities at the sister Bahia Hotel. Children 18 or under stay free. *3999 Mission Blvd., 92109, tel. 619/488–1101, 800/288–0770, or 800/233–8172 in Canada, fax 619/490–3328. 312 rooms. Facilities: restaurant, coffee shop, nightclub, piano bar–lounge, pool, spa, exercise room, watersports rentals, evening bay cruises, gift shop; full kitchens available. AE, D, DC, MC, V.*

San Diego Hilton Beach and Tennis Resort. Spread out on the picturesque grounds of this deluxe resort, low-level bungalows are surrounded by trees, Japanese bridges, and ponds; a high-rise building offers accommodations with lovely views of Mission Bay Park. Rooms in all the buildings are done in attractive contemporary style and have all the expected amenities. The Kids Club Program offers complimentary day care for children over age 5, and the sports facilities on the property are excellent. *1775 E. Mission Bay Dr., 92109, tel. 619/276–4010 or 800/445–8667, fax 619/275–7991. 354 rooms. Facilities: restaurant, coffee shop, lounge, pool, 4 whirlpools, putting greens, 5 lighted tennis courts, exercise room, playground, hotel yacht, shops. AE, D, DC, MC, V.*

$$$ **Bahia Resort Hotel.** This huge complex, on a 14-acre peninsula in Mission Bay Park, offers tastefully furnished studios and suites with kitchens; many have wood-beamed ceilings and attractive tropical decor. The hotel's *Bahia Belle* cruises Mission Bay at sunset, and guests can return for yuks at the on-premises Comedy Isle club. Rates are reasonable for a place so well located—within walking distance of the ocean—and offering so many amenities, including use of the facilities at the Catamaran Hotel. *998 W. Mission Bay Dr., 92109, tel. 619/488–0551, 800/288–0770, or 800/233–8172 in Canada, fax 619/490–3328. 313 rooms. Facilities: restaurant; 2 lighted tennis courts; water-sports, bicycle, and roller-blade rentals; spa, pool, evening bay cruises, comedy club. AE, D, DC, MC, V.*

Crystal Pier Motel. You can drive your car onto the Crystal Pier and park in front of one of this classic motel's blue and white cottages, equipped with kitchenettes and patios overlooking the sea. You'll be lulled to sleep by the gentle lapping of waves against wooden pilings; the cries of sea gulls provide a pleasant wake-up call. A landmark since the 1930s, this place is no longer the bargain it once was, nor does it have the amenities of the other properties in its price category; you're paying for character and a unique proximity to the ocean. But it retains a loyal following nevertheless; call four to six weeks in advance for reservations. Weekly rates are available in winter. *4500 Ocean Blvd., tel. 619/483–6983 or 800/748–5894, fax 619/483–6811. 26 cottages. Facilities: kitchens, parking. 3-night minimum stay June 15–Sept. 15. D, MC, V.*

★ **San Diego Princess Resort.** You'll feel as though you're staying in a self-sufficient village if you book one of the cottages in this 44-acre resort, so beautifully landscaped that it's been the setting for a number of movies. The wide range of amenities includes access to a marina and beaches. All the accommodations have refrigerators and private patios, and a number have bay views. With something for everyone, this hotel is favored by upscale families, particularly during the summer. The hotel underwent a major renovation in 1993–94. *1404 W. Vacation Rd., 92109, tel. 619/274–4630 or 800/344–2626, fax 619/581–5929. 462 cottages. Facilities: 3 restaurants, 6 tennis courts, 5 pools, bicycle and boat rentals, croquet, 18-hole putting golf course, shuffleboard, volleyball courts, jogging path. AE, D, DC, MC, V.*

$$–$$$ **Hyatt Islandia.** Located in Mission Bay Park, one of San Diego's most appealing seashore areas, the Islandia has rooms in several

low-level, lanai-style units, as well as marina suites and rooms in a high-rise building. Many of the tastefully modern accommodations overlook the hotel's gardens and fish pond; others have dramatic views of the bay area. This hotel is famous for its lavish Sunday champagne brunch. In winter, whale-watching expeditions depart from the Islandia's marina. *1441 Quivira Rd., 92109, tel. 619/224–1234 or 800/233–1234, fax 619/224–0348. 423 rooms. Facilities: 2 restaurants, pool, spa, marina with sailboat or sportfishing rentals. AE, D, DC, MC, V.*

\$\$ **Dana Inn & Marina.** This hotel, which has an adjoining marina, is a bargain in the Mission Bay area. If accommodations are not as grand as those in the nearby hotels, they're more than adequate. There are many on-premises sports facilities, and the Dana Inn is within walking distance of Sea World. *1710 W. Mission Bay Dr., 92109, tel. 619/222–6440 or 800/345–9995, fax 619/222–5916. 196 rooms. Facilities: restaurant, pool, spa, marina, boat rentals, 2 lighted tennis courts, shuffleboard, ping-pong. AE, D, DC, MC, V.*

Pacific Shores Inn. One of the better motels in the Mission Bay area, this property is only a half-block from the beach and has nicely decorated rooms. Pets (under 20 lbs) are accepted with a \$50 refundable deposit. *4802 Mission Blvd., 92109, tel. 619/483–6300 or 800/367–6467, fax 619/483–9276. 55 rooms. Facilities: pool. AE, D, DC, MC, V.*

Surfer Motor Lodge. This high rise is right on the beach and directly behind a shopping center with many restaurants and boutiques. Rooms are plain, but those on the upper floors have excellent views. *711 Pacific Beach Dr., 92109, tel. 619/483–7070 or 800/787–3373, fax 619/274–1670. 52 rooms. Facilities: restaurant, cocktail lounge, pool. AE, DC, MC, V.*

\$–\$\$ **Ocean Manor Apartment Hotel.** Some folks have been returning for
★ 20 years to this well-priced Ocean Beach hotel, which rents units by the day (three-day minimum for those with kitchens), week, or month in winter; you'll need to reserve months in advance. Guests at this charming place have included everyone from retired generals to Svetlana Stalin. Located on Sunset Cliffs, Ocean Manor offers lovely views; the beach below has long since washed away, but other beaches are within walking distance and Point Loma is a 10-minute drive away. The comfortable studios and one- and two-bedroom suites are furnished plainly in the style of the 1950s—which is when the amiable owners took over the place. There is no maid service, but fresh towels are always provided. *1370 Sunset Cliffs Blvd., 92107, tel. 619/222–7901 or 619/224–1379. 22 units. Facilities: pool, shuffleboard, ping-pong, garages. MC, V.*

\$ **Mission Bay Motel.** Located a half-block from the beach, this motel offers centrally located, modest units, some with refrigerators. Great restaurants and nightlife are within walking distance, but you may find the area a bit noisy. *4221 Mission Blvd., 92109, tel. 619/483–6440. 50 rooms. Facilities: pool. MC, V.*

Santa Clara Beach and Bay Motel. This small, no-frills motel is a block from the ocean and right in the middle of restaurant, nightlife, and shopping activity in Mission Beach. All the units have refrigerators. Weekly rates are available. *839 Santa Clara Pl., 92109, tel. 619/488–1193. 17 rooms. AE, MC, V.*

Hostels

AYH–Hostel on Broadway (500 W. Broadway, San Diego 92101, tel. 619/525–1531).

American Youth Hostels (335 W. Beach St., San Diego 92101, tel. 619/239–2644).

Banana Bungalow San Diego (707 Reed Ave., Mission Beach 92109, tel. 619/273–3060 or 800/5–HOSTEL).

Elliot–Point Loma AYH Hostel (3790 Udall St., San Diego 92107, tel. 619/223–4778).

Imperial Beach American Youth Hostel (170 Palm Ave., Imperial Beach 92032, tel. 619/423–8039).

Jim's San Diego (1425 C St., San Diego, 92101, tel. 619/235–0234, fax 619/399–4216).

YWCA of San Diego (1012 C St., San Diego 92101, tel. 619/239–0355).

10 The Arts

By Marael Johnson

Revised by Lori Chamberlain

Top national touring companies perform regularly at the Civic Theatre, Golden Hall, Symphony Hall, and East County Performing Arts Center. San Diego State University, the University of California at San Diego, private universities, and community colleges present a wide variety of performing arts programs, from appearances by well-known artists to student recitals. The daily *San Diego Union* lists current attractions and complete movie schedules. The *Reader,* a free weekly that comes out each Thursday, devotes an entire section to upcoming cultural events, as well as current theater and film reviews. *San Diego* magazine publishes a monthly "What's Doing" column that lists arts events throughout the county and reviews of current films, plays, and concerts.

It is best to book tickets well in advance, preferably at the same time you make hotel reservations. There are various outlets for last-minute tickets, though you risk either paying top rates or getting less-than-choice seats—or both.

Half-price tickets to most theater, music, and dance events can be bought on the day of performance at the **TIMES ARTS TIX Ticket Center** (Horton Plaza, tel. 619/238–3810). Only cash is accepted. Advance full-price tickets may also be purchased through ARTS TIX.

Visa and MasterCard holders may buy tickets for many scheduled performances through **Ticketmaster** (tel. 619/278–8497). Service charges vary according to the event, and most tickets are nonrefundable.

Theater

The Blackfriars Theatre (121 Broadway, Suite 203, tel. 619/232–4088). Blackfriars, formerly the Bowery, is acclaimed by critics and theater goers for its premieres of high-quality works by both famous playwrights and soon-to-be-discovered artists.

Coronado Playhouse (1775 Strand Way, Coronado, tel. 619/435–4856). This cabaret-type theater, near the Hotel del Coronado, stages regular dramatic and musical performances. Dinner packages are offered on Friday and Saturday.

Gaslamp Quarter Theatre at the Hahn Cosmopolitan Theatre (444 4th Ave., tel. 619/234–9583). The resident theater company stages comedies, dramas, mysteries, and musicals in the 250-seat Hahn Cosmopolitan Theatre, located in the Gaslamp Quarter.

La Jolla Playhouse (Mandell Weiss Center for the Performing Arts, University of California at San Diego, tel. 619/550–1010). From May to November, look for exciting and innovative presentations, under the artistic direction of Michael Greif. Many Broadway productions, such as *A Walk in the Woods, Big River,* and works by Neil Simon, have previewed here before heading for the East Coast.

La Jolla Stage Company (750 Nautilus St., La Jolla, tel. 619/459–7773). Lavish productions of Broadway favorites and popular comedies are presented year-round in Parker Auditorium at La Jolla High School.

Lawrence Welk Resort Theatre (8860 Lawrence Welk Dr., Escondido, tel. 619/749–3448 or 800/932–9355). About a 45-minute drive from downtown, this famed dinner theater puts on polished Broadway-style productions with a professional cast.

Old Globe Theatre (Simon Edison Centre for the Performing Arts, Balboa Park, tel. 619/239–2255). The oldest professional theater in California performs classics, contemporary dramas, experimental works, and puts on the famous summer Shakespeare Festival at the

Old Globe and its sister theaters, the Cassius Carter Centre Stage and the Lowell Davies Festival Theatre.

RUSE Marquis Public Theater (3717 India St., tel. 619/295–5654). Contemporary, experimental, and original plays are held on the main stage and in the smaller gallery.

San Diego Comic Opera (Casa del Prado Theatre, Balboa Park, tel. 619/231–5714). Four different productions of Gilbert and Sullivan and similar works are given October–July.

San Diego Repertory Theater (79 Horton Plaza, tel. 619/235–8025). San Diego's first resident acting company performs contemporary works year-round on the 550-seat Lyceum stage and in a 225-seat theater that can be rearranged to suit the stage set.

Sledgehammer Theatre (1620 6th Ave., tel. 619/544–1484). One of the cutting-edge theaters in San Diego, Sledgehammer stages avant-garde pieces in St. Cecilia's church.

Starlight Musicals (Starlight Bowl, Balboa Park, tel. 619/544–7827). This series of popular musicals, presented in an outdoor amphitheater from mid-June through early September, is a local summertime favorite.

Sushi Performance and Visual Art (633 9th Ave., tel. 619/235–8466). This nationally acclaimed group provides an opportunity for well-known performance artists to do their thing.

UCSD Theatre (Warren Theatre and Mandell Weiss Theatre, University of California at San Diego campus, La Jolla, tel. 619/534–6467). The students of the University of California at San Diego's theater department take the stage in the theaters used by La Jolla Playhouse in the summer months and present first-rate productions from September to May.

Concerts

Copley Symphony Hall (1245 7th Ave., tel. 619/699–4200). The San Diego Symphony is the only California symphony that has its own concert hall. The performance season runs October–May, with a series of outdoor pop concerts held near Seaport Village during the summer.

Open-Air Theatre (San Diego State University, tel. 619/594–6884). Top-name rock, reggae, and popular artists pack in the crowds for summer concerts under the stars.

Organ Pavilion (Balboa Park, tel. 619/226–0819). Robert Plimpton performs on the giant 1914 pipe organ at 2 PM on most Sunday afternoons and on most Monday evenings in summer. All concerts are free.

Sherwood Auditorium (700 Prospect St., La Jolla, tel. 619/454–2594). Many classical and jazz events are held in the 550-seat auditorium in the San Diego Museum of Contemporary Art. August–May, La Jolla Chamber Music Society presents internationally acclaimed chamber ensembles, orchestras, and soloists. San Diego Chamber Orchestra, a 35-member ensemble, performs once a month, October–April.

Sports Arena (2500 Sports Arena Blvd., tel. 619/224–4176). Big-name rock concerts play to more than 14,000 fans, using an end-stage configuration, so all seats face in one direction.

Spreckels Theatre (121 Broadway, tel. 619/235–9500). This beautiful downtown theater, built more than 80 years ago and designated a landmark in 1972, hosts a wide range of musical events—everything from Mostly Mozart to small rock concerts. Ballets and theatrical productions are also held here. Its good acoustics, as well as its historical interest, make this an appealing place to come for a show of any kind.

Opera

Civic Theatre (202 C St., tel. 619/236–6510). The San Diego Opera draws international artists and has developed an impeccable reputation. The season of five operas runs January–April in the 3,000-seat, state-of-the-art auditorium. English translations of works sung in their original languages are projected on a large screen above the stage.

Dance

California Ballet (tel. 619/560–5676). Four high-quality contemporary and traditional works, from story ballets to Balanchine, are performed September–May. The *Nutcracker* is staged annually at the Civic Theatre; other ballets take place at Poway Center for the Performing Arts (15500 Espola Rd., Poway, tel. 619/748–0505), the Lyceum, and Nautilus Bowl at Sea World.

Issacs McCaleb & Dancers (tel. 619/296–9523). Interpretative dance presentations, incorporating live music, are staged at major theaters and concert halls around San Diego County.

Film

First-run international films are screened at the **Cove** (7730 Girard Ave., La Jolla, tel. 619/459–5404), **Guild** (3827 5th Ave., tel. 619/295–2000), and **Park** (3812 Park Blvd., tel. 619/294–9264) cinemas.

Hillcrest Cinemas (3965 5th Ave., tel. 619/299–2100). Owned and operated by Landmark, the owners of the Guild, Park, Cove, and Ken, this posh new multiplex shuns mainstream Hollywood blockbusters in favor of art and foreign films. You can even get espresso at the snack bar.

Ken Cinema (4061 Adams Ave., tel. 619/283–5909). The roster of art/revival films changes almost every night, and many programs are double bills.

Sherwood Auditorium (*see* Concerts, *above*) regularly hosts foreign and classic film series and special cinema events, including the wildly popular Festival of Animation (January–March).

American Express offers Travelers Cheques built for two.

Cheques *for Two*℠ from American Express are the Travelers Cheques that allow either of you to use them because both of you have signed them. And only one of you needs to be present to purchase them.

Cheques *for Two* are accepted anywhere regular American Express Travelers Cheques are, which is just about everywhere. So stop by your bank, AAA* or any American Express Travel Service Office and ask for Cheques *for Two*.

Pack light.

Take the one number you need for any kind of call, anywhere you travel.

Checking in with your family back home? Calling for a tow truck? When you're on the road, the phone you use might not accept your calling card. Or you might get overcharged by an unknown telephone company. Here's the solution: dial 1 800 CALL ATT.[sm] You'll get flawless AT&T service, competitive calling card prices, and the lowest prices for collect calls from any phone, anywhere. Travel light. Just bring along this one simple number: 1 800 CALL ATT.

11 Nightlife

*By Dan
Janeck*

*Revised by Jon
and Noonie
Corn*

The unbeatable variety of sun-and-surf recreational activities is the prime reason tourists come to San Diego, but most visitors are surprised and delighted by the new momentum the city gains after dark. The highly mercurial nightlife scene is constantly growing—the flavor of the month may be Top 40 or contemporary, reggae, pop-jazz, or strictly rock-and-roll. Live pop and fusion jazz have become especially popular—some say they are the ideal music for San Diego's typically laid-back lifestyle—and they can easily be found at a dozen or so venues throughout the county. Music at local rock clubs and nightclubs ranges from danceable contemporary Top 40 to original rock and new wave by San Diego's finest up-and-coming groups. Discotheques and bars in the Gaslamp Quarter and at Pacific and Mission beaches tend to be the most crowded spots in the county on the weekends, but don't let that discourage you from visiting these quintessential San Diego hangouts. Authentic country-western music is also an option for those willing to go a bit farther afield. And should your tastes run to softer music, there are plenty of piano bars in which to unfrazzle and unwind. Check the free weekly *Reader* for band information or *San Diego* magazine's "Restaurant & Nightlife Guide" for the full range of nightlife possibilities.

California law prohibits the sale of alcoholic beverages after 2 AM. Bars and nightclubs usually stop serving at about 1:40 AM. You must be 21 to purchase and consume alcohol, and most places will insist on current identification. Be aware that California also has some of the most stringent drunk-driving laws in the United States; roadblocks are not an uncommon sight.

Bars and Nightclubs

Cannibal Bar. A tropical-theme bar and nightclub in the Catamaran Resort Hotel, with oldies, contemporary jazz, blues, and swing. *3999 Mission Blvd., Pacific Beach, tel. 619/488–1081. Open Wed.–Sun. 7 PM–2 AM. Entertainment 9 PM–1:30 AM. AE, D, DC, MC, V.*

Cargo Bar. The San Diego Hilton Hotel's nautical-theme bar has a can't-beat view of the bay and a potpourri of entertainment attractions, including a Thursday-night fashion show and Sunday-night salsa. *1775 E. Mission Bay Dr., Mission Bay, tel. 619/276–4010. Open nightly 5 PM–1:30 AM. Entertainment 8:30 PM–1 AM. AE, D, DC, MC, V.*

Club Fifth Avenue. One of the Gaslamp Quarter's newer night spots, this place is fast becoming one of the more popular destinations for San Diego's young professionals. There's a dress code (no jeans, T-shirts, or tennis shoes) on Friday and Saturday night. Entertainment varies nightly, and there is a nominal cover charge. *835 5th Ave., downtown, tel. 619/238–7191. Open Tues.–Sun. 8 PM–2 AM. AE, D, DC, MC, V.*

The Daily Planet. You can't miss this glorified neighborhood bar, painted in neon purple, yellow, and green. The crowd is fun-loving and unpretentious. On weekends at around 9 PM, the pool tables make way for a great DJ and the dance crowd. *1200 Garnet Ave., Pacific Beach, tel. 619/272–6066. Open Mon.–Thurs. 11 AM–2 AM, weekends 9 AM–2 AM. MC, V.*

Diego's. This remodeled Mexican restaurant features a party patio and volleyball court and attracts a festive, sophisticated beach crowd as well as students from nearby San Diego State. *860 Garnet Ave., Pacific Beach, tel. 619/272–1241. Open nightly 9 PM–2 AM. AE, D, MC, V.*

The Green Circle. One of the newer spots in town, this place defies easy classification. But you'll enjoy yourself if you like modern rock played by up-and-coming bands and colorful DJs. *827 F St., Gaslamp Quarter, tel. 619/232–8080. Open Tues.–Sun. 7:30 PM–2 AM. MC, V.*

The Hard Rock Cafe. Part of the international chain, this is a great place to dance and party amid an impressive collection of rock-and-roll memorabilia. *909 Prospect St., La Jolla, tel. 619/454–5101. Open Mon.–Thurs. 11:30 AM–11 PM, weekends 11:30 AM–12:30 AM. AE, D, DC, MC, V.*

Islands Lounge. Tropical decor and lively contemporary music give this lounge in the Hanalei Hotel its unique character and attract a steady stream of regulars. There's live music some weekend nights. *2270 Hotel Circle N, Mission Valley, tel. 619/297–1101. Open Mon.– Thurs. 4 PM–11 PM, weekends 10 AM–1:30 AM. AE, D, DC, MC, V.*

Karl Strauss' Old Columbia Brewery & Grill. The first microbrewery in San Diego draws a downtown crowd to its excellent beers—try the Gaslamp Gold—accompanied by beer-battered fish-and-chips, hefty onion rings, and huge burgers. *1157 Columbia St., downtown, tel. 619/234–2739. Open Sun.–Thurs. 11:30 AM–midnight, Fri. and Sat. until 1 AM. MC, V.*

Megalopolis. This funky little club isn't nearly as large or as flashy as the name may suggest, but an eclectic roster of blues, rock, and folk bands is reason enough to visit. *4321 Fairmount Ave., Kensington, tel. 619/584–7900. Open Tues.–Sat. 8 PM–2 AM. No credit cards.*

Patrick's II. This downtown pub with definite Irish tendencies is a prime place to hear live New Orleans–style jazz, blues, and rock. *428 F St., downtown, tel. 619/233–3077. Entertainment nightly 9 PM–2 AM. No credit cards.*

Princess of Wales. This midtown British pub–style watering hole is the place for Anglophiles in general and groupies of the royals in particular: Hundreds of photos of Princess Di are plastered on the walls. You can order pints of Guinness, Harp, or Black-and-Tans to wash down your platter of fish-and-chips. *1665 India St., downtown, tel. 619/238–1266. Open daily 11 AM–1 AM. MC, V.*

Jazz Clubs

Croce's. The intimate jazz cave of restaurateur Ingrid Croce (singer-songwriter Jim Croce's widow) features superb acoustic-jazz musicians and an interesting menu. Next door, Croce's Top Hat puts on live R&B nightly 9 PM–2 AM. *802 5th Ave., Gaslamp Quarter, tel. 619/233–4355. Open Mon.–Thurs. 8:30 PM–2 AM, Fri.–Sun. 5:30 PM–2 AM. AE, MC, V.*

Elario's. This club, on the top floor of the Summer House Inn, has a sumptuous ocean view and an incomparable lineup of internationally acclaimed jazz musicians every month. *7955 La Jolla Shores Dr., La Jolla, tel. 619/459–0541. Nightly shows at 8:20, 9:45, and 11 PM. AE, DC, MC, V.*

Humphrey's. This is the premier promoter of the city's best jazz, folk, and light-rock summer concert series held out on the grass. The rest of the year the music moves indoors for some first-rate jazz Sunday and Monday. *2241 Shelter Island Dr., tel. 619/523–1010 for taped concert information. Entertainment 8 PM–midnight. AE, D, DC, MC, V.*

The Marine Room. Waves literally crash against the windows here while jazz groups play. *2000 Spindrift Dr., La Jolla, tel. 619/459–7222. Entertainment nightly 6 PM–12:30 AM. AE, D, DC, MC, V.*

Pal Joey's. This comfortable neighborhood bar features jazz and urban blues Friday and Saturday nights. *5147 Waring Rd., Allied*

Gardens, near San Diego State University, tel. 619/286–7873. Enter-tainment 9 PM–1:30 AM. MC, V.

Rock Clubs

Belly Up Tavern. Located in converted Quonset huts, this eclectic live-concert venue hosts critically acclaimed artists who play every-thing from reggae, rock, new wave, Motown, and folk to—well, you name it. Always a fun choice, the Belly Up attracts people of all ages. Sunday nights are usually free and feature local R&B artists. *143 S. Cedros Ave., Solana Beach, tel. 619/481–9022. Open daily 11 AM–1:30 AM. Entertainment 9:30 PM–1:30 AM. MC, V.*

Bodie's. This Gaslamp Quarter bar hosts the best rock and blues bands in San Diego, as well as up-and-coming bands from out of town. *528 F St., tel. 619/236–8988. Open daily 6 AM–2 AM. No credit cards.*

Casbah. This small club showcases rock, reggae, funk, and every other kind of band—except Top 40—every night of the week. *2812 Kettner Blvd., near the airport, tel. 619/294–9033. Live bands at 9:30 nightly. No credit cards.*

Iguanas. Though south of the border in Tijuana, Iguanas is consid-ered a local club for the 18–21 crowd who can't get into San Diego's clubs. Tickets to the concerts by top-name bands that play here are available through Ticketron (tel. 619/278–TIXS); there's also DJ dance music on other nights. A bus shuttles patrons back and forth from the border to the club; the sober and queasy will not want to be on it on the return run. *Pueblo Amigo Shopping Ct., Tijuana, tel. 011–52–66/82–4967. Open nightly 8 PM–2 AM, with concerts beginning at 10. MC, V.*

Old Bonita Store & Bonita Beach Club. This South Bay hangout attracts singles 25–35 and features locally produced rock acts. *4014 Bonita Rd., Bonita, tel. 619/479–3537. Entertainment nightly 8:30 PM–1:30 AM. AE, MC, V.*

Spirit. This original-music club emphasizes the top local alternative and experimental-rock groups. *1130 Buenos Ave., Bay Park, near Mission Bay, tel. 619/276–3993. Open nightly 8 PM–1 AM. No credit cards.*

Winston's Beach Club. Local bands, reggae groups, and, occasion-ally, '60s rock bands play this bowling alley turned rock club. The crowd here can get rowdy. *1921 Bacon St., Ocean Beach, tel. 619/222–6822. Live bands nightly 9 PM–2 AM. MC, V.*

Country-Western Clubs

Big Stone Lodge. The rustic dance hall, formerly a Pony Express station in the last century, now showcases the two-steppin' tunes of the house band, consisting of the owners. If you don't know coun-try-western dances, don't fret; free lessons are given on some nights. *12237 Old Pomerado Rd., Poway, tel. 619/748–1135. Enter-tainment Tues.–Thurs. 8 PM–12:30 AM, Fri. and Sat. 9 PM–1:30 AM, Sun. 5:30 PM–9:30 PM. DC, MC, V.*

The Country Club. Here you'll find live country bands nightly; there are jam sessions on Sunday. *1121 3rd Ave., Chula Vista, tel. 619/426–2977. Live music nightly 8 PM–2 AM. No credit cards.*

In Cahootz. A great sound system, live bands, and a large dance floor make this lively spot a choice destination for cowgirls and -boys and city slickers alike. Free dance lessons (Sun., Mon., Tues., and Thurs. nights), free dinners, and military and ladies nights are among the many incentives this bar provides for you to stop by. *5373*

Mission Center Rd., Mission Valley, tel. 619/291–8635. Open weeknights 5 PM–2 AM, weekends 5:30 PM–2 AM. AE, MC, V.

Leo's Little Bit O' Country. This is the largest country-western dance floor in the county—bar none. Leo's is another fun place to come for free dance lessons. *680 W. San Marcos Blvd., San Marcos, tel. 619/744–4120. Open Tues.–Sat. 4 PM–1 AM, Sun. 5 PM–1 AM. Entertainment 8:30 PM–1 AM, Sun. 6:30 PM–midnight. Closed Mon. MC, V.*

Magnolia Mulvaney's. This is a mainstay for East County residents who come to listen to country music. *8861 N. Magnolia Ave., Santee, tel. 619/448–8550. Open nightly 6:30 PM–1 AM. Entertainment Fri. and Sat. 9 PM–1 AM. AE, MC, V.*

Wrangler's Roost. This is a country-western haunt that appeals to both the longtime cowboy customer and the first-timer. Free dance lessons start at 8 PM. *6608 Mission Gorge Rd., tel. 619/280–6263. Entertainment 9 PM–2 AM. MC, V.*

Zoo Country. Enjoy live music or a DJ seven nights a week at the new hangout for line-dancin', two-steppin' cowpersons. *1340 Broadway, El Cajon, tel. 619/442–9900. Open Tues.–Sun. 5:30 PM–11 PM. AE, D, MC, V.*

Comedy Clubs

Comedy Isle. Located in the Bahia Resort Hotel, this club offers the latest in local and national talent. *998 W. Mission Bay Dr., Mission Bay, tel. 619/488–6872. Shows Wed., Thurs., and Sun. 8:30, Fri. and Sat. 8:30 and 10:30. Reservations accepted. AE, DC, MC, V.*

The Comedy Store. In the same tradition as the Comedy Store in West Hollywood, San Diego's version hosts some of the best national touring and local talent. *916 Pearl St., La Jolla, tel. 619/454–9176. One show Tues.–Thurs. at 8 PM, 2 shows Fri. and Sat. at 8 PM and 10:30 PM. Closed Sun. AE, MC, V.*

The Improv. This is a superb Art Deco–style club with a distinct East Coast feel, where some of the big names in comedy present their routines. *832 Garnet Ave., Pacific Beach, tel. 619/483–4520. One show Sun.–Thurs. at 8 PM, 2 shows Fri. and Sat. at 8 PM and 10:30 PM. Sunday is no-smoking night. AE, MC, V.*

Discos

Characters. This is a beautifully appointed disco inside the La Jolla Marriott Hotel, where out-of-town guests and university students move to a recorded Top 40 beat. *4240 La Jolla Village Dr., La Jolla, tel. 619/587–1414. Open Mon.–Sat. 8 PM–1 AM. AE, DC, MC, V.*

Club Diego's. This flashy discotheque and singles scene by the beach has excellent, nonstop dance music and friendly young (25–35) dancers. *860 Garnet Ave., Pacific Beach, tel. 619/272–1241. Open Tues.–Sun. 9 PM–1:30 AM. AE, MC, V.*

Club Emerald City. Alternative dance music and an uninhibited clientele keep this beach-town spot unpredictable—which is just fine with everyone. *945 Garnet Ave., Pacific Beach, tel. 619/483–9920. Open Mon.–Sat. 8:30 PM–2 AM. Closed Sun. No credit cards.*

Johnny M's. You'll work up a sweat with lawyers and surfers alike at this huge disco. A blues room is open from 10 PM to 1:30 AM, and the DJ plays from 8 PM until 1:30 AM. *801 4th St., Gaslamp Quarter, tel. 619/233–1131. Open Sun.–Thurs. 11 AM–midnight, Fri. and Sat. until 2 AM. AE, D, MC, V.*

Olé Madrid. Slick back your hair and enjoy the loud, continuous beat at this Euro-style disco for the very chic. *755 5th Ave., Gaslamp*

Quarter, tel. 619/557–0146. Open Tues.–Sat. 5 PM–2 AM. Closed Sun. and Mon. AE, MC, V.

For Singles

Dick's Last Resort. On weekends, yuppies, students, and anyone else looking to meet the opposite sex line up to get into this enormous barnlike restaurant and bar. Dick's has live Dixieland music and one of the most extensive beer lists in San Diego. Don't be offended by the surly waitstaff—their "attitudes" are part of the gimmick. *345 4th Ave., downtown, tel. 619/231–9100. Open daily 11 AM–2 AM. AE, MC, V.*

El Torito. Notable happy hours and the central location attract yuppies and students to this Mission Valley Mexican restaurant. *445 Camino del Rio S, tel. 619/296–6154. Open daily 11 AM–2 AM. AE, D, DC, MC, V.*

The U. S. Grant Hotel. This place is the classiest spot in town for meeting fellow travelers while relaxing with a scotch or martini at the mahogany bar. The best local jazz, R&B, salsa, and boogie-woogie bands alternate appearances during the week. It's definitely for the over-30 business set. *326 Broadway, downtown, tel. 619/232–3121. Open daily 11:30 AM–1:30 AM. AE, D, DC, MC, V.*

Piano Bars/Mellow

Hotel del Coronado. The fairy-tale hostelry that has hosted royalty and former presidents features beautiful piano music in its Crown Room and Palm Court, with dance-oriented standards in the Ocean Terrace Lounge. *1500 Orange Ave., Coronado, tel. 619/435–6611. Open daily 10:30 AM–1:30 AM. AE, D, DC, MC, V.*

Top O' the Cove. Show tunes and standards from the '40s to the '80s are the typical piano fare at this magnificent Continental restaurant in La Jolla. *1216 Prospect St., tel. 619/454–7779. Entertainment Wed.–Sun. 8 PM–11 PM. AE, MC, V.*

Westgate Hotel. One of the most elegant settings in San Diego offers piano music in the Plaza Bar. *1055 2nd Ave., downtown, tel. 619/238–1818. Open daily 11 AM–2 AM. Entertainment 8:30 PM–closing. AE, D, DC, MC, V.*

12 Excursions from San Diego

*By Kevin
Brass*

*Revised
by Lori
Chamberlain,
Edie Jarolim,
and Kathryn
Shevelow*

San Diego County is larger than nearly a dozen U.S. states, with a population of more than 2 million—the second-largest county in California. It sprawls from the Pacific Ocean, through dense urban neighborhoods, to outlying suburban communities that seem to sprout overnight on canyons and cliffs. The Cleveland National Forest and Anza Borrego Desert mark the county's eastern boundaries, and the busiest international border in the United States—some 60 million people a year legally cross between Baja California and San Diego—its southern line. To the north, the marines at Camp Pendleton practice land, sea, and air maneuvers in southern California's largest coastal greenbelt, the demarcation zone between the congestion of Orange and Los Angeles counties and the mellower expansiveness of San Diego.

This chapter explores some of the day or longer trips you could schedule to areas outside the city of San Diego—to the North County, to inland and mountain communities, and to the desert.

The San Diego North Coast

To say the north coast area of San Diego County is different from the city of San Diego is a vast understatement. From the northern tip of La Jolla to Oceanside, a half-dozen small communities each developed separately from urban San Diego—and from one another. The rich and famous were drawn early on to Del Mar, for example, because of its wide beaches and thoroughbred horse-racing facility. Just a couple of miles away, agriculture, not paparazzi, played a major role in the development of Solana Beach and Encinitas. Up the coast, Carlsbad still reveals elements of roots directly tied to the old Mexican rancheros and the entrepreneurial instinct of John Frazier, who told people the area's water could cure common ailments. In the late 19th century, not far from the current site of the posh La Costa Hotel and Spa, Frazier attempted to turn the area into a massive replica of a German mineral springs resort.

Today, the north coast is a booming population center. An explosion of development throughout the 1980s turned the area into a northern extension of San Diego. The freeways started to take on the typically cluttered characteristics of most southern California freeways.

Beyond the freeways, though, the communities have maintained their charm. Some of the finest restaurants, beaches, and attractions in San Diego County can be found in the area, a true slice of southern California heritage. From the plush estates and rolling hills of Rancho Santa Fe and the beachfront restaurants of Cardiff to Mission San Luis Rey, a well-preserved remnant of California's first European settlers in Oceanside, the north coast is a distinctly different place.

Arriving and Departing

By Car   Interstate 5, the main freeway artery connecting San Diego to Los Angeles, follows the coastline. To the west, running parallel to it, is Old Highway 101, which never strays more than a quarter-mile from the ocean. Beginning north of La Jolla, where it is known as Torrey Pines Road, Old Highway 101 is a designated scenic route, providing access to the beauty of the coastline.

By Train   **Amtrak** (tel. 619/481–0114 in Del Mar, 619/722–4622 in Oceanside, or 800/872–7245) operates trains daily between Los Angeles, Orange County, and San Diego, with stops in Del Mar and Oceanside. The last train leaves San Diego at approximately 9 PM each night; the last arrival is at approximately midnight.

By Bus **The San Diego Transit District** covers the city of San Diego up to Del Mar, where the **North County Transit District** (tel. 619/722–6283) takes over, blanketing the area with efficient, on-time bus service.

Greyhound (tel. 619/722–1587 in Oceanside, or 800/231–2222) has regular routes connecting San Diego to points north, with stops in Del Mar, Solana Beach, Encinitas, and Oceanside.

By Taxi Several companies are based in North County, including **Amigo Cab** (tel. 619/436–8294) and **Bill's Cab Co.** (tel. 619/755–6737).

By Plane **Palomar Airport** (tel. 619/431–4646), located in Carlsbad 2 miles east of I–5 on 2198 Palomar Airport Road, is a general aviation airport run by the county of San Diego and open to the public. Commuter airlines sometimes have flights from Palomar to Orange County and Los Angeles.

Important Addresses and Numbers

Carlsbad Convention and Visitors Bureau (Box 1246, Carlsbad 92008, tel. 619/434–6093).
Del Mar Chamber of Commerce (1401 Camino del Mar, Suite 101, Del Mar 92014, tel. 619/793–5292).
Oceanside Chamber of Commerce (928 North Hill St., Oceanside 92051, tel. 619/722–1534).

Guided Tours

Civic Helicopters (2192 Palomar Airport Rd., tel. 619/438–8424) offers whirlybird tours of the area. The tours run about $70 per person per half-hour and go along the beaches to the Del Mar racetrack.

Exploring

Numbers in the margin correspond to points of interest on the San Diego North Coast map.

Any journey around the north coast area naturally starts at the beach, and this one begins at **Torrey Pines State Beach,** just south of Del Mar. At the south end of the wide beach, perched on top of
① the cliffs, is the **Torrey Pines State Reserve,** one of only two places (the other place is Santa Rosa Island off the coast of northern California) where the Torrey pine tree grows naturally (*see* Tour 7; La Jolla, in Chapter 3, Exploring San Diego, *for details*). *Tel. 619/755–2063. Admission: $4 per car. Open daily 9–sunset.*

② To the east of the state beach is **Los Penasquitos Lagoon,** one of the many natural estuaries that flow inland between Del Mar and Oceanside. Following Old Highway 101, the road leads into the small village of **Del Mar,** best known for its chic shopping strip, celebrity visitors, and wide beaches. Years of spats between developers and
③ residents have resulted in the **Del Mar Plaza,** hidden by boulder walls and clever landscaping at the corner of Old Highway 101 and 15th Street. The upper level has a large deck and a view out to the ocean, and the restaurants and shops are excellent barometers of the latest in southern California style. A left turn at 15th Street leads to Seagrove Park, a small stretch of grass overlooking the ocean, where concerts are performed on summer evenings. A right

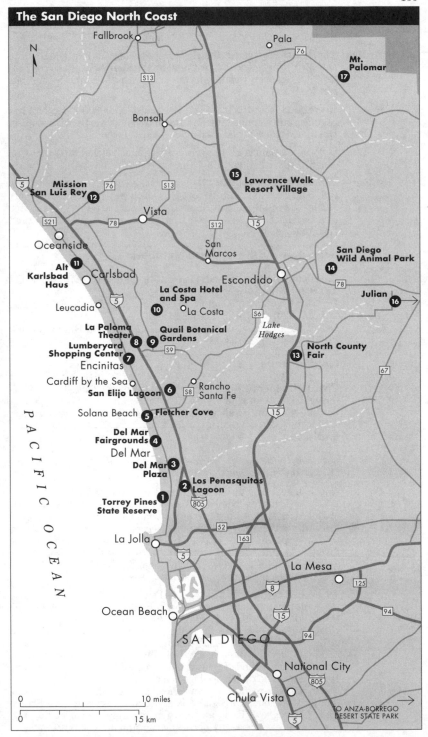

The San Diego North Coast

Fallbrook

Pala

76

Mt. Palomar
17

N

S13

Bonsall

15 Lawrence Welk
Resort Village

5

76

Mission
San Luis Rey
12

S21

Vista

78

S13

S12

15

Oceanside

San
Marcos

San Diego
Wild Animal Park
14

11
Alt
Karlsbad
Haus

Carlsbad

Escondido

78

Julian **16**

5

La Costa Hotel
and Spa

10 La Costa

Leucadia

S6

Lake
Hodges

67

La Paloma
Theater

Quail Botanical
Gardens

8 **9**

Lumberyard
Shopping Center **7**

Encinitas

S9

North County
Fair
13

Cardiff by the Sea

San Elijo Lagoon **6**

S8 Rancho
Santa Fe

Solana Beach **5** Fletcher Cove

15

Del Mar
Fairgrounds **4**

Del Mar

Del Mar **3**
Plaza

2 Los Penasquitos
Lagoon

Torrey Pines
State Reserve **1**

805

La Jolla

52

163

La Mesa

5

8

125

P A C I F I C   O C E A N

Ocean Beach

15

94

SAN DIEGO

94

National City

805

0   10 miles

0   15 km

Chula Vista

5

TO ANZA-BORREGO
DESERT STATE PARK

turn on Coast Boulevard provides access to Del Mar's beautiful beaches, particularly popular with Frisbee and volleyball players.

❹ Less than a half-mile north, Coast Boulevard merges with Old Highway 101. Across the road are the **Del Mar Fairgrounds,** home to more than 100 different events a year, ranging from a cat show to an auto race. *Via de la Valle Rd. exit west from I–5, tel. 619/259–1355 for recorded events line.*

The fairgrounds also host the annual summer meeting of the **Del Mar Thoroughbred Club** (aka "Where the Turf Meets the Surf"). The track brings the top horses and jockeys to Del Mar, along with a cross section of the rich and famous, eager to bet on the ponies. Crooner Bing Crosby and his Hollywood buddies, Pat O'Brien, Gary Cooper, and Oliver Hardy, among others, organized the track in the '30s, primarily because Crosby thought it would be fun to have a track near his Rancho Santa Fe home. Del Mar soon developed into a regular stop for the stars of stage and screen.

During the off-season, horse players can still gamble at the fairgrounds, thanks to a satellite wagering facility. Races from other California tracks are televised, and people can bet as if the races were being run right there. Times vary, depending on which tracks in the state are operating. *Tel. 619/755–1167. Racing season: July–Sept., Wed.–Mon. Post time 2 PM.*

Next to the fairgrounds, on Jimmy Durante Boulevard, is a small exotic bird-training facility, **Freeflight,** which is open to the public. Visitors are allowed to handle the birds—a guaranteed child pleaser. *2132 Jimmy Durante Blvd., tel. 619/481–3148. Admission: $1. Open daily 10–4.*

Following Via de la Valle Road east from I–5 will take you to the exclusive community of **Rancho Santa Fe,** one of the richest areas in the United States. Groves of huge, drooping eucalyptus trees, first imported to the area by a railroad company in search of trees to grow for railroad ties, cover the hills and valleys, hiding the posh estates. The little village of Rancho has some elegant and quaint— and overpriced—shops and restaurants. But it is no accident that there is little else to see or do in Rancho; the residents guard their privacy religiously. Even the challenging Rancho Santa Fe Golf Course, the original site of the Bing Crosby Pro-Am and considered one of the best courses in southern California, is still open only to members of the Rancho Santa Fe community.

Back along the coast, along Old Highway 101 north of Del Mar, is the quiet little oceanside community of **Solana Beach.** A highlight

❺ of Solana Beach is **Fletcher Cove,** located at the west end of Lomas Santa Fe Drive. Early Solana settlers used dynamite to blast the cove out of the overhanging cliffs. Called Pill Box by the locals because of a bunkerlike lifeguard station that overlooks it, the Fletcher Cove beach is easy to reach and features a large parking lot replete with a small basketball court, a favorite of local pickup game players.

❻ To the north, separating Solana Beach from Cardiff, is the **San Elijo Lagoon,** home to many migrating birds. Trails wind around the entire area.

As you continue along Old Highway 101, past the cluster of hillside homes that make up Cardiff and beyond the campgrounds of the San Elijo State Beach, the palm trees of Sea Cliff Roadside Park (Swami's to the locals) and the golden domes of the Self-Realization

Fellowship mark the entrance to downtown **Encinitas.** The Self-Realization Fellowship was built at the turn of the century and is a retreat and place of worship for the followers of a Native American religious sect. Its beautiful gardens are open to the public.

A recent landmark of Encinitas (which was incorporated as a city in 1986, including the communities of Cardiff, Leucadia, and Olivenhain) is the **Lumberyard Shopping Center**, a collection of small stores and restaurants that anchors the downtown shopping area. There is a huge selection of shopping centers inland at the intersection of Encinitas Boulevard and El Camino Real.

An older landmark of Encinitas is the **La Paloma Theater** (471 1st St., near the corner of Encinitas Blvd., tel. 619/436–7469), at the north end of town. Built in the 1920s as a stop for traveling vaudeville troupes, it has served as a concert hall, movie theater, and meeting place for the area ever since. Plays are still being rehearsed and performed here.

Encinitas is best known as the Flower Capital of the World, and although the flower industry is not as prevalent as it once was, the city is still home to Paul Ecke Poinsettias, the largest producer of the popular Christmas blossom. A sampling of the area's dedication to horticulture can be found at the **Quail Botanical Gardens,** home to thousands of different varieties of plants, especially drought-tolerant species. Horticultural lectures are given here, and there are often plant sales. *230 Quail Gardens Dr. (take Encinitas Blvd. east from I–5 and turn left on Quail Gardens Dr.), tel. 619/436–3036. Parking: $1. Open daily 8–5; closed first Mon. of every month.*

Old Highway 101 continues north through **Leucadia** (named after a famous Greek promontory), a small community best known for its small art galleries and stores. At the north end of Leucadia, La Costa Avenue meets Old Highway 101. Following La Costa Avenue east, past the Batiquitos Lagoon, you'll come to **La Costa Resort and Spa** (*see* Lodging, *below*), once famous for its high-profile guests and reputed mafia ties and now noted for its excellent golf and tennis facilities.

La Costa is technically part of the city of **Carlsbad,** which is centered farther north, west of the Tamarack Avenue and Elm Avenue exits of I–5. In Carlsbad, Old Highway 101 is called Carlsbad Boulevard. Large rancheros owned by wealthy Mexicans were the first settlements inland; the coastal area was developed by an entrepreneur, John Frazier, who lured people to the area with talk of the healing powers of mineral water bubbling from a coastal well. The water was found to have the same properties as water from the German mineral wells of Karlsbad—hence the name of the new community. Remnants from the era, including the original well, are found at the **Alt Karlsbad Haus,** a small museum–gift shop carrying northern European wares. *2802A Carlsbad Blvd., tel. 619/729–6912. Open Mon.–Sat. 10–5, Sun. noon–5.*

North of Carlsbad is **Oceanside,** home of Camp Pendleton, the country's largest marine base, as well as a beautiful natural harbor teeming with activity. **Oceanside Harbor** (tel. 619/966–4570) is the north-coast center for fishing, sailing, and all ocean-water sports. Salty fisherman types tend to congregate at Oceanside Pier.

Another highlight of a visit to Oceanside is **The California Surf Museum,** which charts the history of surfing from balsa-wood boards up through the present Fiberglas state-of-the-art. Exhibits change regularly. *308 N. Pacific St., tel. 619/721–6876. Admission free, dona-*

tions appreciated. Open Thurs.–Mon. noon–4, closed. Tues. and Wed., expanded hours in summer.

⑫ Oceanside is also home to **Mission San Luis Rey,** built by Franciscan friars in 1798 to help educate and convert local Native Americans. One of the best-preserved missions in the area, San Luis Rey was the 18th and largest of the California missions. Retreats are still held here, but a picnic area, gift shop, and museum are also on the grounds today. Self-guided tours are available. *4050 Mission Ave. (take Mission Ave. east from I–5), tel. 619/757–3651. Admission: $3 adults, $1 children. Open Mon.–Sat. 10–4:30, Sun. noon–4:30.*

Dining

Given the North Coast's reputation as a suburban area, there is a surprisingly large selection of top-quality restaurants here. In fact, San Diegans often take the drive north to enjoy the variety of cuisines offered in the North County. Prices are for one person and do not include drinks, taxes, or tip.

$30–$50
Del Mar

Tourlas. The restaurant at Del Mar's posh L'Auberge resort has undergone a sea change, with a new name and chef and a shift in cooking style from French to contemporary California. The menu is small but impressive: Such appetizers as corn meal–covered crab cakes might be followed by rack of lamb on couscous or halibut coated in pine nuts. The setting is lovely, and the service is attentive. *1540 Camino del Mar, tel. 619/259–1515. Reservations advised. Jacket advised. AE, D, DC, MC, V.*

Rancho Santa Fe
★

Mille Fleurs. This gem of a French auberge brightens a tiny village surrounded by country estates. Within a mile of Chino's, the county's most famous vegetable farm, where the chef shops daily, this is a most romantic hideaway, with tempting cuisine to enhance the mood. *6009 Paseo Delicias, tel. 619/756–3085. Reservations strongly advised. Jacket advised. AE, D, DC, MC, V No lunch weekends.*

Solana Beach

Frederick's. This husband-and-wife-owned, friendly, relaxed bistro serves traditional French dishes with California-fresh overtones. Leave room for the freshly baked bread and one of the lush desserts. The prix-fixe menu changes weekly. *128 S. Acacia St., tel. 619/755–2432. Reservations strongly advised. Dress: dressy casual. DC, MC, V. Dinner only, closed Sun. and Mon.*

$20–$30
Cardiff

The Chart House. The beach and the sunset above the Pacific are the chief attractions of this surfside dining spot. Entrées include fresh fish, seafood, and beef dishes; there's also a good salad bar. *2588 Rte. 101S, tel. 619/436–4044. Reservations advised. Dress: casual. AE, D, DC, MC, V. Dinner only; Sunday brunch.*

Del Mar

Cilantro's. For a taste of gourmet Mexican and southwestern-style food—creative dishes full of subtle spices—Cilantro's in Del Mar offers a wide variety of unusual creations, including shark fajitas and spit-roasted chicken with a mild chili sauce. The inexpensive tapas menu, with such delicacies as crab tostadas and three-cheese quesadillas, is a little easier on the wallet. *3702 Via de la Valle, tel. 619/259–8777. Reservations advised. Dress: casual. AE, MC, V.*

Epazote. The sister restaurant to Cilantro's, located in the Del Mar Plaza, Epazote serves a similar menu of Cal-Mex cuisine with a southwestern touch. The fresh fish specials, which change daily, are particularly recommended, as are the salads, the selection of imaginative tacos, and the killer margaritas. There's a great ocean view from the patio. *1555 Camino del Mar, tel. 619/259–9966. Reservations advised. Dress: casual to dressy casual. AE, MC, V.*

Il Fornaio. Located within the Del Mar Plaza, this talk-of-the-town ristorante features northern Italian cuisine, such as fresh seafood, homemade pastas, and crispy pizzas. The outdoor piazza affords a splendid ocean view. *1555 Camino del Mar, tel. 619/755–8876. Reservations advised. Dress: casual. AE, DC, MC, V.*

Pacifica Del Mar. Yet another fine Del Mar Plaza restaurant boasting a stunning view, Pacifica Del Mar is related to the downtown and Old Town Pacifica restaurants and, like them, emphasizes an imaginative California cuisine of fresh ingredients prepared with southwestern, Cajun, Italian, and Pacific Rim touches. Start with the scrumptious smoked corn, chicken, and black-bean chowder, and then go on to the grilled prawn salad, blackened catfish, or one of the free-range chicken dishes. Desserts are tasty, and the wine list is excellent. *1555 Camino del Mar, tel. 619/792–0476. Reservations advised. Dress: casual to dressy casual. AE, D, DC, MC, V.*

Under $20
Del Mar

Johnny Rockets. This '50s-style malt-and-burger joint, on the Del Mar Plaza's lower level, dishes up juicy burgers, thick malts, and fries to die for. Booth and counter seating come complete with nickel-a-tune jukeboxes. *1555 Camino del Mar, tel. 619/755–1954. Dress: casual. MC, V.*

Encinitas

Rico's Taco Shop. Short on frills but long on great food, this Mexican fast-food café is a local favorite. Come here for excellent chicken taquitos, carne asada burritos, and the best fish burritos and tacos in town. The owners are friendly and health conscious, too: No lard is used in the recipes. Rico's is open daily for breakfast, lunch, and dinner. *165-L S. El Camino Real, in the Target Shopping Center, tel. 619/944–7689. Dress: very casual. No credit cards.*

Vigilucci's. A welcome addition to the culinary revitalization of First Street in Encinitas, this Italian trattoria has a cozy, bistrolike atmosphere, knowledgeable Italian waiters, and a stylish menu. The pastas are particularly good: Try the *spaghetti al funghetto*, with a fresh mushroom sauce, or the *tagliatelle alla bolognese*, with ground duck, chicken, and veal in a tomato sauce. The locally made bread is excellent, but the wine list needs upgrading. *505 1st St. (Hwy. 101), tel. 619/942–7332. Reservations advised. Dress: casual. AE, D, DC, MC, V. No lunch weekends.*

Solana Beach

California Pizza Kitchen. Bright, noisy, and cheerful, this popular restaurant in Solana Beach's attractive new Boardwalk shopping center produces a selection of designer pizzas from its wood-fired oven, ranging from the conventional to the outlandish. If Caribbean-shrimp, tuna-melt, or moo-shu-chicken pizzas are too exotic for you, try the duck sausage (particularly recommended), the mixed grill vegetarian, or the five-cheese and tomato pizzas. Pastas are good, too, as are the enormous salads. Delivery is available. *437 S. Hwy. 101, tel. 619/793–0999. No reservations. Dress: casual. AE, D, DC, MC, V.*

Chung King Loh. One of the better Chinese restaurants along the coast, Chung King Loh offers an excellent variety of Mandarin and Szechuan dishes. Take-out and delivery services are available. *552 Stevens Ave., tel. 619/481–0184. Reservations advised. Dress: casual. AE, D, DC, MC, V. No lunch Sun.*

Fidel's. Rich in North County tradition, both Fidel's restaurants serve a wide variety of well-prepared Mexican dishes in a low-key, pleasant atmosphere. The original restaurant in Solana Beach, a two-story building with an outdoor patio area, is particularly nice and draws a lively crowd. *607 Valley Ave., tel. 619/755–5292; 3003*

Carlsbad Blvd., Carlsbad, tel. 619/729–0903. Reservations accepted for parties of 8 or more only. Dress: casual. MC, V.

Lodging

The prices below reflect the cost of a room for two people. Many hotels offer discount rates from October to May.

Over $160
Carlsbad

La Costa Hotel and Spa. Don't expect glitz and glamour at this famous resort; it's surprisingly low-key, with low-slung buildings and vaguely southwestern contemporary–style rooms decorated in neutral tones. The sports facilities, especially golf and tennis, are excellent, and La Costa includes such other amenities as supervised children's activities and a movie theater. A variety of nutrition and stress-reduction classes are available. *2100 Costa del Mar Rd., Carlsbad 92009, tel. 619/438–9111 or 800/854–5000, fax 619/438–9007. 480 rooms. Facilities: 5 restaurants, pool, exercise room, golf, 23 lighted tennis courts, beauty spa, massage, hair salon, theater, shops. AE, D, DC, MC, V.*

Del Mar

L'Auberge Del Mar Resort and Spa. Across the street from the Del Mar Plaza and one block from the ocean, L'Auberge is modeled on the Tudor-style Hotel Del Mar, playground for Hollywood's elite in the early 1900s and the original occupant of this site. The inn is filled with dark-wood antiques, fireplaces, and lavish floral arrangements. Spacious rooms and suites are tastefully if not memorably decorated, with beige dominating the color scheme. The grounds are attractively landscaped, with stone paths leading to gazebos and pools; the spa specializes in European herbal wraps and treatments. *1540 Camino del Mar, Del Mar 92014, tel. 619/259–1515 or 800/553–1336, fax 619/755–4940. 123 rooms. Facilities: restaurant, bar, café, 2 tennis courts, 2 pools, whirlpool, beauty spa, exercise machines, yoga, water aerobics. AE, D, DC, MC, V.*

Rancho Santa Fe

Rancho Valencia. The sister hotel to La Jolla's La Valencia, this resort is so luxurious that several high-style magazines have chosen it for fashion backdrops and have named it the most romantic hideaway in the United States. The suites are in red-tile-roofed casitas with fireplaces and private terraces. Tennis is the other draw here, with 18 courts and a resident pro; rates include unlimited use of the courts. *5921 Valencia Circle, 92067, tel. 619/756–1123 or 800/548–3664, fax 619/756–0165. 43 suites. Facilities: restaurant, 18 tennis courts, pool, 2 whirlpools, sauna, croquet. AE, DC, MC, V.*

$100–$160
Carlsbad

Carlsbad Inn Beach Resort. The palm trees seem a bit out of place on the manicured lawn of this sprawling European-style inn, with its gabled roofs and stone supports, but this is Carlsbad after all, where *alte* Germany meets southern California. The public areas and rooms are decorated in appealing Old World style; all the accommodations have VCRs, many offer kitchenettes, and some have fireplaces and private spas. *3075 Carlsbad Blvd., 92008, tel. 619/434–7020 or 800/235–3939, fax 619/729–4853. 60 rooms. Facilities: pool, health club, Jacuzzi, sauna. AE, D, DC, MC, V.*

$60–$100
Carlsbad

Best Western Beach View Lodge. Reservations are essential at this reasonably priced hotel near the beach. A Mediterranean-style low-rise building hosts a variety of attractively decorated rooms with light-wood or whitewashed furnishings; all have refrigerators, and kitchens, private balconies, and fireplaces are also available. Families tend to settle in for a week or more. *3180 Carlsbad Blvd., 92008, tel. 619/729–1151, 800/535–5588 or 800/BEACHVU in CA, fax 619/729–1151. 41 rooms. Facilities: whirlpool, sauna, pool, laundry* *facilities, in-room safes, complimentary Continental breakfast. AE, D, DC, MC, V.*

Del Mar **Stratford Inn.** The inn offers a pleasant atmosphere just outside the center of town and three blocks from the ocean. Rooms are large, with ample closet space and dressing areas; some have ocean views. Suites with kitchenettes are available. Continental breakfast is complimentary. *710 Camino del Mar, 92014, tel. 619/755–1501 or 800/446–7229, fax 619/755–4704. 98 rooms. Facilities: 2 pools, whirlpool, refrigerators in all rooms. AE, D, DC, MC, V.*

Encinitas **Moonlight Beach Hotel.** This folksy, laid-back motel is the closest to the beach at Encinitas. Rooms are basic but spacious and clean; all have kitchenettes. Weekly rates are available. *233 2nd St., 92024, tel. 619/753–0623 or 800/323–1259. 24 rooms. AE, MC, V.*

Radisson Inn Encinitas. This attractively designed low-rise blends nicely into an Encinitas hillside just east of Old Highway 101. Rooms have plush, richly colored rugs and comfy upholstered chairs; some have kitchenettes and/or ocean views. *85 Encinitas Blvd., 92024, tel. 619/942–7455 or 800/333–3333, fax 619/632–9481. 91 rooms. Facilities: pool, whirlpool, restaurant, lounge, complimentary Continental breakfast. AE, D, DC, MC, V.*

Under $60 **Budget Motels of America.** Shag carpeting and kitschy murals deco-
Encinitas rate the rooms at this motel, but the place is clean, low-priced, and convenient to the beach and the freeway. No-smoking rooms are available, and Continental breakfast is included in the room rate. *133 Encinitas Blvd., 92024, tel. 619/944–0260 or 800/795–6044, fax 619/944–2803. 124 rooms. AE, DC, MC, V.*

Leucadia **Pacific Surf.** This motel is clean, comfortable, and near all the shops and restaurants of Encinitas. All rooms have kitchens, and there are discounts for extended stays. *1076 Rte. 101N, 92024, tel. 619/436–8763 or 800/795–1466. 30 rooms. Facilities: laundry. AE, D, DC, MC, V.*

Oceanside **Oceanside TraveLodge.** It's near the beach and centrally located. *1401 N. Hill St., 92054, tel. 619/722–1244 or 800/255–3050, fax 619/722–3228. 28 rooms. Facilities: laundry. AE, D, DC, MC, V.*

Inland North County to Escondido and the Mountains

Even though the coast is only a short drive away, the beach communities seem far removed from the mountain village of Julian or the quiet lakes of Escondido. Inland is the old California, where working farms and ranches are more common than the posh restaurants that mark the coastal landscape. The oak- and pine-covered mountains attracted prospectors seeking their fortune in gold long before tourists headed to the beaches. Home to wineries, old missions, freshwater lakes, and innumerable three-generation California families, the inland area of North County is the quiet, rural sister to the rest of San Diego County; a visit to San Diego wouldn't be complete without at least a drive through this area.

Escondido (aka the Hidden Valley) is a thriving, rapidly expanding residential and commercial city of more than 80,000 people and the center of a wide variety of attractions and destination points. To the south, the three-story, enclosed North County Fair mall is something of a mecca for local shoppers, while animal lovers flock to the nearby Wild Animal Park, an extension of the San Diego Zoo, where animals roam free over the hills. To the north is an attraction of a completely different kind, Lawrence Welk Resort, a museum and resort complex that pay tribute to the late "Mr. Bubbles."

The mountains to the east of Escondido were once a remote outpost of the rugged West. Now they are a favorite spot for hikers, nature lovers, and apple-pie fanatics. Most of the latter head to Julian, an old mining town that is now famous for its annual apple festival. Nearby Cuyamaca Rancho State Park is full of excellent trails and well-preserved picnic and camping areas. To the north, perched in a park atop Mount Palomar, the Palomar Observatory is a haven for stargazers, and it has one of the most famous telescopes in the world.

Arriving and Departing

By Car Escondido sits at the intersection of Route 78, which heads west from Oceanside, and I–15, the inland freeway connecting San Diego to Riverside, 30 minutes to the north of Escondido. Del Dios Highway winds from Rancho Santa Fe through the hills past Lake Hodges to Escondido. Route 76, which connects with I–15 a few miles north of Escondido, veers east to Mount Palomar. Route 78 leads out of Escondido to Julian and Ramona. To reach the mountain areas from San Diego, take I–8 east to Route 79 north.

By Bus **The North County Transit District** (tel. 619/743–6283) has routes crisscrossing the Escondido area.

By Taxi **The Yellow Cab Company** (tel. 619/745–7421) has a base in Escondido.

Important Addresses and Numbers

San Diego North County Convention & Visitors Bureau (720 N. Broadway, Escondido 92025, tel. 619/745–4741).
Julian Chamber of Commerce (2129 Main St., Julian 92036, tel. 619/765–1857).

Exploring

Numbers in the margin correspond to points of interest on the San Diego North Coast map.

⓭ To shopping connoisseurs, **North County Fair** is a paradise, an 83-acre shopping complex with six major department stores and more than 175 specialty shops. *At the intersection of I–15 and Via Rancho Pkwy., tel. 619/489–2332.*

⓮ More than 2,500 animals roam the 1,800 acres of the **San Diego Wild Animal Park,** a zoo without cages. A 50-minute, 5-mile monorail trip is the best way to see the animals, but the park is also a pleasant area to walk around. There are daily bird and trained-animal shows (*see* Other Places of Interest in Chapter 3, Exploring San Diego, *for more details*). *Tel. 619/480–0100. Take I–15 north to Via Rancho Pkwy. and follow the signs. Admission: $17.45 adults, $15.70 senior citizens, $10.45 children 3–12. Admission includes all shows and the monorail tour. Gates open daily 9; call ahead for closing hours, which vary with the season. Parking: $3.*

About a mile east of the Wild Animal Park, on San Pasqual Valley Road, are a monument and museum commemorating the site of the **Battle of San Pasqual.** On December 6, 1846, a troop of Americans, including famous frontier scout Kit Carson, was defeated by a group of Californios (Spanish-Mexican residents of California). This was the Californios' most notable success during the war (21 Americans were killed), but the Americans, with support from Commodore Stockton in San Diego, did regain control of the region. *15808 San Pasqual Valley Rd., Escondido, tel. 619/220–5430. Admission free. Open Fri.–Sun. 10–5.*

Deer Park Vintage Cars and Wine (29013 Champagne Blvd., tel. 619/749–1666), also in Escondido, is a branch of the award-winning Napa Valley Deer Park Winery. Outside are a few select models from a collection of more than 50 vintage convertibles. There is also a delicatessen for impromptu picnics. Other popular local wineries include **Bernardo Winery** (13330 Paseo del Verano N, Rancho Bernardo, tel. 619/487–1866), **Menghini Winery** (1150 Julian Orchards Dr., Julian, tel. 619/765–2072), and **Ferrara Winery** (1120 W. 15th Ave., Escondido, tel. 619/745–7632).

⑮ Following I–15 north past central Escondido leads to the **Lawrence Welk Resort.** Complete with a dinner theater housing a museum of Welk memorabilia, the complex also includes a hotel and two golf courses. *8860 Lawrence Welk Dr., tel. 619/749–3000. Admission free. Museum open daily 10–5, except during dinner theater performances.*

⑯ For more organic pleasures, the small mountain village of **Julian** provides an enchanting glimpse at life in the mountains; to get there from Escondido, take Route 78 east. Gold was discovered in the area in 1869; quartz was unearthed a year later. More than $15 million worth of gold was taken from local mines in the 1870s. Today, this charming mountain town retains many historic false-front buildings from its mining days. When gold and quartz became scarce, the locals turned to growing apples and pears, now the lifeblood of the little town. The pears are harvested in September, the apples in October. The annual Julian Apple Days, first staged in 1909, begin mid-September.

Hour-long tours of an authentic Julian gold mine are offered by the **Eagle Mining Company.** There are also a small rock shop and gold-mining museum on the premises. *C St., 5 blocks east from the center of town, tel. 619/765–0036. Admission: $7 adults, $3 children under 16, $1 children under 5. Tours given daily 10–3, weather permitting.*

Just a few minutes to the south of Julian are the 26,000 scenic acres of **Cuyamaca Rancho State Park** (tel. 619/765–0755). The park's hills feature several varieties of oak and pine trees, small streams, and meadows and provide a quiet escape for nature lovers. Primitive campsites are available. Camping is also permitted in the **Cleveland National Forest** (tel. 619/673–6180) to the south of I–8.

⑰ There are no apples or gold mines on **Mount Palomar**—just one of the world's largest reflecting telescopes. Touring the observatory is a fascinating way to spend an afternoon. The park surrounding the observatory is full of lovely picnic areas and hiking trails. Also, don't forget to stop at Mother's Kitchen, the only restaurant on the mountain, which features some excellent vegetarian dishes. *Take Rte. 76 east from I–15, and follow the signs, tel. 619/742–2119. Admission free. Observatory for self-guided tours open daily 9–4. Closed Christmas and Christmas Eve.*

For those interested in the old missions that pepper the southern California landscape, **Mission San Antonio de Pala,** built in 1816, still serves the Native Americans of the Pala reservation. Displays in a small museum include artifacts from the original mission. *On Rte.*

76 on the way to Mount Palomar, tel. 619/742–3317. Admission: $2 adults, $1 children under 13. Museum and gift shop open Tues.–Sun. 10–3.

Dining

The price categories below are based on the cost of a complete dinner for one, not including beverages, tax, or tip.

$25–$40
Rancho
Bernardo
★

El Bizcocho. In the luxurious dining room of the Rancho Bernardo Inn, El Bizcocho has a well-deserved reputation throughout San Diego County for consistently superb cuisine, with high-quality ingredients and careful preparations. You won't go wrong with anything on the Continental menu, but the roast duck, fresh seafood dishes, and rack of lamb are particularly recommended. A pianist plays nightly. The restaurant also serves an excellent Sunday brunch. *17550 Bernardo Oaks Dr., tel. 619/487–1611. Reservations advised. Jacket required. AE, D, DC, MC, V.*

$15–$25
Escondido

150 Grand Cafe. This recent addition to the Escondido dining scene brings fine cuisine to a city in need of it. An ambitious menu of California-style dishes prepared with a European flair is served in a lovely, comfortable dining room. Try the filet mignon in port wine accompanied by a spinach salad. *150 W. Grand Ave., tel. 619/738–6868. Reservations advised. Dress: casual to dressy casual. AE, D, DC, MC, V. Closed Sun.*

Fallbrook

Le Bistro. Located in the quiet, rural community of Fallbrook, this well-respected restaurant has two dining rooms: The elegant one upstairs specializes in veal and shrimp dishes, and a more casual café downstairs offers patio as well as indoor dining. *119 N. Main St., tel. 619/723–3559. Reservations suggested. Dress: casual to dressy casual. AE, D, DC, MC, V. Upstairs: dinner only, closed Mon.; downstairs: closed Sun.*

San Marcos

Fish House Veracruz. All but the most inveterate fish-haters will be pleased with this very popular restaurant, offering a casual family atmosphere, simple and tasty preparations, and very fresh fish. (The diehards can always head for one of the 15 other restaurants in the shopping center where the Fish House is located). *Suite 124 Old California Row Shopping Center, 1020 San Marcos Blvd., tel. 619/744–8000. No reservations. Dress: casual. AE, D, MC, V. Closed Sun.*

Vista

La Paloma. A popular Mexican restaurant with ambitions, La Paloma was noted in *Gourmet* magazine for its lobster fajitas. The menu is extensive, including well-prepared versions of old favorites along with more unusual dishes such as paella and turkey carnitas. This place is well worth a trip to Vista. *116 Escondido Ave., tel. 619/758–7140. Reservations suggested. Dress: casual. AE, D, DC, MC, V.*

Under $15
Escondido

Hernandez' Hideaway. Isolated on a small road off Valley Parkway near lovely Lake Hodges, this is a popular hangout for local Mexican-food lovers. The ample weekend brunch is particularly popular. *19320 Rancho Lake Dr., tel. 619/746–1444. Reservations advised on weekends. Dress: casual. Full bar. AE, DC, MC, V. Closed Mon.; opens 3 PM weekdays.*

Rancho
Bernardo

Acapulco. Part of a high-quality Mexican restaurant chain with outlets throughout the inland area, these restaurants are large and friendly and serve good margaritas. *16785 Bernardo Center Dr., tel. 619/487–6701; 1020 W. San Marcos Blvd., San Marcos, tel. 619/471–*

2150; 1541 E. Valley Pkwy., Escondido, tel. 619/741–9922. Reserva-tions strongly suggested. Dress: casual. AE, MC, V.

Lodging

Over $185
Rancho
Bernardo

Rancho Bernardo Inn. You can be pampered and relaxed here while enjoying a game on the championship golf course or a sublime Sun-day brunch at El Bizcocho (*see* Dining, *above*). The country-style rooms have large floral bouquets, plush easy chairs, and tiled baths. The health club offers three types of intense massages, and a chil-dren's camp is available in August, on holiday weekends, and during school breaks. *17550 Bernardo Oaks Dr., 92128, tel. 619/487–1611 or 800/854–1065, fax 619/673–0311. 287 rooms. Facilities: 2 restaurants, 2 bars, 2 pools, 12 tennis courts, golf course, fitness center. AE, D, DC, MC, V.*

$109–$139
Rancho
Bernardo

Carmel Highland Doubletree Golf and Tennis Resort. Country living is emphasized at this pale-pink compound bordering a 6,500-acre golf course. The packages for golf, tennis, or fitness regimes are quite reasonable. This is a good spot for a totally relaxing weekend. *14455 Penasquitos Dr., 92129, tel. 619/672–9100 or 800/622–9223, fax 619/672–9166. 172 rooms. Facilities: 2 restaurants, deli, cocktail lounge, golf course, 6 tennis courts, 2 pools, health and fitness center. AE, D, DC, MC, V.*

$50–$125
Escondido

Lawrence Welk Resort. About 15 minutes north of Escondido, this pleasant inn is far from everything except the theater, museum, and golf courses of the complex saluting Welk. The rooms have a south-western flavor, with bleached woods and mauve and turquoise fur-nishings. *8860 Lawrence Welk Dr., 92026, tel. 619/749–3000 or 800/932–9355, fax 619/749–9537. 132 rooms. Facilities: restaurant, shopping, pool, spa, 2 golf courses, tennis, theater. AE, DC, MC, V.*

Fallbrook

Pala Mesa Resort Hotel. The main attraction at this verdant, 205-acre property is the excellent golf course. The large, comfortable rooms were renovated in 1993 in California ranch style, with light maple armoires and mauve marble baths. *2001 Old Hwy. 395, 92028, tel. 619/728–5881 or 800/722–4700, fax 619/723–8292. 133 rooms. Fa-cilities: restaurant, lounge-grill, snack bar, 4 tennis courts, golf course, pool, spa, fitness center. AE, DC, MC, V.*

Julian

Pine Hills Lodge. This secluded mountain lodge, which dates back to 1912, has an on-site dinner theater (Fridays and Saturdays year-round). The rooms are clean but decorated in what the owner dubs early Salvation Army style. Some cabins have fireplaces. *2960 La Posada, 92036, tel. 619/765–1100. 12 cabins with private bath, 6 lodge rooms with shared bath. AE, D, DC, MC, V.*

$72–$92
Julian

Julian Lodge. This bed-and-breakfast near the center of the town is a replica of a Julian hotel that was popular in the late 19th century. The rooms and public spaces are furnished with antiques; on chilly days, guests can warm themselves at the large stove in the lobby. Breakfast is buffet style. *Box 1930, 4th and C Sts., 92036, tel. 619/765–1420 or 800/542–1420. Facilities: upstairs porch. 23 rooms with pri-vate bath. AE, D, MC, V.*

The Desert

Every spring, the stark desert landscape east of the Cuyamaca Mountains explodes with color. It's the blooming of the wildflowers in the Anza-Borrego Desert State Park, less than a two-hour drive from central San Diego. The beauty of this annual spectacle, as well as the natural quiet and blazing climate, lures tourists and natives to the area.

The area features a desert and not much more, but it is one of the favorite parks of those Californians who travel widely in their state. People seeking bright lights and glitter should look elsewhere. The excitement in this area stems from watching a coyote scamper across a barren ridge or a brightly colored bird resting on a nearby cactus or from a waitress delivering another cocktail to a poolside chaise longue. For hundreds of years, the only humans to linger in the area were Native Americans from the San Dieguito, Kamia, and Cahuilla tribes, but the extreme temperature eventually forced the tribes to leave, too. It wasn't until 1774, when Mexican explorer Captain Juan Bautista de Anza first blazed a trail through the area as a shortcut from Sonora to San Francisco, that modern civilization had its first glimpse of the oddly beautiful wasteland.

Today, more than 600,000 acres of desert are included in the Anza-Borrego Desert State Park, making it the largest state park in the contiguous 48 states. It is also one of the few parks in the country where people can camp anywhere. No campsite is necessary; just follow the trails and pitch a tent wherever you like.

Five hundred miles of road traverse the park, and visitors are required to stay on them so as not to disturb the ecological balance of the park. However, 28,000 acres have been set aside in the eastern part of the desert near Ocotillo Wells for off-road enthusiasts. General George S. Patton conducted field training in the Ocotillo area to prepare for the World War II invasion of North Africa, and the area hasn't been the same since.

The little town of Borrego Springs acts as an oasis in this natural playground. Not exactly like Palm Springs—it lacks the wild crowds and preponderance of insanely wealthy residents—Borrego is basically a small retirement community, with the average age of residents about 50. For visitors who are uninterested in communing with the desert without a shower and pool nearby, Borrego provides several pleasant hotels and restaurants.

We recommend visiting this desert between October and May to avoid the extreme summer temperatures. Winter temperatures are comfortable, but nights (and sometimes days) are cold, so bring a warm jacket.

Arriving and Departing

By Car Take I–8 east to Route 79 north. Turn east on Route 78.

By Bus The **Northeast Rural Bus System** (NERBS, tel. 619/765–0145) connects Julian, Borrego Springs, Oak Grove, Ocotillo Wells, Agua Caliente, Ramona, and many of the other small communities with El Cajon, 15 miles east of downtown San Diego, and the East County line of the San Diego trolley, with stops at Grossmont shopping center and North County Fair. Service is by reservation, and buses do not run on Sundays or on some holidays.

Important Addresses and Numbers

For general information about the Borrego and desert areas, contact the **Borrego Springs Chamber of Commerce** (622 Palm Canyon Dr., Box 66, Borrego Springs 92004, tel. 619/767–5555). For details on the state park, phone or write the Visitor Center, **Anza-Borrego Desert State Park** (Box 299, Borrego Springs 92004, tel. 619/767–

5311). During the spring blooming season, a special **wildflower hot-line** (tel. 619/767–4684) gives 24-hour recorded information on what is flowering at the time of your call and what is expected to bloom shortly. For campsite reservations, call **MISTIX** (tel. 800/444–7275).

Exploring

The **Anza-Borrego Desert State Park** is too vast even to consider exploring in its entirety. Most people stay in the hills surrounding Borrego Springs. An excellent underground **Visitor Information Center** (tel. 619/767–5311) and museum are reachable by taking the Palm Canyon Drive spur west from the traffic circle in the center of town. The rangers are helpful and always willing to suggest areas for camping or hiking. A short slide show about the desert is shown throughout the day. For a listing of the interpretive programs scheduled for the year, pick up a copy of the free park newspaper.

One of the most popular camping and hiking areas is **Palm Canyon,** just a few minutes west of the Visitor Information Center. A 1½-mile trail leads to a small oasis with a waterfall and palm trees. If you find palm trees lining city streets in San Diego and Los Angeles amusing, seeing this grove of native palms around a pool in a narrow desert valley may give you a new vision of the dignity of this tree. The Borrego Palm Canyon campground (on the desert floor, a mile or so below the palm oasis) is one of only two developed campgrounds with flush toilets and showers in the park. (The other is Tamarisk Grove Campground at the intersection of Route 78 and Yaqui Pass Road.)

Other points of interest include **Split Mountain** (take Split Mountain Road south from Route 78 at Ocotillo Wells), a narrow gorge with 600-foot perpendicular walls. You can drive the mile from the end of the paved road to the gorge in a passenger car if you are careful (don't get stuck in the sand). Don't attempt the drive in bad weather, when the gorge can quickly fill with a torrent of water; even if the sky is clear when you arrive, check ahead at the visitor center to find out if current road condition allow for a safe trip.

On the way to Split Mountain (while you are still on the paved road), you'll pass a grove of the park's unusual **elephant trees** (10 feet tall, with swollen branches and small leaves). There is a self-guided nature trail; pick up a brochure at the parking lot.

You can get a good view of the Borrego Badlands from **Font's Point,** off Borrego–Salton Seaway (S22). The badlands are a maze of steep ravines that are almost devoid of vegetation and are best navigated by a four-wheel-drive vehicle.

In **Borrego Springs** itself, there is little to do besides lie or recreate in the sun. The challenging 18-hole Rams Hill Country Club course is open to the public (tel. 619/767–5000), as is the more modest course at the Borrego Roadrunner Club (tel. 619/767–5374). Borrego Resorts International Tennis (tel. 619/767–9748) has courts that are open to the public, as does La Casa del Zorro (tel. 619/767–5323). One of the best and most appreciated deals in town is the Borrego Springs High School pool (tel. 619/767–5337), at the intersection of Saddle and Cahuilla roads and open to the public during the summer.

Most people prefer to explore the desert in a motorized vehicle. While it is illegal to drive off the established trails in the state park, the **Ocotillo Wells State Vehicular Recreation Area** (tel. 619/767–5391), reached by following Route 78 east from Borrego, is a popular haven for off-road enthusiasts and those who drive vehicles that are not street legal. The sand dunes and rock formations are challenging as well as fun. Camping is permitted throughout the area, but water is not available. The only facilities are in the small town (really no more than a corner) of Ocotillo Wells.

To the east of Anza-Borrego is the Salton Sink, a basin that (although not as low as Death Valley) consists of more dry land below sea level than anywhere else in this hemisphere. The Salton Sea is the most recent of a series of lakes here, divided from the Gulf of California by the delta of the Colorado River. The current lake was created in 1905–7, when the Colorado flooded north through canals meant to irrigate the Imperial Valley. The water is extremely salty, even saltier than the Pacific Ocean, and it is primarily a draw for fishermen seeking corbina, croaker, and tilapia. Some boaters and swimmers also use the lake. The state runs a pleasant park, with sites for day camping, recreational vehicles, and primitive camping. *Take Rte. 78E to Rte. 111N, tel. 619/393–3059.*

Bird-watchers will love the **Salton Sea National Wildlife Refuge.** A hiking trail and observation tower make it easy to spot the dozens of varieties of migratory birds stopping at Salton Sea. *At the south end of Salton Sea, off Rte. 111, tel. 619/348–5278.*

Dining

Quality, not quantity, is the operable truism of dining in the Borrego area. Restaurants are scarce and hard to find, and many close on holidays during the summer, but the best are high quality. Prices are based on the cost of a complete meal for one, not including beverage, tax, or tip.

$10–$20   **Chinese Panda Restaurant.** The only business in a Quonset hut in Borrego Springs, this friendly Chinese restaurant serves tasty versions of Mandarin and Szechuan dishes. *818 Palm Canyon Dr., tel. 619/767–3182. Reservations accepted. Dress: casual. MC, V. Closed Mon. and Aug.*

Rams Hill Country Club. This top-notch Continental restaurant offers a copious Sunday brunch. *1881 Rams Hill Rd., tel. 619/767–5006. Reservations accepted. Dress: casual; jacket required on Sat. AE, MC, V. Closed for dinner Mon.–Wed., July–Oct. 1.*

Under $10   **Mi Tenampa Cafe.** It may seem odd to find good Mexican seafood in the desert, but no stranger, perhaps, than this low-key restaurant's location—just off Christmas Circle. *747 Palm Canyon Dr., no tel. No reservations. Dress: casual. No credit cards. Closed Mon. and Tues.*

Lodging

If camping isn't your thing, there are two very nice resorts near Borrego Springs that offer fine amenities minus the overdevelopment of Palm Springs. Prices are based on the cost of a room for two. In the summer months, rates drop by as much as 50%.

$145–$370   **Ram's Hill Country Club.** Those who want a vacation dedicated to golf can rent fully furnished one-, two-, or three-bedroom homes adjacent to a posh country club. A two-night minimum stay is required. *1881 Rams Hill Rd., Box 664, Borrego Springs 92004, tel. 619/767–5028 or 800/423–0947, fax 619/767–4418. 60 units. Facilities: restaurant, snack bar, golf course, 7 tennis courts, pool, Jacuzzi. AE, MC, V.*

$80–$495 **La Casa del Zorro.** This is a small, low-key resort complex in the heart of the desert. You need walk only a few hundred yards to be alone under the sky, and you may well see roadrunners crossing the highway. There are 17 different types of accommodations, set in comfortable one- to three-bedroom ranch-style houses complete with living rooms and kitchens; some three-bedroom suites have private pools, while other suites come with baby grand pianos. The elegant Continental restaurant puts on a good Sunday brunch. *3845 Yaqui Pass Rd., 92004, tel. 619/767–5323 or 800/824–1884, fax 619/767–5963. 77 suites, 94 rooms, 19 casitas. Facilities: restaurant, 6 lighted tennis courts, 3 pools, whirlpool, bicycles. AE, D, DC, MC, V.*

$75–$130 **Palm Canyon Resort.** This is one of the largest properties in the area, with a hotel, an RV park, a restaurant, and recreational facilities. *221 Palm Canyon Dr., 92004, tel. 619/767–5342 or 800/242–0044 in CA only, fax 619/767–4073. 44 rooms. Facilities: restaurant, RV spaces, 2 pools, 2 whirlpools, general store, laundromat. AE, D, DC, MC, V.*

13 Tijuana, Rosarito Beach, and Ensenada

By Maribeth Mellin

Since you've come as far as the southwesternmost city in the United States, take advantage of the opportunity and go *un poquito mas allá* (just a bit farther) and experience Mexico. Just 18 miles south of San Diego lies Baja California, a 1,000-mile-long stretch of beaches, desert, and hills that has long been a refuge for Californians with an urge to swim, surf, fish, and relax in a country unlike their own.

Tijuana, at the international border, is the most popular destination for day-trippers, who come for the souvenir shopping, sports events, and sophisticated Mexican dining. Laid-back Rosarito Beach, 18 miles south of Tijuana on the Pacific Coast, attracts travelers in search of a more mellow Mexico. Ensenada, a major port, combines many elements of Tijuana and Rosarito, but also retains its own character.

It is possible to visit Tijuana, Rosarito Beach, and Ensenada in a long, busy day. Begin by bypassing Tijuana and heading straight for the toll road to Rosarito Beach, about a 40-mile drive south. Once in Rosarito, stop at the gracious Rosarito Beach Hotel for breakfast, take a short walk on the beach in front of the hotel, and check out a few of the shops on Boulevard Juárez. Return to the toll road just south of the hotel and continue south for 45 miles to Ensenada. Take your time along this stretch of road, and exit at Salsipuedes and El Mirador to admire the view.

In Ensenada, park at the Plaza Marina on the waterfront and do your exploring on foot. Spend an hour or two wandering along Avenida López Mateos and its side streets, where you may find bargains on leather goods and jewelry in high-quality shops. Hussongs bar is an essential stop for rowdy types; culture-seekers should tour the Riviera del Pacifico, a former gambling palace built in the 1920s. Return to the waterfront for a quick run through the fish market and a snack of fish tacos, and try to be back on the road by early afternoon—and to save room for a lobster lunch at Puerto Nuevo, about 10 miles south of Rosarito.

If you finish lunch by mid-afternoon, you'll be able to reach Tijuana before nightfall. Once in the city, park in a lot by Calle 2A, the road that ties the highway to the border; walk up Calle 2A to Avenida Revolución, finish your souvenir shopping, and have dinner at a restaurant on the way back to your car. It's smart to wait until after 7 PM to cross the border, when rush-hour traffic has diminished.

A more leisurely tour would include an overnight stay in Rosarito Beach. By doing so, you can spend the morning in Tijuana seeing the sights and pricing possible purchases. Check into your hotel in Rosarito in the early afternoon, then visit the beach or the shops. Dine in Rosarito or Puerto Nuevo, get to bed early, and start off to Ensenada in the morning. Spend a half-day there, then head back to Tijuana, where you can pick up that last tacky souvenir from a salesman along the border traffic lines.

Essential Information

Official Requirements

Passports and Tourist Cards

U.S. citizens entering Mexico by road are required to have proof of citizenship: The only acceptable proof of citizenship is either a valid passport or an original birth certificate plus a photo ID. Tourist cards are not needed unless you are traveling south of Ensenada or

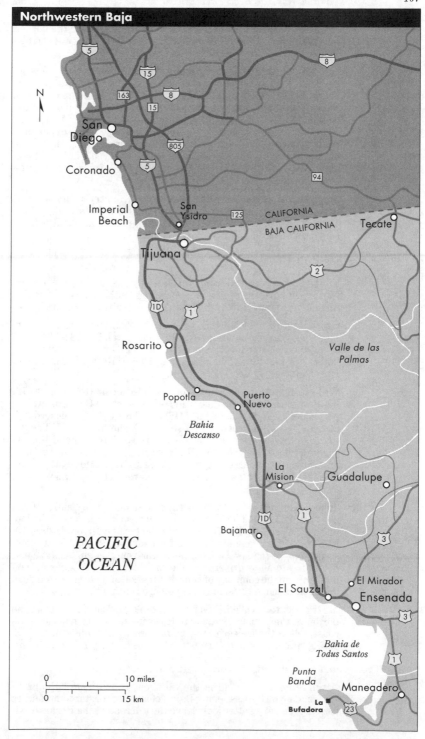

N

San Diego

Coronado

Imperial Beach

San Ysidro

Tijuana

Tecate

CALIFORNIA

BAJA CALIFORNIA

Rosarito

Valle de las Palmas

Popotla

Puerto Nuevo

Bahia Descanso

La Mision

Guadalupe

PACIFIC OCEAN

Bajamar

El Sauzal

El Mirador

Ensenada

Bahia de Todus Santos

Punta Banda

La Bufadora

Maneadero

0   10 miles

0   15 km

are planning to stay longer than 72 hours. Otherwise, tourist cards can be obtained from the information booth just inside the border. Passports are required of non-U.S. citizens for reentry at the San Ysidro or Otay Mesa border crossings.

Customs U.S. residents may bring home duty-free up to $400 worth of foreign goods, as long as they have been out of the country for at least 48 hours. Each member of the family is entitled to the same exemption, regardless of age, and exemptions may be pooled. Included in the allowances for travelers 21 or older are one liter of alcohol, 100 cigars (non-Cuban), and 200 cigarettes. Only one bottle of perfume trademarked in the United States may be imported. There is no duty on antiques or works of art more than 100 years old. Anything exceeding these limits will be taxed at the port of entry and may be taxed in the traveler's home state.

Since Mexico is considered a "developing" country, many arts and handicrafts may be brought back into the United States duty-free. You will need to declare the items and state their value and use, but they won't count against your $400 limit.

Getting There

Tijuana can be reached from San Diego by bus, trolley, or car; from there, you have the option of continuing south by bus or car. The 67-mile trek from Tijuana to Ensenada takes about 2½ hours by car.

By Bus **Greyhound** (tel. 619/239–9171 or 800/231–2222) serves Tijuana from San Diego several times a day. **Mexicoach** (tel. 619/232–5049) has several daily departures from the Santa Fe Depot to Tijuana. For listings of bus lines connecting San Diego, Rosarito Beach, and Ensenada, *see* Guided Tours, *below.*

Within Baja, **Autotransportes de Baja California** (tel. 66/85–8472) has first-class buses to Tijuana and other points in Baja. **Autotransportes del Pacífico** (tel. 66/86–9045) and **Tres Estrellas de Oro** (tel. 66/86–9186) offer second-class service throughout Baja. The Tijuana central bus station is at Calz. Lázaro Cárdenas and Bd. Arroyo Alamar (tel. 66/80-9060). In Rosarito Beach, the bus station is on Avenida Juárez across from the Rosarito Beach Hotel (no phone). Ensenada's bus station is at Avenida Riveroll between Calles 10 and 11 (tel. 617/8–6770).

By Car Take I–5 or Route 805 to the border crossing in San Ysidro. If you are visiting **Tijuana** for the day, consider parking in one of the lots on the U.S. side and walking across the border. If you do drive in, be sure to purchase Mexican auto insurance, available at many stands before the last U.S. exit. U.S. car-rental companies are just beginning to allow drivers to take their cars into Mexico, but you must inform the company of your destination and purchase Mexican auto insurance at the same time you are renting the car.

Mexico Route 1, called Ensenada Cuota (toll road), runs from the border at the Tijuana crossing to Rosarito and Ensenada along the coast; follow the ROSARITO, ENSENADA signs. Each toll is about U.S. $2.50, and there are three toll booths between Tijuana and Ensenada. The road is in good condition, but parts of it are often under construction, so drive with care.

Although the toll road is the quickest route from Tijuana to Ensenada, you bypass seeing Baja's charming coastal communities close up. To get a better look, leave the toll road at the Rosarito exit and travel Old Ensenada Highway (Ensenada Libre, the free road), a bit rough in spots but perfectly serviceable.

Beaches, restaurants, and other locations along the coast are often designated by the number of kilometers they are located from the beginning of the peninsular highway. A restaurant with an address of Km 55, therefore, would be 21 miles down the road; look for roadside markers to indicate these locations (to convert kilometers to miles, multiply by .621: km × .621 = mi).

Rosarito Beach is 18 miles south of Tijuana on the coast. You can tour Rosarito Beach proper on foot, which is a good idea on weekends, when Boulevard Juárez has bumper-to-bumper traffic. To reach Puerto Nuevo and other points south, continue on Boulevard Juárez, also called Ensenada Libre, through town and south.

Ensenada is an easy city to navigate; most streets are marked. If you want to get to the waterfront area, stay with alternate Route 1 as it travels along the fishing pier and becomes Boulevard Costero, also known as Lázaro Cardenas.

By Boat   **Starlite Cruises** (tel. 800/488–7827) offers one-day cruises from San Diego to Ensenada, with gambling on board. **Royal Caribbean** (tel. 800/772–7272) has four-day cruises from Los Angeles to Ensenada.

By Trolley   The bright red **San Diego Trolley** (tel. 619/233–3004) runs to the border and is the most convenient transportation for a day trip from San Diego to Tijuana. Trolleys depart from the station on Kettner Boulevard, across the street from the Santa Fe Depot in downtown San Diego, every 15 minutes during the day (every 30 minutes after 9 PM). The trip costs $1.75 and takes about 45 minutes. Once you reach the border, you must walk across a long freeway overpass to reach the pedestrian entrance into Mexico. There are taxis on the Mexican side of the border to take you to your destination.

By Taxi   Taxis (called *rutas*) will drive you from downtown Tijuana, at Calle Madero and Calle 3, to Rosarito. The drivers usually won't leave until they have four passengers. The fare should be under $10 per person. In Ensenada, the central taxi stand (*sitio*) is located on López Mateos by the Bahia Hotel (tel. 617/8–3475). Be sure to negotiate the price before the taxi starts moving. Destinations within the city should cost $10 or less.

Guided Tours

From the U.S.   **Baja California Tours** (6986 La Jolla Blvd. 204, La Jolla, CA 92037, tel. 619/454–7166) offers comfortable, informative bus trips throughout Baja and can arrange special-interest tours. Vans depart daily from San Diego to Ensenada; midweek transportation-and-hotel packages are a real bargain. The company also offers customized Tijuana tours, including visits to private homes and tours of art galleries and artists' studios.

Five Star Tours (1050 Kettner Blvd., San Diego, CA 92101, tel. 619/232–5049) provides transportation from the Amtrak station in downtown San Diego to the main drag in Tijuana. Buses leave both locations at intervals throughout the day, returning to San Diego as late as 9 PM on weekends.

Gray Line Tours (1775 Hancock St., San Diego, CA 92110, tel. 619/491–0011 or 800/331–5077) arranges shopping and sightseeing tours on air-conditioned buses. Combination tours of Ensenada and San Felipe, including transportation, hotel, dinner, and one night in both Ensenada and San Felipe, are available. Make reservations two weeks in advance.

San Diego Mini Tours (1726 Wilson Ave., National City, CA 91950, tel. 619/477–8687) has frequent departures throughout the day from San Diego hotels to Avenida Revolución in Tijuana and back and connections with a Mexican-operated trolley tour of Tijuana.

In Mexico   **Gordo's Sportsfishing** (Sportsfishing Pier, Ensenada, tel. 617/8–2190) operates whale-watching trips from December through February. The half-day trip, which goes to La Bufadora and Isla Todos Santos, costs $35 per person.

Servicios Turisticos (Av. Septiembre 213-B, tel. 66/86–1725; Viajes Harold, Av. Revolución 608, tel. 66/88–1111) offers assistance with tours of Tijuana and beyond.

In Ensenada, half-day bus tours of Ensenada and the surrounding countryside are available for $20 from **Viajes Guaycura** (López Mateos 1089, tel. 617/8–3718).

Important Addresses and Numbers

To call Baja Norte from the United States, dial 011–52, the area code, and the number. The area code for Tijuana has been changed from 668 to 66; the following number should have six digits. The area code for Rosarito Beach is 661, and for Ensenada, 617.

Getting information or arranging reservations is infinitely easier for most people in the United States than in Mexico. Whenever possible, make inquiries and/or reservations before you enter Mexico, through travel agents or other tourist information centers.

Tijuana/Baja Information (7860 Mission Center Court, No. 202, San Diego, CA 92108, tel. 619/299–8518 or 619/298–4105, 800/225–2786, or 800/522–1516 in CA) handles reservations and provides valuable information about the area.

Tijuana   A tourism office (tel. 66/83–1310), just past the border crossing, has maps, newspapers, and English-speaking clerks. Other tourist-information booths are located at the foot of Calle 1, just after the pedestrian overpass across the border; at the airport; and at the intersection of Avenida Revolución and Calle 4. **The Attorney General for the Protection of Tourists Hotline** (tel. 66/88–0555) helps with tourist complaints and problems on weekdays.
Chamber of Commerce. The English-speaking staff is very helpful, and maps and many brochures are available. *Av. Revolución and Calle Comercio (Calle 1A becomes Calle Comercio as you head east toward the river), tel. 66/85–8472. Open daily 9–7.*
Main telephone office. *Calle Pio Pico, between Calles 10 and 11.*
Main post office and telegraph office. *Corner of Av. Negrete and Calle 11, tel. 66/85–2682.*
U.S. Consulate. *Tapachula 96, Colonia Hipódromo, just behind the Tijuana Country Club, tel. 66/86–3886.*

Rosarito   There is a **tourist information** office just south of La Quinta (Bd. Juárez, tel. 661/2–0200).

Ensenada   **Convention and Visitors Bureau** (Av. López Mateos and Av. Espinoza, tel. 617/8–2411).
Police (Ortiz Rubio and Libertad, tel. 617/9–1751).
Hospital (Av. Ruíz and Calle 11, tel. 617/8–2525).
Post Office (Av. Juárez 1347).
Red Cross (tel. 617/8–1212).

State Tourism Office (Av. López Mateos 1305, tel. 617/6–2222).

Emergencies   A three-digit emergency dialing system is in effect throughout Baja Norte—for police, dial 134; Red Cross, 132; fire department, 135.

Tijuana

As Mexico's fourth-largest city, Tijuana can no longer be called a border "town." The border crossing at Tijuana is the busiest in the United States. Residents of San Diego and Tijuana go back and forth regularly to work, shop, dine, and visit family and friends. The dollar is as common as the peso, and Spanish and English blend into the border language of Spanglish, easing communication.

Before the turn of the century, when Tijuana became a recreational center for southern Californians, it was a ranch populated by a few hundred Mexicans. In the 1920s, Prohibition caused the city to boom: Americans seeking alcohol, gambling, and more fun than they could find back home flocked across the border, spending freely. Tijuana became the entry port for what some termed a "sinful, steamy playground," frequented by Hollywood stars and the idle rich.

When Prohibition was repealed, the flow of travelers from the north slowed to a trickle for a while, but Tijuana still captivated those in search of the sort of fun that was illegal or just frowned upon at home. The ever-growing number of servicemen in San Diego kept Tijuana's sordid reputation alive. Before the toll highway to Ensenada was finished in 1967, travelers going south drove straight through downtown Tijuana, stopping along Avenida Revolución and its side streets for supplies and souvenirs.

In the 1970s and '80s, Avenida Revolución, once lined with brothels and bars, underwent tremendous rehabilitation. Today the avenue is lined with shops and restaurants, all catering to tourists. Park benches and shade trees on brick paths winding away from the traffic encourage visitors to linger and watch the scenery.

The city's population has mushroomed—from 300,000 in 1970 to nearly 2 million today. Tijuana's instant neighborhoods of migrants and immigrants from throughout Latin America spread into canyons and dry riverbeds, over hillsides, and onto ocean cliffs. The city's infrastructure is incapable of keeping up with the surges in population: During the torrential rains in the winter of 1993, for example, floods and mud slides devastated entire sections of Tijuana and northern Baja, leaving thousands homeless. But the tourism sectors remained relatively intact even during the deluge, and visitors continued to shop for sombreros and serapes in the rain.

Tijuana's tourist attractions have remained much the same throughout the century. Betting on greyhounds is legal and popular at the Agua Caliente Racetrack, and the impressive El Palacio Frontón (Jai Alai Palace), where betting is also allowed, draws crowds of cheering fans to its fast-paced matches. Some of Mexico's greatest bullfighters appear at the oceanfront and downtown bullrings; some of Latin America's most popular musicians and dancers perform at the Cultural Center; and there are an extraordinary number of places in town that provide good food and drinks.

Shopping is one of Tijuana's other main draws. From the moment you cross the border, people will approach you or call out and insist that you look at their wares. If you drive, workers will run out from

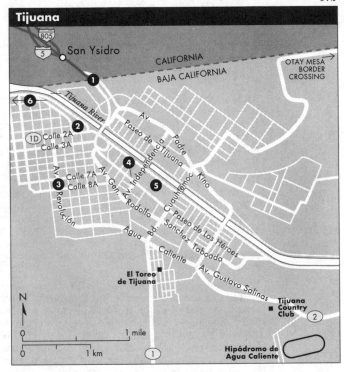

auto-body shops to place bids on new paint or upholstery for your car. All along Avenida Revolución and its side streets, shops sell everything from tequila to Tiffany lamps; serious shoppers can spend a full day searching and bargaining for their items of choice. If you intend to buy food in Mexico, get the U.S. customs list of articles that are illegal to bring back, so your purchases won't be confiscated.

Exploring Tijuana

Numbers in the margin correspond to points of interest on the Tijuana map.

❶ At the **San Ysidro Border Crossing,** a pedestrian walkway travels through the Viva Tijuana dining and shopping center and an adjacent lineup of stalls filled with the full spectrum of souvenirs, and **❷** then goes up Calle 2 into the center of town. **Mexitlan,** a museum-entertainment-shopping center, has scale models of the major archaeological and cultural landmarks throughout Mexico, restaurants and shops featuring authentic cuisine and folk art, and frequent performances by folkloric dancers and musical groups. *Av. Ocampo between Calles 2 and 3, tel. 66/38–4101 or 619/685–3628 in San Diego. Admission: $3.25 adults. Open Tues.–Fri. 10–6, weekends noon–8 (extended hours in summer).*

Calle 2 intersects **Avenida Revolución,** lined with designer-clothing shops and restaurants, all catering to tourists. Many shopping arcades open onto Avenida Revolución; inside the front doors are mazes of small stands with low-priced pottery and other handicrafts.

❸ **El Palacio Frontón (Jai Alai Palace)** is on Avenida Revolución between Calles 7a and 8a. The magnificient Moorish-style palace is an exciting place for watching and betting on fast-paced jai alai games (*see* Spectator Sports, *below*).

Time Out Among the many restaurants along Avenida Revolución, **La Especial** (Av. Revolución 718, tel. 66/85–6654) is a favorite for Mexican food that hasn't been fancied up for the tourists.

Between Boulevard Agua Caliente and the border is the **Río Tijuana** area, which runs parallel to the river. With its impressive Cultural Center and shopping complex, this section of town, along Avenida Paseo de los Héroes, is fast becoming Tijuana's Zona Rosa.

❹ The **Cultural Center,** designed by the same architects who created Mexico City's famous Museum of Anthropology, introduces thousands of visitors to Mexican history. The Omnimax Theater features a cinematic tour of Mexico (which has become somewhat outdated); a bookstore has an excellent selection on Mexican history, culture, and arts in Spanish and English. Guest artists appear at the center regularly. The restaurant is a good place to relax and absorb all you've seen. It's about a 20-minute walk from Avenida Revolución to the Cultural Center, and you must cross some very busy thoroughfares: You're best off taking a taxi. *Paseo de los Héroes and Av. Independencia, tel. 66/84–1111. Admission to the museum: $1.60; museum and Omnimax Theater: $5.50 for English-language shows, $2.30 for Spanish. Open daily 11–7; the English-language version of the film* El Pueblo del Sol *is presented daily at 2 PM.*

❺ Long, wide sidewalks lead from the Cultural Center to **Plaza Río Tijuana,** on Paseo de los Héroes, landscaped with shade trees and flowers. The enormous shopping complex houses good restaurants, department stores, and hundreds of shops. The plaza has become a central square of sorts, where holiday fiestas are held. Smaller shopping centers are opening all along the Paseo de los Héroes; Plaza Fiesta and Plaza de Zapatos are two of the finest.

❻ The **Playas Tijuana** area, at the oceanfront, is slated next for development. For now, the area is a mix of modest and expensive residential neighborhoods, with a few restaurants and hotels. The long, isolated beaches are visited mostly by locals.

Shopping

The traditional shopping strip is Avenida Revolución, between Calles 1 and 8, lined with shops and arcades that display a wide range of crafts and curios. Bargaining is expected on the streets and in the arcades, but not in the finer shops. **Sanborn's** carries beautiful crafts from throughout Mexico, excellent baked goods, and chocolates from Mexico City. The **Drug Store, Maxim's, Dorian's,** and **Sara's** have good selections of clothing and imported perfumes. **Tolan,** across from the Jai Alai Palace at Avenida Revolución, has an impressive variety of high-quality crafts. **Benetton, Guess, Eduardo's,** and **Ralph Lauren Polo** carry sportswear and resortwear. **La Gran Bota** has great cowboy boots; **Espinosa,** with branches on Avenida Revolución and in the Cultural Center, purveys fine silver, brass, and gold jewelry.

The Avenida Revolución shopping area spreads down Calle 1 to the pedestrian walkway leading from the border. The shops in **Plaza Revolución,** at the corner of Calle 1 and Avenida Revolución, stock good-quality crafts. Begin shopping at the stands along the border-crossing walkway, comparing prices as you travel toward Avenida Revolución. You may find that the best bargains are closer to the border, and you can pick up your piñatas and serapes on your way out of town.

Plaza Río Tijuana is described in Exploring Tijuana, above, as is **Mexitlán** on Avenida Ocampo, which stocks folk art from throughout Mexico. **Pueblo Amigo** on Boulevard Paseo de los Héroes is a fanciful pseudocolonial marketplace with boutiques. **Plaza Fiesta,** on Paseo de los Héroes across from Plaza Río Tijuana, has a collection of boutiques, jewelry stores, and stained-glass shops. Next door, the **Plaza de los Zapatos** sells designer shoes imported from throughout the world.

Spectator Sports

Bullfights Bullfights, considered artistic spectacles, not sporting events, feature skilled matadors from throughout Mexico and Spain. They are held at **El Toreo de Tijuana** (Av. Agua Caliente, just outside downtown, tel. 66/85–2210 or 619/232–5049 in San Diego) on Sundays at 4, May–September. In July and August, you can also see fights at the **Plaza de Toros Monumental** (Playas Tijuana area, Ensenada Hwy., tel. 66/85–2210 or 619/232–5049 in San Diego) on Sundays at 4.

Greyhound Races At the **Hipódromo de Agua Caliente,** still reminiscent of the glamorous years when Hollywood stars gambled here, horse racing was phased out in 1993, but greyhounds race nightly (except Tuesday) at 7:45 and afternoons at 2:30 on Mondays, Wednesdays, and Fridays. In the Foreign Book area, gamblers can bet on races taking place in California and shown at Caliente on TV monitors. *Bd. Agua Caliente at Salinas, tel. 66/81–7811 or 619/231–1919 in San Diego.*

Jai Alai An ancient Basque sport, fast-paced jai alai is in some ways similar to handball but uses a long, curved basket strapped to the competitor's wrists. The Moorish-style **Palacio Frontón** is a good place to be introduced to this exciting game. *Av. Revolución and Calle 8, tel. 66/88–0125 or 619/231–1919 in San Diego. Admission: $3–$5. Closed Wed.*

Dining

There is no shortage of good eating in Tijuana, from *taquerías* (taco stands) to gourmet and Continental restaurants; Avenida Revolución resembles one long food court with places for every taste and budget. Street nightlife often becomes rowdy, with tourists demonstrating the effects of potent Mexican margaritas. Seafood is abundant; beef and pork are common, both grilled and marinated as *carne asada* and *carnitas* (marinated pork). Dress is casual, although T-shirts and shorts are frowned upon in the evening, and reservations are not required unless otherwise noted. Some restaurants add a 15% service charge to the bill. Highly recommended restaurants are indicated by a star ★.

Category	Cost*
$$$$	over $20
$$$	$15–$20
$$	$8–$15
$	under $8

*per person for a three-course meal, excluding drinks and service

$$$$ **La Casa de Alfonso.** Since it opened in the spring of 1993, this Basque-Spanish restaurant has drawn rave reviews from both sides of the border. Owner Alfonso Casas Quintas spent two years transforming a private home into a series of gorgeous dining rooms, and the yard into a romantic patio. The Spanish chef excels with his paella Valenciana, roasted baby goat, and salmon with seafood sauce. Spanish and Mexican wines are available, and the patries are not to be missed. *Esteban Cantú 2007 in the Zona Río, tel. 66/81–8955. Reservations suggested. Jacket suggested. Closed Sun. MC, V.*

$$$ **El Taurino.** Walk a few blocks west of Avenida Revolución and you're
★   in the true downtown Tijuana, where residents work, shop, and eat. One of their favorite spots is this cozy steakhouse. Request a menu in English and zero in on the beef selections, especially the New York steak, called *cabreria.* Shrimp and lobster are also good choices, and all come with soup or salad. *Calle 6 #7531, tel. 66/85–7075. MC, V.*

★   **Pedrín's.** One of Tijuana's best seafood restaurants overlooks the Jai Alai Palace from a second-story garden room. Entrées come with deep-fried fish appetizers, fish chowder, salad, and a sweet after-dinner drink. Recommended are *rajas shrimp,* with melted cheese and green chilies, and grilled lobster. *Av. Revolución 1115, tel. 66/85–4052. AE, MC, V.*

$$ **La Fonda Roberto's.** By far the best restaurant in Tijuana for tradi-
★   tional cuisine from the many culinary regions of Mexico. Try the meats with spicy achiote sauce and many varieties of mole. Portions are small, so order liberally and share. *Old Ensenada Hwy. (also called Calle 16 de Septiembre), near Bd. Agua Caliente in the Siesta Motel, tel. 66/86–1601. MC, V.*

★   **La Leña.** The sparkling clean, white dining room in La Leña faces an open kitchen where chefs grill unusual beef dishes, like *gaonera,* a tender fillet stuffed with cheese and guacamole, while women prepare fresh tortillas. *Bd. Agua Caliente 4560, tel. 66/86–2920; Av. Revolución between Calles 4 and 5. AE, MC, V.*

La Taberna Española. The mainstay of Plaza Fiesta's multiethnic cafes, this Spanish tapas bar attracts a youthful, sophisticated crowd. A sampling of *tapas* (appetizers) might include octopus in its own ink, a plate of spicy sausages, a wedge of Spanish tortilla with potatoes and eggs, and fava beans. Sit at the outdoor tables for a better view of the crowd waiting in line. *Plaza Fiesta, Paseo de los Héroes 10001, tel. 66/84–7562. No credit cards.*

Tía Juana Tilly's. Popular with both tourists and locals looking for revelry and generous portions of Mexican specialties, this is one of the few places where you can get *cochinita píbil,* a Yucatecán specialty made of roast pig, red onions, and bitter oranges. Part of the same chain is Tilly's Fifth Ave., catercorner to the original on Avenida Revolución. *Av. Revolución at Calle 7, tel. 66/85–6024. AE, DC, MC, V.*

$ **Carnitas Uruapan.** At this large, noisy restaurant, patrons mingle at long tables, toasting one another with chilled *cervezas* (beer). The main attraction is carnitas, sold by weight and served with home-made tortillas, salsa, cilantro, guacamole, and onions. *Bd. Díaz Ordaz 550, tel. 66/81–6181; Paseo de los Héroes at Av. Rodriguez, no tel. No credit cards.*

Lodging

Tijuana's hotels are clustered downtown, along Avenida Revolución; near the country club on Boulevard Agua Caliente; and in the Río Tijuana area on Paseo de los Héroes. There are ample accommodations for all price levels, and a number of new hotels are under construction. **Baja Information** (7860 Mission Center Court, Suite 202, San Diego, CA 92108, tel. 619/298–4105 or 619/299–8518; 800/225–2786 in the U.S.; 800/522–1516 in CA, AZ, and NV; fax 619/294–7366) can reserve hotel rooms. **Baja Lodging Services** (4659 Park Blvd., San Diego, CA 92116, tel. 619/491–0682) makes hotel, condo, and private-home reservations throughout Baja. Highly recommended lodgings are indicated by a star ★.

Category	Cost*
$$$$	over $90
$$$	$60–$90
$$	$25–$60
$	under $25

*All prices are for a standard double room, excluding service charge and sales tax (10%).

$$$$ **Gran Hotel.** The two mirrored towers of the hotel, which often hosts
★ parties for Tijuana's elite, are the city's most ostentatious landmarks. The rooms on the club floors are particularly extravagant, with separate seating areas, king-size beds, and astounding views of Tijuana's sprawl. *Bd. Agua Caliente 4558, 22450, tel. 66/81–7000, 619/284–7593 in CA or 800/546–4030, fax 66/81–7016. 422 rooms with bath. Facilities: restaurant, nightclub, health club, tennis courts, pool, travel agency. MC, V.*

$$ **Corona Plaza.** The interior of this building, which looks like a non-descript office tower, is surprisingly pleasant. Rooms, furnished in handsome bleached wood, overlook an atrium lobby and restaurant. For less noise and more air, ask for a second- or third-floor room near the pool. The bullring is within walking distance; other attractions are just a short taxi ride away. *Bd. Agua Caliente 1426, 22450, tel. 66/81–8183, fax 66/81–8185. Facilities: restaurant, pool. AE, MC, V.*

La Villa de Zaragoza. La Villa is a well-maintained, brown stucco motel with a good location—near the Jai Alai Palace and one block from Avenida Revolución. It has the nicest rooms downtown in this price range. *Av. Madero 1120, 22000, tel. 66/85–1832. 42 rooms. Facilities: restaurant, parking. MC, V.*

The Arts and Nightlife

Tijuana has toned down its Sin City image; much of the action now takes place at the **Jai Alai Palace** and the racetrack. Several hotels, especially the **Lucerna** and **Gran Hotel,** feature live entertainment.

rooms. The less extravagant rooms are comfortable and decorated with folk art. A waterfall cascades into the pool, and a good restaurant overlooks the gardens. *Av. López Mateos and Av. Guadalupe, tel. 617/6–4070, fax 617/6–4939; reservations in the U.S.: Box 4C, San Ysidro, CA 92073. 150 rooms and suites. Facilities: restaurant, cocktail lounge, 2 pools, hot tub, disco, convention facilities, shops, cable TV. AE, MC, V.*

$ **Joker Hotel.** A bizarre, brightly colored mishmash of styles makes it hard to miss this hotel, conveniently located for those traveling south of Ensenada. Spacious rooms have private balconies, satellite TV, and phones. *3 mi south of Ensenada on Rte. 1, 22880, tel. and fax 617/6–7201; reservations in the U.S.: 3085 Beyer Blvd., A-105, San Diego, CA 92154. 20 rooms. Facilities: pool, whirlpool. MC, V.*

Nightlife

Ensenada is a party town for college students, surfers, and other young tourists. **Hussong's** and **Papa's and Beer** on Avenida Ruíz are rowdy at night. Most of the expensive hotels have bars and discos that are less frenetic.

La Taberna Española (Bd. Costero 1982) is a great place to gather for a night-long feast of tapas and sangria and a flamenco show. **Smitty González,** on Avenida Ryerson, attracts devoted disco dancers. **Joy's Discotheque,** at Avenidas López Mateos and Balboa, is popular with the locals.

Index

Personal Itinerary

Departure *Date*

Time

Transportation

Arrival *Date*   *Time*

Departure *Date*   *Time*

Transportation

Accommodations

Arrival *Date*   *Time*

Departure *Date*   *Time*

Transportation

Accommodations

Arrival *Date*   *Time*

Departure *Date*   *Time*

Transportation

Accommodations

Personal Itinerary

Arrival *Date*   *Time*

Departure *Date*   *Time*

Transportation

Accommodations

Arrival *Date*   *Time*

Departure *Date*   *Time*

Transportation

Accommodations

Arrival *Date*   *Time*

Departure *Date*   *Time*

Transportation

Accommodations

Arrival *Date*   *Time*

Departure *Date*   *Time*

Transportation

Accommodations

Personal Itinerary

Arrival	*Date*	*Time*
Departure	*Date*	*Time*
Transportation		

Accommodations

Arrival	*Date*	*Time*
Departure	*Date*	*Time*
Transportation		

Accommodations

Arrival	*Date*	*Time*
Departure	*Date*	*Time*
Transportation		

Accommodations

Arrival	*Date*	*Time*
Departure	*Date*	*Time*
Transportation		

Accommodations

Addresses

Name

Address

Telephone

Name

Address

Telephone

Name

Address

Telephone

Name

Address

Telephone

Name

Address

Telephone

Name

Address

Telephone

Name

Address

Telephone

Name

Address

Telephone

Name

Address

Telephone

Name

Address

Telephone

Name

Address

Telephone

Name

Address

Telephone

Name

Address

Telephone

Name

Address

Telephone

Name

Address

Telephone

Name

Address

Telephone

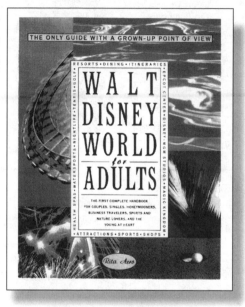

Fodor's Travel Guides

Available at bookstores everywhere, or call 1–800–533–6478, 24 hours a day.

U.S. Guides

Alaska

Arizona

Boston

California

Cape Cod, Martha's Vineyard, Nantucket

The Carolinas & the Georgia Coast

Chicago

Colorado

Florida

Hawaii

Las Vegas, Reno, Tahoe

Los Angeles

Maine, Vermont, New Hampshire

Maui

Miami & the Keys

New England

New Orleans

New York City

Pacific North Coast

Philadelphia & the Pennsylvania Dutch Country

The Rockies

San Diego

San Francisco

Santa Fe, Taos, Albuquerque

Seattle & Vancouver

The South

The U.S. & British Virgin Islands

USA

The Upper Great Lakes Region

Virginia & Maryland

Waikiki

Walt Disney World and the Orlando Area

Washington, D.C.

Foreign Guides

Acapulco, Ixtapa, Zihuatanejo

Australia & New Zealand

Austria

The Bahamas

Baja & Mexico's Pacific Coast Resorts

Barbados

Berlin

Bermuda

Brittany & Normandy

Budapest

Canada

Cancún, Cozumel, Yucatán Peninsula

Caribbean

China

Costa Rica, Belize, Guatemala

The Czech Republic & Slovakia

Eastern Europe

Egypt

Euro Disney

Europe

Florence, Tuscany & Umbria

France

Germany

Great Britain

Greece

Hong Kong

India

Ireland

Israel

Italy

Japan

Kenya & Tanzania

Korea

London

Madrid & Barcelona

Mexico

Montréal & Québec City

Morocco

Moscow & St. Petersburg

The Netherlands, Belgium & Luxembourg

New Zealand

Norway

Nova Scotia, Prince Edward Island & New Brunswick

Paris

Portugal

Provence & the Riviera

Rome

Russia & the Baltic Countries

Scandinavia

Scotland

Singapore

South America

Southeast Asia

Spain

Sweden

Switzerland

Thailand

Tokyo

Toronto

Turkey

Vienna & the Danube Valley

Special Series

Fodor's Affordables

Caribbean

Europe

Florida

France

Germany

Great Britain

Italy

London

Paris

**Fodor's Bed &
Breakfast and
Country Inns Guides**

America's Best B&Bs

California

Canada's Great
Country Inns

Cottages, B&Bs and
Country Inns of
England and Wales

Mid-Atlantic Region

New England

The Pacific
Northwest

The South

The Southwest

The Upper Great
Lakes Region

The Berkeley Guides

California

Central America

Eastern Europe

Europe

France

Germany & Austria

Great Britain &
Ireland

Italy

London

Mexico

Pacific Northwest &
Alaska

Paris

San Francisco

**Fodor's Exploring
Guides**

Australia

Boston &
New England

Britain

California

The Caribbean

Florence & Tuscany

Florida

France

Germany

Ireland

Italy

London

Mexico

New York City

Paris

Prague

Rome

Scotland

Singapore & Malaysia

Spain

Thailand

Turkey

Fodor's Flashmaps

Boston

New York

Washington, D.C.

Fodor's Pocket Guides

Acapulco

Bahamas

Barbados

Jamaica

London

New York City

Paris

Puerto Rico

San Francisco

Washington, D.C.

Fodor's Sports

Cycling

Golf Digest's Best
Places to Play

Hiking

The Insider's Guide
to the Best Canadian
Skiing

Running

Sailing

Skiing in the USA &
Canada

USA Today's Complete
Four Sports Stadium
Guide

**Fodor's Three-In-Ones
(guidebook, language
cassette, and phrase
book)**

France

Germany

Italy

Mexico

Spain

**Fodor's
Special-Interest
Guides**

Complete Guide to
America's National
Parks

Condé Nast Traveler
Caribbean Resort and
Cruise Ship Finder

Cruises and Ports
of Call

Euro Disney

France by Train

Halliday's New
England Food
Explorer

Healthy Escapes

Italy by Train

London Companion

Shadow Traffic's New
York Shortcuts and
Traffic Tips

Sunday in New York

Sunday in San
Francisco

Touring Europe

Touring USA:
Eastern Edition

Walt Disney World and
the Orlando Area

Walt Disney World
for Adults

**Fodor's Vacation
Planners**

Great American
Learning Vacations

Great American
Sports & Adventure
Vacations

Great American
Vacations

Great American
Vacations for Travelers
with Disabilities

National Parks and
Seashores of the East

National Parks
of the West

**The Wall Street
Journal Guides to
Business Travel**

At last — a guide for Americans with disabilities that makes traveling a delight

0-679-02591-X $18.00 ($24.00 Can)

This is the first and only complete guide to great American vacations for the 35 million North Americans with disabilities, as well as for those who care for them or for aging parents and relatives. Provides:

- Essential trip-planning information for travelers with mobility, vision, and hearing impairments

- Specific details on a huge array of facilities, along with solid descriptions of attractions, hotels, restaurants, and other destinations

- Up-to-date information on ISA-designated parking, level entranceways, and accessibility to pools, lounges, and bathrooms

AT LAST

YOUR OWN PERSONALIZED LIST
OF WHAT'S GOING ON IN THE
CITIES YOU'RE VISITING.

KEYED TO THE DAYS WHEN
YOU'LL BE THERE, CUSTOMIZED
FOR YOUR INTERESTS,
AND SENT TO YOU BEFORE YOU
LEAVE HOME.

GET THE INSIDER'S PERSPECTIVE. . .

UP-TO-THE-MINUTE
ACCURATE
EASY TO ORDER
DELIVERED WHEN YOU NEED IT

Now there is a revolutionary way to get customized, time-sensitive travel information just before your trip.

Now you can obtain detailed information about what's going on in each city you'll be visiting <u>before</u> you leave home—up-to-the-minute, objective information about the events and activities that interest you most.

Your Itinerary:
Customized reports available for 160 destinations

Travel Updates contain the kind of time-sensitive insider information you can get only from local contacts – or from city magazines and newspapers once you arrive. But now you can have the same information before you leave for your trip.

The choice is yours: current art exhibits, theater, music festivals and special concerts, sporting events, antiques and flower shows, shopping, fitness, and more.

The information comes from hundreds of correspondents and thousands of sources worldwide. Updated continuously, it's like having your own personal concierge or friend in the city.

You specify the cities and when you'll be there. We'll do the rest — personalizing the information for you the way no guidebook can.

It's the perfect extension to your Fodor's guide and the best way to make the most of your valuable travel time.

Use Order Form on back or call 1-800-799-9609

s
ag
air t
tour o
9902 E
Regent's P
The annua
in this anci
domain of Re
tion as Joe Pap
worthwhile. It's
the perfomances
Tickets are usually a
venue. Alternate tic
mances are cancelled
given. For more informa
Open-Air Theatre, Inner C
NW1 4NP Open Air Theat
Tel: 935-5756. Ends: 9-11-93.
International Air Tattoo
Held biennially, the world's
military air display in
demostra-
tions, milita
bands

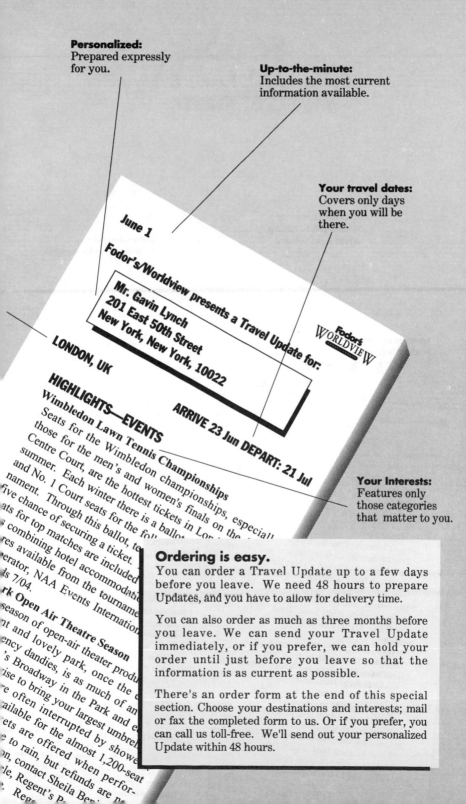

Personalized:
Prepared expressly for you.

Up-to-the-minute:
Includes the most current information available.

Your travel dates:
Covers only days when you will be there.

June 1

Fodor's/Worldview presents a Travel Update for:

Mr. Gavin Lynch
201 East 50th Street
New York, New York, 10022

Fodor's
WORLDVIEW

LONDON, UK

ARRIVE 23 Jun DEPART: 21 Jul

Your Interests:
Features only those categories that matter to you.

HIGHLIGHTS—EVENTS

Wimbledon Lawn Tennis Championships

Seats for the Wimbledon championships, especiall
those for the men's and women's finals on the
Centre Court, are the hottest tickets in Lon
summer. Each winter there is a ballot
and No. 1 Court seats for the fol
nament. Through this ballot, to
five chance of securing a ticket.
ats for top matches are included
combining hotel accommodat
res available from the tourname
erator, NAA Events Internation
ls 7/04.

rk Open Air Theatre Season

season of open-air theater produ
nt and lovely park, once the e
ency dandies, is as much of an
's Broadway in the Park and e
ise to bring your largest umbrel
re often interrupted by showe
ailable for the almost 1,200-seat
ets are offered when perfor-
e to rain, but refunds are n
on, contact Sheila Beri
le, Regent's P
. Reg

Ordering is easy.

You can order a Travel Update up to a few days before you leave. We need 48 hours to prepare Updates, and you have to allow for delivery time.

You can also order as much as three months before you leave. We can send your Travel Update immediately, or if you prefer, we can hold your order until just before you leave so that the information is as current as possible.

There's an order form at the end of this special section. Choose your destinations and interests; mail or fax the completed form to us. Or if you prefer, you can call us toll-free. We'll send out your personalized Update within 48 hours.

**Special concerts—
who's performing
what and where**

**One-of-a-kind,
one-time-only events**

**Special interest,
in-depth listings**

Children — Events

Angel Canal Festival

The festivities include a children's funfair, entertainers, a boat rally and displays on the water. Regent's Canal. Islington. N1. Tube: Angel. Tel: 267 9100. 11:30am-5:30pm. 7/04.

Blackheath Summer Kite Festival

Stunt kite displays with parachuting teddy bears and trade stands. Free admission. SE3. BR: Blackheath. 10am. 6/27.

Megabugs

Children will delight in this infestation of giant robotic insects, including a praying mantis 60 times life size. Mon-Sat 10am-6pm; Sun 11am-6pm. Admission 4.50 pounds. Natural History Museum, Cromwell Road. SW7. Tube: South Kensington. Tel: 938 9123. Ends 10/01.

Childminders

This establishment employs only women, providing nurses and qualified nannies to

Music — Jazz & Blues

Tito Puente's Golden Men of Latin Jazz

The father of mambo and Cuban rumba king comes to town. Royal Festival Hall. South Bank. SE1. Tube: Waterloo. Tel: 928 8800. 8pm. 7/15.

Georgie Fame and The New York Band

Riding a popular tide with his latest album, the smoky-voiced Fame and his keyboard are on a tour yet again. The Grand. Clapham Junction. SW11. BR: Clapham Junction. Tel: 738 9000. 7:30pm. 7/07.

Jacques Loussier Play Bach Trio

The French jazz classicist and colleagues. Kenwood Lakeside. Hampstead Lane. Kenwood. NW3. Tube: Golders Green, then bus 210. Tel: 413 1443. 7pm. 7/10.

Tony Bennett and Ronnie Scott

Royal Festival Hall. South Bank. SE1. Tube: Waterloo. Tel: 928 8800. 8pm. 7/11.

Santana

Royal Festival Hall. South Bank. SE1. Tube: Waterloo. Tel: 928 8800. 8pm. 7/12.

Count Basie Orchestra and Nancy Wilson Trio

Royal Festival Hall. South Bank. SE1. Tube: Waterloo. Tel: 928 8800. 8pm. 7/14.

King Pleasure and the Biscuit Boys

Royal Festival Hall. South Bank. SE1. Tube: Waterloo. Tel: 928 8800. 6:30 and 9pm. 7/16.

Al Green and the London Community Gospel Choir

Royal Festival Hall. South Bank. SE1. Tube: Waterloo. Tel: 928 8800. 8pm. 7/13.

BB King and Linda Hopkins

Mother of the blues and successor to Bessie Smith. Hopkins meets up with "Blues Boy" ...th Bank. SE...

Music — Classical

Marylebone Sinfonia

Kenneth Gowen conducts music by Puccini and Rossini. Queen Elizabeth Hall. South Bank. SE1. Tube: Waterloo. Tel: 928 8800. 7:45pm. 7/16.

London Philharmonic

Franz Welser-Moest and George Benjamin conduct selections by Alexander Goehr, Messiaen, and some of Benjamin's own compositions. Queen Elizabeth Hall. South Bank. SE1. Tube: Waterloo. Tel: 928 8800. 8pm.

London Pro Arte Orchestra and Forest Choir

Murray Stewart conducts selections by Rossini, Haydn and Jonathan Willcocks. Queen Elizabeth Hall. South Bank. SE1. Tube: Waterloo. Tel: 928 8800. 7:45pm. 7/...

Kensington Symphony Orchestra

...ducts Dvorak's Dm...

Here's what you get . . .

Detailed information about what's going on — precisely when you'll be there.

Show openings during your visit

Handy pocket-size booklet

Reviews by local critics

Exhibitions & Shows—Antique & Flower

Westminster Antiques Fair

Over 50 stands with pre-1830 furniture and other Victorian and earlier items. Thu-Fri 11am-8pm; Sat-Sun 11am-6pm. Admission 4 pounds, children free. Old Royal Horticultural Hall. Vincent Square. SW1. Tel: 0444/48 25 14. 6-24 thru 6/27.

Royal Horticultural Society Flower Show

The show includes displays of carnations, summer fruit and vegetables. Tue 11am-7pm; Wed 10am-5pm. Admission Tue 4 pounds, Wed 2 pounds. Royal Horticultural Halls. Greycoat Street and Vincent Square. SW1. Tube: Victoria. 7/20 thru 7/21.

Hampton Court Palace International Flower Show

Major international garden and flower show taking place in conjunction with

Theater — Musical

Sunset Boulevard

In June, the four Andrew Lloyd Webber musicals which dominated London's stages in the 1980s (Cats, Starlight Express, Phantom of the Opera and Aspects of Love) are joined by the composer's latest work, a show rumored to have his best music to date. The 1950 Billy Wilder film about a helpless young writer who is drawn into the world of a possessive, aging silent screen star offers rich opportunities for Webber's evolving style. Soaring, aching melodies, lush technical effects and psychological thrills are all expected. Patti Lupone stars. Mon-Sat at 8pm; matinee Thu-Sat at 3pm. In-person sales only at the box office; credit card bookings, Tel: 344 0055. Admission 15-32.50 pounds. Adelphi Theatre. The Strand. WC2. Tube: Charing Cross. Tel: 836 7611. Starts: 6/21.

Leonardo A Portrait of Love

A new musical about the great Renaissance artist and inventor comes in for a London pre-... tested by a brief run at Oxford's Old ... The work explores ...

Spectator Sports — Other Sports

Greyhound Racing: Wembley Stadium

This dog track offers good views of greyhound racing held on Mon, Wed and Fri. No credit cards. Stadium Way. Wembley. HA9. Tube: Wembley Park. Tel: 902 8833.

Benson & Hedges Cricket Cup Final

Lord's Cricket Ground. St. John's Wood Road. NW8. Tube: St. John's Wood. Tel: 289 1611. 11am. 7/10.

Business-Fax & Overnight Mail

Post Office, Trafalgar Square Branch

Offers a network of fax services, the Intelpost system, throughout the country and abroad. Mon-Sat 8am-8pm, Sun 9am-5pm. William IV Street. WC2. Te...

Fodor's WORLDVIEW
TRAVEL UPDATE

London, England
Arriving: June 23
Departing: July 21

Interest Categories

For your personalized Travel Update, choose the categories you're most interested in from this list. Every Travel Update automatically provides you with *Event Highlights* - the best of what's happening during the dates of your trip.

1.	**Business Services**	Fax & Overnight Mail, Computer Rentals, Photocopying, Protocol, Secretarial, Messenger, Translation Services

Dining

2.	**All Day Dining**	Breakfast & Brunch, Cafes & Tea Rooms, Late-Night Dining
3.	**Local Cuisine**	In Every Price Range—from Budget Restaurants to the Special Splurge
4.	**European Cuisine**	Continental, French, Italian
5.	**Asian Cuisine**	Chinese, Far Eastern, Japanese, Other
6.	**Americas Cuisine**	American, Mexican & Latin
7.	**Nightlife**	Bars, Dance Clubs, Casinos, Comedy Clubs, Ethnic, Pubs & Beer Halls
8.	**Entertainment**	Theater—Comedy, Drama, English Language, Musicals, Dance, Ticket Agencies
9.	**Music**	Country/Western/Folk, Classical, Traditional & Ethnic, Opera, Jazz & Blues, Pop, Rock
10.	**Children's Activities**	Events, Attractions
11.	**Tours**	Local Tours, Day Trips, Overnight Excursions, Cruises
12.	**Exhibitions, Festivals & Shows**	Antiques & Flower, History & Cultural, Art Exhibitions, Fairs & Craft Shows, Music & Art Festivals
13.	**Shopping**	Districts & Malls, Markets, Regional Specialities
14.	**Fitness**	Bicycling, Health Clubs, Hiking, Jogging
15.	**Recreational Sports**	Boating/Sailing, Fishing, Golf, Ice Skating, Skiing, Snorkeling/Scuba, Swimming, Tennis & Racquet
16.	**Spectator Sports**	Auto Racing, Baseball, Basketball, Boating & Sailing, Football, Golf, Horse Racing, Ice Hockey, Rugby, Soccer, Tennis, Track & Field, Other Sports

Please note that interest category content will vary by season, destination, and length of stay.